Science & Christianity
Four Views

edited by Richard F. Carlson

InterVarsity Press
Downers Grove, Illinois

InterVarsity Press
P.O. Box 1400, Downers Grove, IL 60515
World Wide Web: www.ivpress.com
E-mail: mail@ivpress.com

InterVarsity Press® *is the book-publishing division of InterVarsity Christian Fellowship/USA*®*, a student movement active on campus at hundreds of universities, colleges and schools of nursing in the United States of America, and a member movement of the International Fellowship of Evangelical Students. For information about local and regional activities, write Public Relations Dept., InterVarsity Christian Fellowship/USA, 6400 Schroeder Rd., P.O. Box 7895, Madison, WI 53707-7895.*

Scripture quotations in chapters one and three, unless otherwise indicated, are taken from the Holy Bible, New International Version®*.* NIV®*. Copyright* ©*1973, 1978, 1984 by International Bible Society. Used by permission of Zondervan Publishing House. All rights reserved.*

Scripture quotations in chapters two, four and the postscript, unless otherwise indicated, are taken from the New Revised Standard Version of the Bible, *copyright 1989 by the Division of Christian Education of the National Council of the Churches of Christ in the USA. Used by permission. All rights reserved.*

Figure 1 on page 253 is provided courtesy of Fred Hereen, Daystar Publications. Used with permission.

Cover illustration: James L. Amos/Photo Researchers, Inc.

ISBN 0-8308-2262-3

Printed in the United States of America ∞

Library of Congress Cataloging-in-Publication Data

Science & Christianity: four views/edited by Richard F. Carlson.

   p. cm.
Includes bibliographical references.
ISBN 0-8308-2262-3 (paper: alk. paper)
   1. Religion and science. I. Title: Science and Christianity. II. Carlson, Richard F.,
1936-
BL240.2.S3228 2000
261.5'5—dc21

                                                      00-040949

19	18	17	16	15	14	13	12	11	10	9	8	7	6	5	4	3	2	1
15	14	13	12	11	10	09	08	07	06	05	04	03	02	01	00			

To my dear wife, Sandy

Acknowledgments

I would like to thank my wife, Betty, for her encouragement during this project. WAYNE FRAIR

I am grateful to my wife, Susan, for her patience during the writing and rewriting of our chapter. I am greatly appreciative to Richard Bube of Stanford University who introduced me to this area of study. Finally, I acknowledge the contributions of my colaborers at Carnegie Mellon University and the University of Pittsburgh in the course "Christianity and Science": John Dolan, Robert Griffiths, Kevin Kelly, David Laughlin, Barry Luokalla, Alan Love and David Snoke. GARY PATTERSON

I would like to thank Dr. Finn R. Pond and the Rev. Dr. William J. Pugliese for their helpful comments on my chapter. JEAN POND

I dedicate my essay to Dave Weyerhaeuser, a mentor, friend and spiritual father who now stands in the presence of him "in whom are hidden all the treasures of wisdom and knowledge" (Col 2:3 NIV). I thank my colleague Bill Dembski for help in researching parts of this essay and for his work on our joint article "Fruitful Interchange or Polite Chitchat? The Dialogue Between Science and Religion" (*Zygon*, September 1998) from which comes the conception of epistemic support developed here. I also thank Steve Dilley, Erik Larson, Matt Lockard and Bill Kvasnikoff for their research assistance and the Discovery Institute's Center for the Renewal of Science and Culture for research support. STEPHEN C. MEYER

There are many people who have contributed to this book. I have found that the gentle exercise of slow jogging or walking—either alone or with friends—has brought many concepts to mind which have found their way into this book. I especially wish to thank Bill and Marybeth Maury-Holmes for being a sounding board and a source for feedback and new ideas as we have walked together. Bill and another friend, Dr. Thurman Rynbrandt, were particularly helpful in the writing of my postscript. I have enjoyed working with the editorial staff at InterVarsity Press, and in particular, I am grateful to Rodney Clapp and Drew Blankman for their encouragement, counsel and assistance. I have subjected my students in theology and science classes, both at the University of Redlands and at Fuller Theological Seminary, to the various stages of this manuscript. I am grateful for the many helpful comments from these students. And of course, without the outstanding writing done by the contributors to this book—Wayne Frair, Gary D. Patterson, Jean Pond, Stephen C. Meyer and Howard J. Van Till —this book would not exist. My grateful thanks for the job well done by each of them.

Finally, I wish to acknowledge the contribution that Sandy, my dear wife, has made to me through her encouragement, patience and enthusiasm for this project. It is to her that I gratefully dedicate this book.

RICHARD F. CARLSON

Introduction
Richard F. Carlson

For many serious Christians the so-called creation controversy, sometimes referred to as the evolution versus creation issue, shows no signs of being resolved or disappearing. At least part of the reason for this state of affairs is that the issues are subtle and involve a number of specialized disciplines such as natural science (physics, biology, geology and cosmology), systematic theology, biblical studies and philosophy (including philosophy of science). Very few people have had experience or have a background in all of these areas. But for a person to understand creation-evolution issues, it is necessary (or at least very helpful) for that person to have some acquaintance or experience in each of these areas.

In addition, the peculiarities of the historical sequence of development in the natural sciences (in particular, in earth science and biology) and in modern philosophy have played a role in setting the stage for possible conflicts with Christianity. Even the particular individuals who chose to become involved in the issues, especially in response to Darwinism, have played a crucial role in the determination of the current "state of the game" in the United States in particular.

Let me make one thing clear from the beginning. I am convinced that there is no *single distinctly Christian viewpoint* on matters of the relationship of natural science and Christian faith. There are, however, *distinct viewpoints held by Christians,* and these distinct viewpoints are found in particular Christian subcultures, subtraditions and groups, but these groupings cut across all sorts of Christian boundaries. One thing shared in common by

Christians concerned with these matters is that all viewpoints try to answer the same question: *How is Christian faith related to developments in contemporary natural science, especially to biology, earth science and cosmology?* And how do I, as I try to be a faithful Christian believer, respond to the pronouncements of contemporary science? Is science a help or a hindrance to belief? Or is science related at all to belief?

Another question I have pondered is the following: is it possible to identify a single key issue in the creation-evolution debate? I think the answer to that question may be yes, and if the answer is yes, then a strong case can be made that the key issue is this: *How does a faithful Christian read the Bible?* If this is not the single key issue, then I believe that it is among a small handful of key issues. I have discussed this with a number of Christians who hold a wide variety of viewpoints on this and related matters, yet there seems to be agreement on at least one fundamental point—nearly everyone I have discussed this with holds a very high view of the Bible and wants to take the Bible seriously. But this positive attitude toward the Bible does not always result in agreement on creation-evolution issues. What appears to divide many Christians here is not their high view of the Bible *but how they read the Bible and then apply it to questions which arise in the science-faith arena.*

A fairly recent (May 1995) presentation on the Public Broadcasting System, "In the Beginning—The Creationist Controversy" examined the status of the creation-evolution issue in the United States. Three principal positions were presented—two Christian positions and a position associated principally with scientists who did not identify themselves as Christian believers. I would classify all three positions in one way or another as having a significant or at least some element of *conflict.*

What do I mean by this? None of the scientists on this particular presentation takes religion seriously; each scientist sees religion in conflict with science; and each scientist regards science rather than religion as the avenue to truth, with at least one of them regarding science as the *only* avenue to truth. I classify this position of scientific preeminence or scientific imperialism by the term *scientism* or *scientific materialism,* and I will immediately dismiss this position as a viable possibility for any Christian believer. This position will not be discussed in any detail in this book as my purpose here is to present only the principal positions that Christian believers hold, especially in the United States.

The two Christian positions in the PBS presentation are variations of what could be called *creationism*, which in a certain sense are also conflict positions. As in the case of scientific materialism, creationists see at least a certain amount of conflict between Christian belief and science, but in the case of creationism it is Christianity that is preeminent. However, advocates of these positions accept some scientific work and some scientific theories but find themselves rejecting other scientific conclusions. Creationism could be simply defined as a belief system that places principal or final authority in the Bible, many times (but not always) in terms of a literal reading of the Bible that is regarded as inerrant or infallible. In any conflict arising between scientific and theological conclusions, the science is taken to be defective or incomplete or inadequate or at least suspect, for the Bible is seen to be free from any error and is the final authority in all matters concerning faith. Over the years there have been a number of variations of creationism including differing views on the age of the universe (and earth), differing views on whether or not some evolution has occurred (although no creationist believes that humankind has descended from some earlier subhuman form) and differing views on the historical actuality of the flood associated with Noah.[1] The variety of creationism depicted on the PBS presentation is a six-day creation followed later by a literal flood of forty days involving Noah and a complete covering of the earth by water.

Currently, two forms of creationism are playing important roles in the United States. One form, the form represented in the PBS presentation, is usually referred to as *creationism*—young-earth, anti-Darwin and literal interpretation, inerrant Bible creationism (a thoroughly antiscience position), represented by such organizations as the Creation Research Society and the Institute for Creation Research.

A variation of creationism (or at least a distant cousin)—usually called *intelligent design*—was also presented on the PBS program. This is a relatively recent development by people such as Phillip Johnson, Michael Behe, William Dembski, Stephen Meyer and others. In this latter form of

---

[1]For a fascinating account of the history of creationism in the United States, see Ronald Numbers, *The Creationists* (Berkeley: University of California Press, 1993).

creationism, two areas of contemporary science are generally under attack—Darwinism and chemical evolution. Especially in the writings of Phillip Johnson contemporary Darwinism is dismissed as invalid science.[2] In the PBS presentation Johnson was the only representative of this position, and he concentrated his critical remarks on evolutionary science in particular but also mainstream science, which he classifies as being metaphysically naturalistic in general. But in the writings of others in this group the scientific idea of chemical evolution (the formation early in the history of the development of life on our earth of crucial molecules and assemblies of molecules necessary for the development of life) is strongly attacked both from the scientific side and also in terms of questioning the philosophical foundations of the entire scientific enterprise. This group advocates an alternative to current scientific theoretical accounts of certain data sometimes under the label of *intelligent design,* sometimes under the label of *qualified agreement,* advocating that the best way to explain the scientific data is to extend science beyond a purely naturalistic methodology and to posit a designer as the only satisfactory way to explain how, for instance, the first proteins were assembled, with the implication that the designer is a transcendent Being. In this book this position will be referred to as *qualified agreement,* for advocates of this position do accept much of contemporary science, including contemporary cosmology and physics, reserving their criticisms mainly toward contemporary Darwinism and theories of chemical evolution.

I believe that the PBS presentation was accurate as far as it went in identifying the three positions discussed so far—the three conflict positions. But I am convinced that this is not the entire story; I am convinced that there are additional possible ways to see the creation-evolution controversy and that *there exist additional possible positions for Christians to consider,* positions that some Christian believers do hold at the present time. In contrast with the three conflict positions, advocates of these additional positions, while also taking their Christianity very seriously, tend to be more accepting of the results of science; that is, they do not see contemporary science as the threat to Christian faith that supporters of the two creationism positions hold.

---

[2]For example, see Johnson's books such as *Darwin on Trial* (Downers Grove, Ill.: Inter-Varsity, 1993); and *Reason in the Balance* (Downers Grove, Ill.: InterVarsity, 1995).

The first of these additional positions is *independence,* where even though both science and Christianity are valued in themselves, each enterprise is seen as parallel and hence not interacting. Here there is no common ground that science and Christian theology share, and hence there is no possibility for conflict. This has been a popular position in the past and remains a viable position for many Christian believers. For example, Langdon Gilkey argued from this position in the Arkansas textbook trial in 1982.

The position which I believe completes the spectrum of creation-evolution positions is a more complete form of integration than found in the intelligent design position. Here integration varies from what could be called hypothetical consonance to full integration in which Christianity and science work together as partners and must influence each other. Here again there is an appreciation for both Christianity and essentially all of the achievements of science. In this category people ask what each enterprise might contribute to a question, and the contribution from each enterprise is valued. Here people look for those places where there can be dialogue between the two enterprises. Hence, science is not seen as a threat to faith but something that can enhance faith. Also, Christian theology is seen as an enterprise that can inform science. Supporters of this position take developments in theology and science seriously in the sense that they do not hesitate to use both as tools in trying to understand our universe and our lives in general. And here people tend to accept contemporary scientific conclusions regarding the age of the universe (15 billion years or so), the slow development over time of what we now experience on earth, and the evolutionary development of life from very simple beginnings (a few chemicals). This is a position in which Christian theology and science work in *partnership* in theorizing about important and relevant matters.

I realize that the science-theology (or creation-evolution) pie can be cut in many ways. But I believe that my identification of the four positions just discussed does an adequate job of representing the main possible positions for contemporary Christians. That there are as many as four distinct positions may be a surprise to some, but I am convinced that each of the four positions is a distinct position, and there is a sizable community of serious Christian believers to be found in each camp. I am also aware that there has been vigorous (sometimes even nasty and heated) discussion between

adherents of the various Christian positions. Whereas I fully agree that all
Christians should reject (and know the reasons for this rejection) the anti-
Christian position of scientism, I also am convinced that too much bad feeling has existed among Christian believers who find themselves opposed to
other Christian believers from differing creation-evolution camps. And
finally, but of crucial importance, I am also aware (as implied by the PBS
presentation) that not all Christian believers are aware of all of the Christian viewpoints.

There is, I believe, a subtle danger—a danger that partially motivates
this book. Most people recognize the fact of the extraordinary success modern Western science has enjoyed over the past three hundred years, a science that (interestingly) had its roots in medieval Christianity. What is a bit
ironic is that too many people regard science as the only road to truth, concluding that religion (in particular, Christianity) has no relevance to our
contemporary lives, and that our dependence on science has replaced our
need for God. As Christians try to sort out the relationship of their religion
to the culture in which they find themselves immersed, and in particular
the relationship of their religion to the scientific culture, I am convinced
that it is crucial that these believers become aware of the best thinking by
Christian scholars who have devoted themselves to wrestling with the question of the relationship of contemporary natural science to their Christian
faith. To that end I feel that it would be helpful for Christian believers to
have before them a clear presentation of each of the four Christian
options, presented by Christian thinkers, each of whom is an advocate of
one of these positions. This is the purpose of this volume.

Each of the four types or viewpoints is represented in this book by articulate spokespersons. For the purposes of this book what I will refer to as
the traditional creationism viewpoint is portrayed jointly by Drs. Wayne
Frair and Gary Patterson. Dr. Frair has recently retired as chair of the biology department at King's College (New York) and for several years (1986-
1993) was president of the Creation Research Society, one of the principal
advocates of creationism in the United States if not the entire world. Dr.
Patterson is professor of chemical physics and polymer science at Carnegie
Mellon University (Pittsburgh), and his honors include fellowship in the
American Physical Society. Their position rests on an inerrant Bible as
their primary source of knowledge and secondarily on what they term *effec-*

tive science. Whereas each coauthor has an appreciation for a number of aspects of contemporary science, they especially find some crucial aspects of neo-Darwinism and the idea of the origin of life on earth through chemical evolution to be scientifically suspect. Yes, there are areas of conflict between science and Christianity, but most of the crucial conflicts are resolved because they see the science in these cases to be defective. However, even though they regard the Bible as completely authoritative and inerrant, they do not advocate an entirely consistently literal reading of the Bible. While I do not want to unfairly criticize advocates of creationism, I note that relatively few active scientists are supporters of this position. As a result, as creationists Frair and Patterson are somewhat in a unique position, having earned Ph.D. degrees in science (biology—Frair) and (chemical physics—Patterson). Hence, as serious and well-regarded scientists they indeed have a true appreciation of contemporary science; they are, after all, professional practicing and teaching scientists. And as a result their judgments regarding contemporary science may well be taken a bit more seriously than those with less experience or training in science.

In chapter two Dr. Jean Pond, professor of biology at Whitworth College (Washington), fully accepts all aspects of Christianity and contemporary natural science, including evolutionary geology, biology and cosmology. But she sees science and Christian theology operating in two distinct and nonoverlapping arenas; she regards them as independent enterprises, and because of this *independence* there is no possible conflict between the two.

In chapter three Dr. Stephen Meyer, associate professor of philosophy at Whitworth College, advocates a position related to intelligent design as represented by Phillip Johnson on the PBS presentation. Here contemporary scientific data from cosmology and physics (data that are used to support the idea that our universe is exquisitely "fine-tuned" for the emergence of carbon-based life here on earth) are used to build a new philosophical argument for the existence of a transcendent intelligent designer. In addition, the lack of an adequate (or complete) scientific understanding of how primitive life initially arose on our earth is also used to build an independent argument for intelligent design. In my opinion this is a type of conflict position, for Meyer sees science as a metaphysically naturalistic enterprise and as an alternative to a Christian worldview. And yet he happily uses the "fine-tuning" scientific data and much of contemporary cosmology, physics and chemistry to support both his conclusions on design and their call for a new philosophical argument for the existence of God. Hence, except for his rejection of chemical evolution (and perhaps also neo-Darwinism), Meyer is in agreement with much of contemporary science. As a result I will label this position *qualified agreement.*

The final major presentation is found in chapter four by Dr. Howard Van Till, recently retired as professor of physics and astronomy at Calvin College (Michigan). As is the case with Jean Pond, Van Till values and accepts both Christian theology and contemporary science as valid enterprises, with these two enterprises as working together to formulate a more comprehensive picture of reality than either can do alone. He sees no threat to Christianity from science. In particular, Van Till sees the picture that modern biology has given us in terms of the development of life forms, including humans, as a depiction of how God endowed the universe with potentiality at creation. So Van Till sees science and theology as working together in *partnership* and not in any way in conflict with each other.

Each of the four positions—*creationism, independence, qualified agreement,* and *partnership*—that are presented in the following four chapters, are positions a significant number of serious Christian believers hold. Hence, my conclusion is that there is no one "Christian" position. Quite frankly, each position can be criticized in one way or another. Perhaps one of these positions, maybe with some modification, may eventually emerge as the consensus Christian position. But for now there is diversity, and it is my opinion that it is beneficial for Christians to be aware of all of the major positions before settling into one of them. And hence, the purpose of this book is to put these positions on the table, each of which is a preferred alternative to the atheistic materialistic position of scientism or metaphysical naturalism.

1 Creationism
An Inerrant Bible & Effective Science

Wayne Frair & Gary D. Patterson

This chapter was written by two Christians who share a personal faith in Jesus Christ. We also share a lifelong commitment to science as an effective approach to searching for an understanding of the observable world and as a profitable way to "work with our hands" (1 Thess 4:11, 12). The senior author (Wayne Frair) was the head of the biology department at The King's College (now emeritus). His collaborator is professor of chemical physics and polymer science at Carnegie Mellon University. He spent the early years of his career in the chemical physics department at AT&T Bell Laboratories.

We met at Camp-of-the-Woods in the Adirondack Mountains of New York, where Dr. Frair teaches a seminar on science and Christian faith. We discovered that we share a large number of presuppositions about the nature of science, scientific practice and the way scientific knowledge is obtained. These basic tenets are presented in parts one and two of this chapter. We also found that we share a common view on the authority of the Bible and its relevance to Christian faith and practice. The nature of theology and its approach to knowledge are the complementary section in parts one and two. We believe that scientists can be Christians and that Christians can contribute valuable insights to the practice of science. The relationship between science and Christian faith is discussed in part three. Wayne Frair was the president of the Creation Research Society from 1986 to 1993. He is a coauthor of the book *A Case for Creation* (1983). Gary Patterson has cotaught an academic course in the philosophy department at Carnegie Mellon University on Christianity and science, with support from the Templeton Foundation.

In part four the principles developed in parts one through three are applied to several issues of current interest. The "beginning" and the age of the universe are considered in section A. The subject of physics and the underlying levels of description used in the Bible and in science comprise section B. The subject of chemistry and the nature of the material world are explored in section C. The origin and biology of life are discussed in section D. And finally, the relationship of human history to the God of history is presented in section E.

The range of conclusions reached by scientists who subscribe to an inerrant view of the Bible is very large indeed. The conclusions presented by us here are within this set of positions, but we strongly reject any scholarly program that ignores the clearly established data and conclusions of science or that rejects the authority of the Bible. Within these parameters we are convinced that profitable discussion of presuppositions, the current status of the data, experimental procedures, methods of data analysis, interpretations of the data and the details of the conclusions can proceed. Both scientific and theological activities must be open to thorough examination and discussion. The present volume is evidence that a very wide range of conclusions is still possible! The common ground is a full commitment to the reality of the observable universe and to the saving grace of Jesus Christ.

Part 1: Aims of Natural Science and Christian Theology

A. What is science? Science is a human activity. One broad definition of science is the formal study of the observable world. Early scientific activity was concerned with those phenomena that could be observed directly by humans using the five senses of touch, taste, sight, smell and hearing. But many of the modern advances in science are associated with observations carried out with the aid of instruments such as telescopes and microscopes. One important concept associated with the process of observation is the protocol that allows any scientist to verify any reported observation. If other scientists cannot repeat the observations and obtain similar results, the phenomenon or data will be viewed with skepticism. Two recent examples of unverified phenomena are polywater and cold fusion.

The enterprise of scientific observation is guided by a conceptual framework that organizes previous observations and suggests profitable directions for further study. For example, the Egyptian astronomer Ptolemy (second century A.D.) adopted a frame of reference for the description of the heavens with the earth as the center, hence the name *geocentrism*. This approach did a very good job of accounting for the known observations of the night sky and was employed for hundreds of years. One of the most important improvements associated with the heliocentric (sun-centered) theory of the solar system was the ease with which more planetary bodies could be included in the model. The observational revolution inaugurated by the telescope required a more flexible theory to interpret new observations and to suggest new searches. The fruitful interplay between theory and observation continues unabated in astronomy. The current conceptual framework for astronomy is based on the idea that there is no special place in the universe. Stephen Hawking expresses this concept in the form: The universe has no boundaries, but it is finite in extent.[1]

Science is motivated by the full range of human emotions and ambitions, and the history of science is replete with examples of human greed. Scientists rarely live up to the characterization of detached objectivity as suggested in school textbooks. However, the scientific enterprise has been extremely successful over time in extending the scope of its activity. One reason for this outcome is the self-correcting nature of science and engineering. Better observations and better conceptual frameworks tend to produce better outcomes. Another common motivation for scientific activity is personal prestige. Early scientists were employed in the courts of kings and princes. They were expected to accurately explain the world experienced by the kingdom and to make correct predictions. Failure was often punishable by banishment or death. The need to avoid error is often a strong motive to find the truth. Unfortunately, there also are all too many examples of cases where scientists were employed to provide supposed authority for particular worldviews derived apart from a firm observational base. Scientists today are not immune from the same kinds of pressure that are

---

[1]Stephen Hawking, *Black Holes and Baby Universes* (New York: Bantam, 1993), chapter 9.

observed in the history of all societies. However, the faith of a typical scientist is that in the long run the establishment of a sound observational database and the creation of corresponding conceptual frameworks will allow humans to understand the world in which we live and will provide the knowledge needed to solve the ongoing material problems of human existence.

The history of science is not a record of monotonic steady progress. The ability to carry out new observations often awaits the introduction of new technology. The ability to interpret known observations often awaits the development of new conceptual frameworks. However, many episodes can be summarized in terms of an increasing concord between the known observations and the conceptual framework used to understand and organize those observations. Celestial mechanics could account for the observed trajectories of the objects in the solar system in terms of the concept of gravity and the mathematical formalism of Newtonian mechanics—or could it? The orbit of Mercury showed small deviations from the classical predictions. Could this observational discrepancy be explained as an experimental artifact? There are many such errors (or artifacts) littering the pages of scientific journals. Could a minor improvement in classical mechanics rectify the problem? The solution actually involved a scientific revolution. What is mass? What is space? What is time? What is gravity? The whole conceptual framework was recreated by Einstein in order to describe an experimental situation that was far removed from everyday experience. Today almost everyone knows the equation $E=mc^2$, but very few people understand Einstein's theory of relativity. The price of improved science is often a radical departure from the comfortable world of unaided human observations and intuitive common sense notions of physical reality.

Another common activity engaged in by scientists is speculative theory. The goal of such work is to explore and extend our understanding of physical reality. One early Greek model of matter proposed that all substances are composed of four elementary forms: earth, air, fire and water. However, no universally accepted protocol was established to measure the composition of an unknown substance in terms of the four elements. More modern efforts have been able to analyze most of the substances on earth in terms of their atomic composition and structure. Detailed protocols have been established to identify particular atoms. Speculative theory has established the range of atoms that could exist, and many atoms not found in the earth have been created by nuclear reactions. The creation of new substances is another important aspect of science. While some creative activity is serendipitous, the existence of good speculative theory directs creative efforts and helps to interpret apparently accidental discoveries.

B. What is theology? Theology is also a human activity. A broad definition of theology is: the study of God and his relationship to his created world. There are several key concepts that underlie this endeavor. First, "God is spirit" (Jn 4:24). Although a common challenge from atheists is to provide material evidence of God, the five senses are not sensitive to the Spirit. Second, "no one has ever seen God" (Jn 1:18). The search for God is not carried out with the same tools used in science. One essential tool for the study of God is faith. Third, "without faith it is impossible to please God, because anyone who comes to him must believe that he exists and that he rewards those who earnestly seek him" (Heb 11:6). God is not the conclusion to an argument but the premise on which all theology is based.

Information about God is received by revelation. "No one has ever seen God, but God the One and Only, who is at the Father's side, has made him known" (Jn 1:18). The primary source of revelation for the Christian is the Bible. Everything we infer about the relationship of God to the created world is interpreted in terms of the biblical context. It is "by faith we understand that the universe was formed at God's command" (Heb 11:3). Merely scanning the heavens does not lead to a direct observation of God. However, studying the stars has been found to be a profoundly satisfying activity for Christians who recognize that "the heavens declare the glory of God" (Ps 19:1). Christian astronomers have no reason to suppose that the universe has existed forever or that it will continue indefinitely. The Bible tells us that God is the Lord of history and that all created things, including the universe, have a history.

The initial act of God in creating the universe out of nothing is followed by the sustaining providence of God (Col 1:17). The ongoing activity of God is summarized in Jesus' words "My Father is always at his work to this very day, and I, too, am working" (Jn 5:17). Any view of God that restricts his activity to one or a few miracles at the dawn of time is inconsistent with the biblical view of God's incessant involvement with his created world. Rather than occasionally intruding on the universe, God is constantly at work, and the Bible helps us to recognize God's activity. The Bible explicitly identifies many specific acts of God in the history of the world. For "now we see but a poor reflection as in a mirror" (1 Cor 13:12), but the light of faith reveals God's presence in the history of the universe and humankind.

The Bible is God's Word to humans, but it is written in the form of human language. This means that it must be interpreted to be understood. The scholarly activity known as hermeneutics is highly valued by any Christian who seeks to understand the relationship of God to his creation. Interpretation of written documents is not a cut-and-dried procedure. Grant Osborne has described the process as an iterative protocol called the hermeneutical spiral.[2] After the philological and grammatical issues have been examined, and after the biblical and historical contexts have been established, proposed interpretations are subjected to comparisons with our knowledge base and revised accordingly. No text can be interpreted in isolation. The process of biblical interpretation must continue as long as the church is still on earth.

Theology is also motivated by the full range of human emotions and ambitions. While Christians should be guided by the principle of "speaking the truth in love" (Eph 4:15), the practice of theology has not produced the same level of consensus as is sometimes observed in science. One problem is the lack of agreement on the database. While for most Christians the historicity of Jesus Christ is beyond question, unfortunately even this central concept is rejected by some modern biblical scholars and theologians. One of the key problems is the impossibility of separating the presentation of Jesus Christ from the performance of miracles. If we cannot believe that God incarnate is constantly performing miracles, we will find it difficult to believe in miracles at all. If there are no miracles, the Bible is a fraud. If we reject the Bible as God's revelation to humanity, where will we look for our spiritual database?

The overall aim of science is to understand the observable world and to utilize this knowledge for the benefit of humankind. The overall aim of Christian theology is to understand the Bible and to use this knowledge to worship God, to enjoy his benefits, to serve his creation and to proclaim his

---

[2]Grant R. Osborne, *The Hermeneutical Spiral* (Downers Grove, Ill.: InterVarsity Press, 1991).

salvation to a lost and perishing world. Merely solving the material problems of existence will not benefit the people of this world in eternity. Only by leading them to Jesus will we fulfill the purpose presented in the Bible. This ultimate purpose must be remembered by all Christians as they carry out the scientific enterprise and by all Christian theologians as they interpret the Bible and analyze the present history of our world.

Part 2: Obtaining Knowledge in Science and Theology
A. Scientific epistemology. Scientific knowledge can be obtained in many ways, but it is most satisfying when the phenomenon under consideration can be explained in terms of other observable phenomena. One of the most powerful physical theories is thermodynamics. The essence of thermodynamics is the relationship between measurable macroscopic properties of physical systems. The fundamental quantities of thermodynamics such as temperature, pressure, heat and work are defined operationally in terms of one another. The macroscopic properties also can be explained in terms of more microscopic measurable properties using the theory of statistical mechanics. Then the quantities invoked are less familiar to us and are harder to imagine. One example is the potential energy of interaction between two atoms or molecules. This quantity can be explained in terms of even more microscopic quantities and the theory of quantum mechanics, at least in principle.

Every observation can be reported at many levels of description. The level chosen may vary with the goal of the exposition or with the intended audience. The description may vary with the chosen frame of reference. On human length and mass scales the notions of Cartesian space and separable time allow us to live our normal lives. But we cannot make sense of the whole universe from this perspective. On human length and mass scales the notions of classical mechanics imply that we can predict with certainty the past and future of a system that we know exactly in the present. These ideas fare poorly in the microscopic world of electrons and other elementary particles. We now know they fare poorly even in the terrestrial world of weather prediction. A scientist must choose the appropriate contextual framework in which to observe the world—the one that allows the results to be interpreted. Without a context, observations that fall outside the predictive ability of the current standard model will not be recognized.

One goal of speculative theory is to be able to express concepts in mathematical form. The exceptional success of mathematical equations in the description of the created world has been noted by many scientists.[3] But sometimes there are solutions of the mathematical equations that have no correspondence in physical reality. One goal of experimental science is to establish the limits of validity of mathematical theory. Creating the conditions in the laboratory that correspond with the assumptions of the theory is a challenge. One use of well-established theory is to help identify artifacts in reported measurements. The frequency of invalid experimental results is well-known to scientists but often not advertised. Theory and experiment are complementary activities in the healthy practice of science. Untested theory and uninterpreted observations are not profitable science.

One of the foundations of modern science is the ability to create in the laboratory the well-controlled conditions necessary to make reliable observations and to test theories. However, there are many phenomena that cannot be studied directly on earth. Observations of the extraterrestrial universe have become very useful in the study of high energy physics because phenomena in this realm have occurred or are occurring in this energy range. There is a general belief in science that the basic properties of matter are the same whenever and wherever they are studied. This belief suggests the possibility that observations made in the present will allow reliable information to be gained about the past and will allow predictions of the future. Any such efforts are subject to uncontrolled uncertainties, but humankind seems to have a great thirst for plausible explanations for phenomena that go beyond that which is directly observable. A plausible explanation invokes only processes that are known to operate and a history that has enough evidence to support it. Forensic science, as is used in crime laboratories, depends on these principles. The study of origins requires this kind of science. One example of this approach is the dating of objects based on their atomic and molecular composition. In order for this procedure to be valid, it is necessary to have historical data on the composition of known objects from each era. Since modern analytical techniques were not available at the time of manufacture for ancient objects, the more usual procedure is to carry out analyses in the present on objects that have been

---

[3]See Kitty Ferguson, *The Fire in the Equations* (Grand Rapids, Mich.: Eerdmans, 1994).

dated by other techniques and to develop an empirical database to be used to date objects of unknown provenance. While there is an inherent circularity associated with such procedures, many fields have progressed and obtained consistent results that are viewed as reliable.

The issue of scientific epistemology is an area of intense current activity. Proper protocols and valid conceptual frameworks are usually developed and accepted by specific working communities of scientists. What is acceptable in one field may not be approved in another. It often is difficult for nonscientists to appreciate the intellectual heterogeneity of science. But most scientists believe that they can detect pseudoscience, at least in their own field. Any scientist who wishes to work in a particular area has an obligation to be in intellectual touch with the appropriate working community. Isolation is usually the worst enemy of science because it is assumed that valid science is the same at all times and in all places.

B. Christian epistemology. As noted above, Christian theology starts with the Bible. The text of the Bible is now accepted by the scholarly community with a high degree of consensus. The Masoretic text of the Old Testament and the current Nestle-Aland version of the New Testament provide a sound textual base for study and interpretation.

The practice of hermeneutics is also highly developed. The book by Osborne cited above is a good example. In order to interpret the text the full context must be determined. The literal words of Scripture have been the subject of exhaustive scholarly work, and the grammatical structure of the text has been established with a high degree of consensus. Newer approaches have examined the literary style with more tools; the Bible is not a flat text that reads like a textbook exposition. For example, some of the most profound poetry is found in the Bible. Because the issues are so foundational and deal with subjects that are beyond our normal experience, figurative language is used in many passages. An amazing variety of literary genre, or literary styles, is found in the Bible—from history to narrative, parable, proverb and prophecy. The biblical authors carefully chose a particular literary style to fit the purpose for which a given passage was intended in the life of the original readers. Hence, one cannot assume that every biblical passage uses language in a strictly referential (literal) way.

In spite of the potential misuse of this tool, establishing the cultural, social and historical context of a particular biblical text is essential for a proper understanding. The words meant something to the people who first read them, and it is critical that we find out what that was. Words change meaning over time, and the entire context of a passage must be determined to understand the actual message to those for whom it was originally intended. Only then can we ask what the passage might mean to us today. Christians must use the best tools because they are servants of the Most High God. The use of defective hermeneutical protocols will not advance the cause of Christ.

Although the Bible is the primary source of theological knowledge, other ways of obtaining spiritual insight have been suggested. One proposed source of spiritual knowledge is subjective personal experience. Early efforts in science were often characterized by subjective impressions, but greater progress occurred when more objective protocols were established and followed. The Bible is more than a collection of personal recollections; it was inspired by the Holy Spirit, who provides the ultimate conceptual framework! It was received by the people of God; a collective judgment was added to the claim of the authors that the words were from God, and it has stood the test of time as the principal reliable source of spiritual knowledge.

Another proposed source of spiritual knowledge is observation of the created world. This approach often is called natural theology. One of the most important insights in science is that there are no bare facts; all observations occur in some context. In the practice of theology observations of the created world must be carried out in a biblical context if a reliable interpretation is to be obtained. We derive our theology from the Bible, but if we have accurately formulated the principles of God's action in his created world, observations of that world can be interpreted in terms of our theology. God's ways are not our ways, and we cannot trust our own intuitive ideas about God to guide our observation of his world. Nor can we trust the popular prejudices or philosophical dogmas of our society. We can trust the Holy Spirit to guide our paths as we exercise faith in Jesus Christ and observe the world he has created. We are still capable of error in observation and interpretation, but we are not alone!

Part 3: Relation of Science and Christian Theology

The Bible is an essential part of the practice of science for a Christian. It provides the context for the study of God's creation. A portion of Psalm 8 affords a good example:

> When I consider your heavens,
>   the work of your fingers,
> the moon and the stars,
>   which you have set in place,
> what is man that you are mindful of him,
>   the son of man that you care for him?
> You made him a little lower than the heavenly beings
>   and crowned him with glory and honor.
> You made him ruler over the works of your hands;
>   you put everything under his feet. (Ps 8:3-6)

Only by understanding the proper place of humankind in the purposes of God can we correctly apply the consequences of science.

For example, the study of astronomy has produced a profound insecurity in many scientists because the vastness of space seems to leave no significant place for humankind.[4] We are significant because God has declared humans to be so. By faith we can have peace in a universe that contains quasars and black holes! And we can rejoice in the study of the myriad of complex phenomena created by God. We worship the Creator, not the cosmos.

The study of geology has driven many scientists to question the significance of a species that they believe has existed for a trivial fraction of the age of the earth. The Bible tells us that the earth was formed for the express purpose of providing a home for humankind (Is 45:18). The significance of humankind is not based on our worthiness or on our longevity but on God's purposes revealed in the Bible. We worship the Creator, not Gaia (Mother Earth).

The study of biology also has left many scientists confused about the place of humankind in the animal kingdom. Without the clear revelation that we are unique because we are made in the image of God (Gen 1:27), science provides no context for acting as the responsible rulers of the animal kingdom. With the confidence inspired by the knowledge that we are

---

[4]Robert Jastrow, *God and the Astronomers* (New York: W. W. Norton, 1978).

stewards of God's creation, we are free to explore the wonderfully complex world that God has made. We worship our Creator, not his creatures (Rom 1:25).

The purpose of theology is to systematize our understanding of the Bible and to bring us into proper communion with God. A consideration of those revelations in the Bible that relate to the physical world can deepen our understanding and devotion. However, we should not expect to find quantum mechanics in the Bible. One devotional approach to the text seeks to establish concord between the current standard models of physical reality and current interpretations of the biblical text. Several Israeli physicists (Orthodox Jews) have taken a leading role in this endeavor.[5] Since both science and theology are human activities, and since there have been substantial changes in both the standard models of science and the interpretation of some biblical passages, no effort of this type can be considered final or even unique. But some contemporary research scientists have claimed that their faith was strengthened by such meditations.

Another level of analysis of the text seeks to discern general principles that can be understood in the human context. Humans live in a world where light is very important; light is a creation of God. Humans live in a world where both land and sea are very important; the current configuration of the earth is a creation of God. Humans live in a world where times and seasons are in a delicate balance; God is the architect of the current world order. Humans live in a world where plant life is essential for human life and well-being; God is the master gardener. Humans live in a world where other creatures constitute essential factors for our survival; God created the terrestrial zoo. Every aspect of human existence must be understood in relationship to God, and the Bible reveals those relationships.

There is much that occurs in our world that is beyond our direct notice. The Bible does not discuss the creation of bacteria; it does not present the kinetic theory of gases; and it does not introduce the wave theory of the electron. It does not tell us how God made Adam from the dust of the earth, but it does alert us to the fact that chemically humankind is made of the

---

[5]See Nathan Aviezer, *In the Beginning* (Hoboken, N.J.: KTAV, 1990); Gerald L. Schroeder, *Genesis and the Big Bang* (New York: Bantam, 1990), and *The Science of God* (New York: Free Press, 1997).

same stuff as the rest of God's creation. Modern biology tells us that humans share the same basic genetic material as other types of life. The Bible tells us that we are related by dominion to all life as God the creator's personal representative. Some scientists affirm that because of the long history of life, humankind is beyond freedom and dignity; yet, it was not science that compelled this conclusion. Materialistic presuppositions provided the impetus for these assertions. Without a source of knowledge of the place and significance of humans in the universe, unrestrained speculation inspired by the results of scientific investigation often produces arrogance or nihilism. Science will not be able to solve the problems of the human spirit or relationships. Only faith in Jesus Christ and trust in his Word, the Bible, will suffice for this need.

The understanding of the Bible has changed from the founding of the church in the first century to the present. For a number of centuries Christian theology was strongly influenced by Greek thought, and Christians during that period tried to make sense out of the Bible using familiar concepts. But Greek science and philosophy are not truly conformal with the Bible, and works by authors such as Origen (third century A.D.) make amusing reading today. Jesus addressed the fundamental issue metaphorically in terms of wine and wineskins (Mt 9:17); a person cannot put new wine in old wineskins. Christians during the Enlightenment also tried to force the Bible into their temporally determined modes of thought. And, of course, we do the same today! However, at any given time the best hermeneutics uses the best knowledge base and philosophical framework available. Skeptical analysis in the nineteenth century confidently denigrated the Bible as scientifically and historically inaccurate. However, by the late twentieth century archaeological and historical research have affirmed the biblical record much more than they have supported the challenges of biblical critics. Christians can only benefit from sound scholarship that produces a true understanding of science and history, since only when we have a valid knowledge base can we accurately interpret the Bible. We do God no favors by turning our faces from the light. The Bible cannot be interpreted properly apart from the valid tools of scholarly analysis. Evangelical believers must support the best analysis because we have pledged to obey the Bible; we actually care what it means!

The basic premise of our analysis is that the Bible is an inerrant revelation from God. It is then vital for Christians to learn what the Bible means and to apply that knowledge to every aspect of human existence. We also assert that physical reality may be observed by humans and that a valid database can be compiled. It is then the responsibility of scientists to learn what the data mean and to apply that knowledge to solve the material problems of human existence. In the next section a number of topics of current interest will be considered within this framework. The current state of scientific knowledge will be briefly summarized and the theoretical framework used to understand this data will be discussed. The significance of these results for our understanding of the Bible will be assessed, and the relevance of the Bible for our application of the scientific conclusions will be presented.

Part 4: Topics of Current Interest
There are many issues wherein science and Christian theology have contributed to our considerations, and in this section we specifically address some of them. The current state of discussion in science is summarized for each topic and the interaction with Christian theology is presented from the perspective outlined above.

   A. Cosmology and the Bible—The beginning and the age of the universe. The conceptual framework that includes a beginning for the physical universe has been strongly resisted by scientists ever since Aristotle. So it is not some philosophical presuppositions that have led to the popular belief in the big bang theory for the beginning of the universe. Even this particular model has had its opponents, among whom are those who have preferred to deny a beginning.[6] A good summary of the basic ideas of this model can be found in *The First Three Minutes by Steven Weinberg (1993)* or in *A Brief History of Time* by Stephen Hawking (1988). Recent work on this topic has focused on the so-called inflationary process that is believed to have produced the remarkable but not perfect homogeneity in the temperature and mass distribution of the universe. Concepts of "the beginning" from various perspectives transcend the intuitive commonsense notions of most people,[7]

---

[6]Jastrow, *God and the Astronomers.*
[7]Stephen Hawking and Roger Penrose, *The Nature of Space and Time* (Princeton, N.J.: Princeton University Press, 1996).

but a beginning there was. Hawking confesses to deep distress on this subject,[8] but his scientific insights could be a major advance in the description of the earliest moments.

The clear statement of the Bible is that "In the beginning God created the heavens and the earth" (Gen 1:1). This concept is amplified in Hebrews, "By faith we understand that the universe was formed at God's command, so that what is seen was not made out of what was visible" (Heb 11:3). Of even greater note we find in Colossians that the scope of creation includes things "visible and invisible" (Col 1:16). Colossians also addresses the initial activity of the Son, Jesus Christ, in the creation of all things and the continuing activity of the Son in the maintenance of all things (Col 1:17). Global descriptions found in the Bible form the proper context for the overall scientific enterprise. Even though the theory of general relativity does not follow from reading the Bible, neither does it contradict it. A deep understanding of space-time strengthens our appreciation of God's universe, which now is understood to be one whole without a boundary.[9] This concept has been pictured or modeled by likening it to the surface of a balloon. The balloon expands, but the surface remains one surface without a boundary. We cannot visualize a three-dimensional world without a boundary, but Hawking assures us that this is the best description of the universe on a cosmic scale.[10] Hallelujah!

The finite size and limited age of the universe can be verified by anyone on a clear night: the sky is mostly black, whereas a very old universe of infinite size would be characterized by a bright sky at all times! Since the current scientific conception of the age of the universe is based on the observation that the universe is expanding,[11] at some finite time in the past the distance between objects would become small in this model. The scientific estimate for this time is approximately 15 billion years. There are substantial uncertainties regarding this date, but it is still well outside Bishop Ussher's biblical estimate of a few thousand years for the age of the universe. Many Christians believe that the scientific estimate for the age of the universe may not be outside what could be understood on the basis of bib-

---

[8]Hawking, *Black Holes*, chapter 9.

[9]Hawking and Penrose, *Nature of Space and Time*.

[10]Hawking, *Black Holes*.

[11]John North, *Astronomy and Cosmology* (New York: W. W. Norton, 1995).

lical comprehension. Because the observations of the stars and the interpretation of their spectra involve many assumptions, we should remain cautious about dogmatism regarding our conclusions.

The understanding of the age of the universe as virtually equivalent to the genealogical age of the first *adam* (human) is a popular Christian position, but it is not universally adopted by all Christians who believe in an inerrant Bible. The detailed exegesis of the early chapters of Genesis by Blocher is a good example of serious modern scholarly work.[12] There have been many attempts to achieve concordance between the current scientific consensus and current biblical interpretations of Genesis, and these views have changed over time. The hermeneutical spiral would suggest that we consider the findings and conclusions of astronomers before reaching our conclusions.

The whole issue of space-time and the perspective of the Bible will be addressed in the next section. However, some concordist attempts to deal with Genesis 1 and the age of the universe recently have been inclined toward appealing to general relativity.[13] It is certain that Moses was not thinking of proper time or global frames of reference when he wrote Genesis, but the text of Genesis 1 was not determined by direct observation. Exactly how God revealed Genesis 1 is not known, but no person was an eyewitness of the events presented there. The more we discover, the clearer it is that Genesis is just as relevant today as it was when it was revealed to Moses. Modern astronomy has served to help clarify our appreciation of God's actions in creating the universe.

B. Physics and the Bible. The twentieth century indeed experienced a revolution in the description of the physical universe.[14] The world looks pretty continuous to the unaided eye, but microscopes have revealed structure on smaller length scales. Powerful probes have revealed the atomic structure of matter on earth. More powerful probes have revealed the structure of the atom itself, and even more powerful probes have explored the structure of the nucleus of the atom. Even nuclear particles have been shown to have

---

[12]Henri Blocher, *In the Beginning* (Downers Grove, Ill.: InterVarsity Press, 1984).

[13]Gerald L. Schroeder, *The Science of God: The Convergence of Scientific and Biblical Wisdom* (New York: Broadway Books, 1998).

[14]Robert P. Crease and Charles C. Mann, *The Second Creation* (New York: Macmillan, 1986).

internal structure.[15] Light looks continuous to us, but certain experiments have revealed that light particles (called photons) arrive one at a time. Light has no rest mass, but light particles with sufficient energy can create particles with rest mass. Whatever happened to Newton's simple clockwork picture of the universe?

The appropriate level of description of the physical universe is often determined by the phenomenon being examined. There is no point in adopting the frame of reference of the internal structure of the nucleus if macroscopic phenomena are being observed! One of the key elements of craft competence in physics is the ability to choose the most convenient perspective for each problem. While each level of description should not contradict any other, it is often the case that one level of description cannot simply be reduced to a lower level. Dogmatic reductionism is philosophical nonsense and bad science!

Not only has the microscopic world been discovered, but also the picture of the extraterrestrial world has changed radically in the last hundred years.[16] Taken as a whole, the universe is remarkably uniform, with an ambient temperature everywhere in space close to 2.7K. But on a local scale enormous fluctuations occur. Very hot places exist, and there are believed to be strange regions like quasars and black holes. So in order to make sense of the large-scale structure of the universe, the theory of general relativity is necessary. At present there are many popular presentations of general relativity,[17] but most people (including professional scientists) still find the detailed structure of the theory difficult to grasp. A few key concepts may help at least to reassure the reader that Einstein is comprehensible. Physicists now believe that the total energy of the universe is constant, and Einstein realized that mass is simply a measure of the local energy: $E=mc^2$. The presence of mass determines the nature of the local geometry of space. The concept that there is some absolute Cartesian frame of reference that determines all the geometry in the universe has been shown experimentally to be incorrect. It is very hard for humans on the earth to appreciate this fact, but understanding the Bible is much easier if there is no edge to the universe! All of space and all of time

---

[15]J. C. Polkinghorne, *The Particle Play* (Oxford: Freeman, 1979).
[16]North, *Astronomy and Cosmology.*
[17]Hans C. Ohanian and Remo Ruffini, *Gravitation and Spacetime* (New York: W. W. Norton, 1994).

are contained *within* the universe created by God. There is no such thing as an independent space or independent time.

Einstein also realized that nothing in the universe can travel faster than the speed of light in a vacuum, c. The speed of light is measured to be the same by any observer in any frame of reference. One consequence of this fact is that there is no such thing as absolute time. The passing of time for any observer depends on the frame of reference. The existence of relativistic time also leads to new ideas about the simultaneity of events. Since information cannot be exchanged instantly but only at the speed of light, the relative ordering of events depends on where the observer is located and the relative velocity of the phenomenon being observed. Time appears to pass more slowly the faster our time-measuring devices go. This is called time dilation. It actually is observed in the world of elementary particle physics, where muons created in the upper atmosphere reach the surface of the earth because they are traveling fast enough to increase their apparent lifetime (the average time for them to decay to other particles). Some helpful books that continue the current discussion of the nature of time include *About Time* by Paul Davies (1995) and *Creation and Time* by Hugh Ross (1996).

The description of the world in terms of the classical mechanics of Isaac Newton dominated both the eighteenth and nineteenth centuries. A rigid determinism was often claimed to be a necessary implication of the mechanics of Newton, which in many cases was extended to all of thought. But the development of quantum mechanics shattered the uncomfortable world of Descartes and Laplace, where nothing was left to chance and God was excluded as a direct influence in the physical world. The empirical observations that led to the foundation of quantum mechanics leave no doubt that the energy spectra of matter are dominated by discrete rather than continuous energy states at the fundamental level. Physicists agree that the quantum description of matter (e.g., discrete states) is highly reliable; however, the philosophical implications of the theory of quantum mechanics are still being debated more than seventy years after the establishment of the quantum theory. When small distances and particles with small mass are involved, quantum effects are dominant, and paradoxical conclusions are all too common.[18] While most people do not think in quantum terms on a daily basis,

---

[18]J. C. Polkinghorne, *The Quantum World* (London: Longman, 1984).

our bodies continue to carry out quantum processes that are the basis of life. All chemistry is quantum mechanical at its basic level.

Macroscopic (large scale) systems are now known that display chaotic behavior, where the future development of the system cannot reliably be predicted from the present state because small random changes that cannot be excluded lead to large and unpredictable changes in the system.[19] Weather prediction is a well-known example. The exquisite sensitivity of the macroscopic world to the details of the environment and the inherent probabilistic character of the microscopic world have revolutionized our understanding of the physical world. The future is now much more open than some philosophers and scientists in the past claimed it would be. The development of quantum mechanics and chaotic dynamics helps us to appreciate much more fully the wonderful world that God has created.[20] Christians should welcome every new insight gained from physics!

The Bible was written before the advent of modern or even medieval science, but the prevailing views and understanding of ancient Middle Eastern culture are reflected in the text. The scientific statements found in the Bible can be verified by any person who chooses to observe the world with the five senses in the geographical region described in the text. The sun is observed to rise in the east and to set in the west. The horizon forms a circle around the observer. The heavens are above and the earth is below. This very human frame of reference makes complete sense for all people because the phenomenological language is meaningful to men and women of the past, present and future. The notion that the stars are billions of miles away makes no sense to the unaided eye in the context of everyday life. Distances on the earth referred to in the Bible were measured relative to the range of typical experience of people of that day. The advent of sea travel extended the range quite a bit, but the whole world was still viewed on the scale of the ancient Middle East and the immediately surrounding countries. Jerusalem was seen to be the center of the universe, and all distances were reckoned relative to the temple!

Time in the Bible is reckoned relative to Adam. The history of the universe is not measured with a cosmic clock but with reference to the life

---

[19]James Gleick, *Chaos* (New York: Heinemann, 1988).
[20]J. C. Polkinghorne, *Quarks, Chaos and Christianity* (New York: Crossroad, 1997).

span of humankind. No real history existed before God made humans "in his image." Time for humankind is often regulated by events in the heavens: the day depends on the rising and setting of the sun, the month on the phases of the moon and the year on the celestial seasons. But where did the week come from? God created time as a gift to humankind and the sabbath as a special reminder of who created time. Attempts to modify the length of the week have not succeeded, and the seven-day cycle of life is one more evidence of the influence of God in our lives.

C. Chemistry and the Bible. Chemistry is the study of matter and its changes, and it all started when the elements were formed during the period of creation. The fabrication of atoms with higher atomic numbers from hydrogen and helium is a delicately balanced process. Even atheists marvel at the enormous number of quantities that must have extremely precise values to lead to nucleosynthesis.[21] The current model identifies exploding stars as the celestial chemical factories for heavy atoms.

The existence of atoms is not sufficient to yield life because life requires molecules. Current research has identified many molecules in interstellar space and as constituents of meteorites, and interestingly there is an especially large amount of water associated with the Oort cloud beyond Pluto. Under the right conditions, including those in space, atoms combine to form molecules. Cosmochemistry has become a recognized field of research.

Large molecules (macromolecules) are required for life as we understand it, but the interstellar universe is not the right kind of place for the formation of large molecules. Although the earth's magnetic field protects us from the high energy ions emitted by the sun, molecules in space are subject to the full force of the solar wind. A special environment is required for the formation and stabilization of macromolecules. High temperatures favor small molecules; so the earth needed to be at the appropriate temperature before life could be sustained. Life requires highly concentrated solutions of molecules, but at the present time no one has been able to demonstrate how this could have occurred spontaneously. The current popular notion that chemistry leads inevitably to life is based on nothing more than unsupported conjecture. Life requires molecules that are cata-

---

[21]David Arnett, *Supernovae and Nucleosynthesis* (Princeton, N.J.: Princeton, 1996).

lytic (which promote more rapid chemical reactions). Although it has been speculated that RNA molecules were the ubiquitous primeval catalysts,[22] no actual mechanism has been identified by which RNA molecules could have been formed on the earth. Given the difficulty modern chemists have in reproducing the molecules of life, it requires remarkable faith to believe that they arose spontaneously under the hostile conditions that are believed to have existed on earth during the suggested time period!

The core of the earth is still partially molten. If the earth were actually more than four-billion-years old and if cooling occurred primarily by thermal radiation, then the earth should have fully solidified long ago. It currently is believed that the liquid condition is maintained by radioactivity within the core where there are energetic neutrons, electrons, alpha particles (helium nuclei) and gamma rays (photons) constantly being produced. The detailed physics that leads to radioactivity is now well-understood, and the basic phenomenology has been described in detail. The rate at which nuclear chemical reactions occur has been measured for virtually all the known elements.[23] Radioactive clocks have been used to help gain insight into the scale of the history of the earth, and geochemistry also has become an important field of science. While there are many factors that are not known with great precision, and there are many assumptions that are used in the reconstruction of the geological history of the earth, sound exegesis requires that the evidence of geology be considered in the interpretation of biblical texts. The stones do cry out, but what do they say?

The Bible contains interesting information about certain technological uses of chemistry in ancient Middle Eastern cultures. The direct descendants of Cain were metalworkers (Gen 4:22). The practice of chemistry was well-developed in Egypt, and the children of Israel practiced the art of the apothecary (Ex 30:25). Appeal to theory is absent, as would be expected in a work written in the centuries before Christ, but the chemical details can be verified by anyone (Prov 25:20).

 The process of winemaking was understood completely at a practical level. Thus the first miracle of Jesus was understood to be outside the nor-

---

[22]Christian deDuve, *Vital Dust* (New York: BasicBooks, 1995).
[23]Gerhart Friedlander et al., *Nuclear and Radiochemistry* (New York: Wiley-Interscience, 1981).

mal practice (Jn 2:9). No chemist of the first century could instantly make wine out of pure water, but the Creator of water and alcohol could accomplish this feat by divine command. We worship the maker of matter, not the matter itself. Pure materialism is the basest of beliefs.

D. Biology and the Bible. Modern biologists have discovered remarkable things about the world of living creatures *(nephesh chai)*. The basis of all life is the cell. While it is simple to conceive how a molecule of water could be formed in the outer reaches of a star, it is much more difficult to imagine how a cell could be formed by spontaneous processes. The popular notion that cells just arose at a certain stage in the earth's history is based on a number of highly speculative scenarios, none of which have been supported by experimental evidence. In the following we will consider the factors necessary to form a cell.

A cell is defined by a mechanically and chemically stable boundary called a cell membrane. It is a simple matter to assemble homogeneous vesicles if water and phospholipids are shaken together in a test tube. But the membrane of an actual cell does much more than just define the boundary. The cell membrane actively transports ions and molecules from the inside to the outside and from the outside to the inside. Without the active transport of the cell membrane, the object would not be alive. The chemical concentrations inside the cell are very different from the composition of the surrounding solution. Merely establishing an equilibrium between the primeval soup and the inside of the cell will not produce life.

Active transport requires a source of energy. In fact all the active processes of life require a source of energy. The proposed process by which the first cells obtained and utilized energy is completely unknown. Plants today can capture the energy of light in a process called photosynthesis. Current scientific models of the earth during the time when the first cells are believed to have appeared are characterized by a very low solar energy flux and a largely translucent atmosphere.[24] What source of energy is available under these conditions? It has been proposed that the chemistry of sulfur and iron could have provided the necessary energy.[25] But in order to utilize this energy, sophisticated systems of enzymes are required. The

---

[24]Preston Cloud, *Oasis in Space* (New York: W. W. Norton, 1988).
[25]deDuve, *Vital Dust.*

large number of extremely rare and highly concentrated compounds necessary to initiate metabolism spontaneously transcends normal levels of credulity. Honesty requires substantial humility on the part of any spontaneous model for the origin of metabolism.

A cell needs to be sensitive to its environment. This sensitivity must reside in the cell membrane since it is the surface that is in contact with the outside world. Food must be transported from the outside to the inside and waste products must be transported from the inside to the outside. Ions must be specifically identified and transported in the correct direction. The enormous amount of detection and control information necessary for the life of the simplest single celled organism strongly suggests that it did not arise by purely random processes.

A living cell is not just a solution contained in a membrane boundary. The interior architecture of the simplest living cell is a marvel of complexity. The surface area of the interior membranes of the cell is very much larger than the surface area of the exterior cell membrane. There are many interior organelles with specific functions and even with their own DNA. A common analogy that fully applies to the present subject is that it would be just as likely for a tornado ripping through a junkyard to produce a fully functioning 747 jet as it would be for random processes to produce all the interior structures of a cell!

Many cells are capable of active motility. Some cells move by a type of swimming motion involving flagella or cilia. Other cells move by deforming their shape in nonrandom ways. The chemistry and biology of actin (the active protein involved in cell motility) is truly a wonder. Actin filaments can be assembled and degraded with remarkable speed inside a cell. While random processes do yield many types of self-assembly, specific self-assembly to produce motion in the direction determined by the cell membrane is far too complicated a process to be random. There are many interlocking processes that are necessary to achieve the desired movement: energy transport, raw material synthesis, raw material transport, enzyme synthesis, enzyme transport, and so on. A truly random process would slow down and stop as the system approached equilibrium. What random process keeps the cell on task as it continuously carries out the actin ballet?

Cells are capable of reproduction. The biology of mitosis is now well-known. The choreography of DNA duplication, organelle segregation and cell division is far too finely tuned to have been the result of unconnected random mutations. How does the cell know that both DNA strands must be duplicated instead of merely making an RNA template suitable for protein synthesis? The precision of the control mechanisms in a cell suggests strongly that they were designed. In spite of rationalist rantings, the macroscopic design arguments of Paley (1802) have never been refuted. Design in nature does not prove that there is a God, but it certainly does establish that the biology we do know is not characterized entirely by random processes! For those who believe the Bible's clear assertion that God is the designer as well as the fabricator of life, the wonders of biology are no surprise. Brave defenses of nineteenth century Darwinism cannot cover the basic fact that the world of life exhibits such exquisite complexity that the inference of a designer is most compelling.

In contrast to the scientific viewpoint, the Bible presents God as the creator and sustainer of life (Ps 104). The earth is claimed to be the planned home of plants and animals. The marvelous relationships between flora and fauna that we now call ecology were ordained by God. The study of other creatures is encouraged as an example of God's current active concern for their welfare, as noted in Matthew 6:26-30.

While humankind shares dust *(aphar)* with the earth and breath *(ruach)* with the animals, we are more than matter and metabolism. The Bible tells Christians that "the Spirit himself testifies with our spirit that we are God's children" (Rom 8:16). Any view that restricts us to nothing but molecules in motion is less than Christian. The deepest understanding of humankind does not come from physics, chemistry or biology.

E. History and the Bible. Although some contemporary views of history question the concept of objectivity, we believe that events actually happened in the past. We even believe that it is possible to gain a measure of certainty as to what they were and so are convinced that there is a field of scholarly endeavor known as historiography. Modern academic history has suffered from two devastating but quite different trends. Atheistic rationalism views the data of history through such a strong ideological filter that many well-attested events are rejected because they violate the presuppositions of the historian. For example, since miracles *cannot* occur, miracles *do not* occur. While a healthy skepticism is essential in all historical work, there are times when the historical evidence must be at least considered, even though the event is difficult to understand or believe under a particular set of presuppositions. Pure skepticism is neither good science nor good philosophy. The other current, counterproductive trend is the assertion that all written history is necessarily myth, which means that it was produced to convince the reader, but the objective veracity of the details is lacking. Valid insights from the sociology of knowledge have been fallaciously extended to deny the objectivity of all written texts. It follows that since all previously written histories are mythical, the job of the contemporary scholar is to reimagine history. We categorically reject this postmodern perversion of the honorable science of history. Good historical research is hard work, and the raw data must be analyzed carefully to reach valid conclusions. But we assert that valid histories can be written, and we assert that the facile work of many current postmodern historians is an insult to all previous generations of historians!

When the science of history is applied to the Bible, many secular historians immediately give up and move on. If they are interested in subjects that are covered in the Bible, they tend to ignore completely the biblical evidence and instead choose to reimagine their own version of the past. *The History of Israel* by Martin Noth (1930) is a typical example. However, for those who believe that the Bible is inerrant, in order to properly interpret the Scripture it is necessary to consider all the external historical evidence as well as internal biblical evidence. The passage of time in the late twentieth century has been very kind to the biblical data regarding its reciting of the history of the nation of Israel. Fanciful histories concocted by unbelieving scholars have been largely discredited by recent archaeological and philological research, while the biblical record has been confirmed.

Biblical history starts with a man and woman who can communicate verbally and conceptually with God. Adam and Eve were not primitive people. The subsequent history is measured chronologically relative to the first "adam," and secular evidence of human culture during the time frame inferred from the genealogies of the Bible (4000-3000 B.C.) confirms the existence of language, farming, metallurgy and domesticated animals (Gen 4:2, 22). Our spiritual parents were not savages. In particular, they were not pagans; they worshiped God. The Bible is basically silent regarding the extent and nature of other beings with similarities to humans. The focus is

on the race of creatures that were chosen by God to communicate with him
and to worship him.

While the setting and the scenario of Genesis 3 may be difficult for
some scholars to believe, for there is no direct external evidence to support
the events recorded there, the rest of the Bible treats the Fall of humankind
as a historical event. We choose to accept the witness of the Bible for this
key happening. Failure to accept the historicity of the Fall has disastrous
consequences for all theology. The sad history of humankind is certainly
consistent with a fallen race. There have been more atrocities committed in
the twentieth century than in any preceding one-hundred-year period. The
levels of morality common today parallel those reported for the world just
prior to the flood of Noah. While the problem of evil helps to keep philosophers employed, the assertion that moral evil has no historical roots is completely inconsistent with Scripture.

Another central event in the early chapters of Genesis is the Noachian
flood. A helpful treatment of this subject is *The Biblical Flood* by Davis
Young (1995). The understanding that the biblical text is focused on the
direct descendants of Adam and the local geographical area could help to
make sense of the external evidence. Both epistles of Peter clearly present
Noah as a historical character and the Flood as an important part of the
history of humankind. Sound interpretation of the relevant texts requires
consideration of both the internal textual evidence and the external geological and historical evidence.

Abraham was revered throughout the ancient Middle East, not just by
the Jews, and there is compelling external evidence for a historical Abraham. In addition to his wealth and political power, which were acknowledged by the surrounding tribes, God chose to reveal himself to Abraham
in a special way. However, theophanies (direct appearances of God to men)
are out of the question for atheistic scholars. God also chose Abraham to
receive prophecies about the future of his descendants and the world as a
whole (Gen 12:2). Prophecy is even more repulsive to rationalists. If there is
a God, and if he has communicated with humankind, then prophecy must
be accepted as a possibility. The Bible is filled with prophecies, but if apparent prophecies are only dishonest redactions, then our faith is in vain. If
solid textual evidence exists that the written word preceded the historical
events by many years, then skeptical disparagement of prophecy must yield

to the evidence, however distasteful this might be for some. The prediction of the coming of the Messiah in Daniel 9 is a strong example of fulfilled prophecy.

The Bible asserts that Jesus was literally the Son of God. The historicity of the incarnation is an oxymoron for a number of scholars, including some who claim to be Christians! It has even become fashionable to deny that Jesus ever existed,[26] but the external evidence fully supports the Bible's record of a historical Jesus. However, the Jesus presented in the Bible is often unacceptable to people in the modern world. He was always in communion with his Father in heaven (except for the brief period on the cross); he knew the thoughts of all people; he knew the future; he calmed storms and raised the dead. The internal biblical evidence has not convinced some scholars that such a person ever actually existed. One scholarly approach is to attempt to demythologize the text and to try to discover the authentic historical data behind the supposedly corrupt text. Many scholars give up in disgust! Jesus really was the person presented in the text of the Bible, and there is no point in trying to reimagine a Jesus made in our latest politically correct image. Anyone who would worship a God made in their own image is deluded. But if Jesus really did do and say the things attributed to him, what will become of the nonnegotiable presuppositions of the rationalists?

While the incarnation is offensive to atheists, the resurrection is an outrage. It even enrages certain Protestant theologians. But the historical evidence makes the resurrection of Jesus Christ one of the best attested events in antiquity. The Bible is unequivocal in its presentation of the historicity of this event. The apostle Paul concludes, "and if Christ has not been raised, our preaching is useless and so is your faith" (1 Cor 15:14). The key criterion for a miracle is not its explanation, but its attestation.

According to the Bible, history not only has a beginning, but also it has an end. Peter summed up many themes in the following passage.

> First of all, you must understand that in the last days scoffers will come, scoffing and following their own evil desires. They will say, "Where is this 'coming' he promised? Ever since our fathers died, everything goes

---

[26]James D. G. Dunn, *The Evidence for Jesus* (Louisville, Ky.: Westminster Press, 1985).

on as it has since the beginning of creation." But they deliberately forget that long ago by God's word the heavens existed and the earth was formed out of water and by water. By these waters also the world of that time was deluged and destroyed. By the same word the present heavens and earth are reserved for fire, being kept for the day of judgment and destruction of ungodly men.

But do not forget this one thing, dear friends: With the Lord a day is like a thousand years, and a thousand years are like a day. The Lord is not slow in keeping his promise, as some understand slowness. He is patient with you, not wanting anyone to perish, but everyone to come to repentance.

But the day of the Lord will come like a thief. The heavens will disappear with a roar; the elements will be destroyed by fire, and the earth and everything in it will be laid bare. (2 Pet 3:3-10)

The prediction of future judgment is followed by the announcement of "a new heaven and a new earth" (2 Pet 3:13). Science will become obsolete; theology will not be needed in the presence of God himself; but the Word of the Lord will endure forever!

Part 5: Concluding Remarks—A Case for Creation

The fundamental Christian position that God is Creator of all things is based on the unanimous testimony of the Bible. Many specific verses have been cited in support of this view, and it has been our intention to keep the Bible in clear view throughout this chapter. We believe that a Christian does not need to abandon a biblical perspective in order to carry out effective science. Accurate exegesis and reliable interpretation of the Bible along with valid scientific conclusions are the goal of all scientists who are Christians.

It is clear that not all interpretations of the Bible are consistent with all conclusions asserted by scientists. It is our hope that the rejection of invalid biblical exegesis and interpretation along with unsubstantiated scientific assertions will continue in the arena of science and religion. Many controversies have resulted from the conflict between unsound interpretations of the Bible and unsupported or even incorrect conclusions presented in the name of science. The resulting polarization has never been resolved by choosing one bad position over another. A genuine search for solutions requires a willingness to consider possibilities outside the narrow positions that sometimes emerge in such debates. There is much work to be done in both biblical exegesis and some fields of science, but it is our conviction that a proper understanding of the Bible will be consistent with all valid scientific observations of the world in which we live.

Astronomy remains one of the most dynamic and exciting fields in current science. New observations of the most distant celestial objects continue to challenge current concepts. Christians should humbly consider whether the latest proposed scientific conclusions are invalid results that come about because some scientists use atheistic presuppositions in doing their science, or whether these conclusions are based on sound scientific methodology that includes reproducible observations of the heavens. Christians are under no obligation to acquiesce to the assumption that there is no God, but when the scientific conclusions do not depend on such presuppositions, we should carefully consider the evidence and the arguments that lead to a given scientific position. We also should carefully examine our approach to biblical exegesis and interpretation. We are convinced that a productive Christian approach is to consider the work of skillful and faithful biblical exegetes such as Henri Blocher who provide detailed evidence and careful discussions of the nature and meaning of the biblical text. We find Blocher's treatment of the early chapters of Genesis to be helpful in sorting out some of the relevant issues of creation and science. Our conclusion and conviction is that astronomy and the study of the cosmos is not a threat to Christian faith. The more we discover about the heavens, the more we appreciate the Creator of the heavens.

Another area of intense current activity is the earth sciences. Our planet is now understood to be a very dynamic system with multiple coupled subsystems. The degree of complexity revealed by the precise observations now being carried out is an eloquent witness to the Creator of the earth. The reconstructed history of the earth reveals the degree to which our planet was prepared systematically for the appearance of life as we know it. Christians should be wary of attempts to use the current scientific consensus on some issues as an argument in favor of atheism, but the misuse of science should not be employed as an excuse to reject the sound scientific observations and carefully reasoned conclusions that dominate the actual work in this field. Most of the naive and simplistic notions that characterized the great controversies of eighteenth- and nineteenth-century geology have been discarded in favor of models that have a clear basis in observation. Christian earth scientists can provide a continuing encouragement to focus on what can be observed and to be skeptical of arguments that are based on "what must have happened." The more we learn about the earth, the more we appreciate the Creator of the earth. Our own faith has been increased by our study of our planet.

The life sciences are now growing rapidly as new technologies enable new observations and investigations. Many old conclusions or theories that were based on speculation have been replaced by more accurate pictures based on actual observations. The more we learn about earth life forms—all plant life and living creatures—the more we appreciate the Creator of life. While the Christian belief in God as the Creator of life is established on clear exegesis of the Bible, the external evidence only strengthens this position. Christian life scientists should welcome all new observations of the structure and function of living organisms. Yet, they serve as ballasts in the scientific community by displaying a healthy skepticism when scientific arguments are based primarily on assumptions and not on actual observations. As the life sciences emerge from the period when consensus was based primarily on the opinions of experts to the phase where key experiments are cited in support of new ideas, Christians can follow the latest developments with increasing admiration. It is our conviction that a compelling case can be made for the creation of life—the very complex structure and highly regulated functions of biological organisms have all the appearances of being created.

While we have presented a positive case that the observed biological world is consistent with the concept of creation, it is also important for us to address the prevailing view in the life sciences that life arose by chance and that natural selection provides a filter that leads necessarily to the appearance of more complex life forms over time. Christian life scientists can play an important role in distinguishing the valid observations and organizing principles that guide current research from atheistic presuppositions that hinder or even preclude progress in some areas. This will promote a more effective search for new concepts to help understand the structure and function of biological organisms.

When the philosophical presupposition of a world governed entirely by chance is applied to specific proposed histories of the formation of life on earth, the probabilities calculated are so low that they cease to have meaning in the context of ordinary life. Attempts to appeal to situations like a state lottery—producing a winner using a clear protocol even though the *a priori* probability of a particular person winning is low—illustrate the vast difference between human attempts to understand the biological world in terms that are familiar to us and the unimaginably small probabilities that emerge from detailed calculations. The statistical approach to the formation of life has been a dismal scientific failure.

The current biological consensus on dating the appearance of the first cells creates another major problem for the view that life formed over a very long time period due to purely random events. It appears that living cells were formed as soon as the earth cooled enough to form significant amounts of liquid water. Attempts to explain this phenomenon illustrate a parallel strategy in the current practice of biology—the appeal to necessity. It is argued that since cells are observed, it is highly likely that there are mechanisms that lead to the formation of living organisms from nonliving matter. This proposition has also been expressed by proposing that the principles of chemistry lead inevitably to biology.

Research at the interface of chemistry and biology need not be wedded to atheistic presuppositions, but when concrete results are rare, there is a temptation to cover gaps in understanding with appeals to necessity. Attempts to understand what constitutes the essential elements of biological life at the cellular level do not conflict with the view that God is the author of life, and success in this scientific program will only increase our appreciation of God's activity in creation.

A consideration of the differences between single cell and multicell organisms requires new concepts to explain the mechanisms of biological development. Currently, this is an especially active field of research, and further progress is eagerly anticipated. It is often assumed that the capacity for multicellular development was acquired by chance, but such a complicated biological system would require a highly unlikely or even impossible history of formation if only random events were postulated. The beautifully orchestrated development of the simplest multicell organisms looks more like a ballet than like a mob scene. It is our conviction that the Christian desire for a detailed understanding of the structure and function of these creatures provides the best context in which to study them, but the actual observations and the induced relationships between them constitute the scientific enterprise. An appeal to atheism does not lead to any actual observations, nor does a prejudice against well crafted biological subsystems aid in the identification of the interacting parts.

The abrupt appearance of large numbers of apparently new life forms at the Cambrian explosion presents a challenge to a model of biological history characterized by minute changes occurring over long periods of time. The Darwinian approach to this problem is rooted in the nineteenth-century emphasis on uniformitarian processes. The notion that only small, slow changes are possible has been rejected in astronomy and the earth sciences. It is time for the introduction of highly nonlinear processes into biology. This research field is still in its infancy, but the explanation of large changes in biology requires a willingness to consider new possibilities. The Christian assertion that God had a direct role in the creation of new life forms (kinds) is based on an interpretation of the Bible which emphasizes the continuing activity of the Creator in the history of earth. This perspective does not address how one particular kind of animal could be changed into a very different type, but an appeal to atheism also offers no guidance on this question. Such a complex problem will require a truly multidisciplinary approach if any progress is to be made. New understanding must be data driven as new observations enabled by new technologies are reported. It is our conviction that every new discovery in the life sciences will only increase our appreciation of the Creator of life.

The rapid increase in sophistication in the earth and life sciences has created an ethical crisis. Science itself provides no basis for deciding what ought to be done. Christian scientists can provide a clear voice that identifies the actual source of ethical pronouncements made in the name of science. As humankind's ability to do great good as well as great harm has increased, the need for clear ethical principles is even greater. The biblical perspective has two crucial components. First, the earth and all living things have been created by God. Second, the Bible clearly states in Genesis 1—2 that humanity has been ordained by God to care for creation in a nurturing and preserving sense. These components provide the basis for the central ethical principle for all issues involving our environment and our fellow creatures. If Christians are to be heard on these issues, they must be able to speak intelligently at the cutting edge of current science. Christian scientists should exercise the utmost diligence as representatives of the Creator of the physical and biological worlds to know and understand the best scientific observations and models.

The final area to be considered is the human sciences. The Christian position asserts that language was created by God for the benefit of humankind and that in addition to communicating with one another this ability allows communion with God himself. Christian human scientists can serve to resist the persistent efforts to dehumanize our race by reducing humankind to nothing more than a naked ape. God has created humans in his image and no attempt to formulate a human science entirely apart from this perspective will be fully adequate. However, considerable progress has been made in fields like cognitive psychology, where reproducible observations have been organized into general principles. Christian scientists can help to distinguish those aspects of human behavior and civilization that are based on sound observations from mere speculations based on political prejudices. In a field where the scientist as observer is also part of the group being observed, Christians can take the lead in identifying the influence of the observer on the nature of the reported observations. While difficulties associated with carrying out research in the human sciences must be clearly faced, this is an area where Christians have the most to offer. The more we learn about how God has formed us, the more we marvel. What makes us human is that we are created by God in his image.

Creation by God is the unifying concept that pervades all work by Christian scientists. It is the basis for our life and work. By observing the created world we answer the question, What has God wrought?

An Independence Response

Jean Pond

I find myself in agreement with much of what Wayne Frair and Gary Patterson describe as the way science works. From a basic belief in the "reality of the observable universe" to their comments on the self-correcting nature of science (p. 20), they have given a clear exposition of the traditional operation of the scientific enterprise. I also appreciate their description of the complexities of biblical hermeneutics, an area of limited familiarity to me.

The authors spend several pages (pp. 40-42) discussing some of the complex structures and activities of modern cells. Space precludes a general discussion here of how these structures and activities might have evolved, but I will comment on one thing: natural selection incorporates random elements, but it is *not* a random process. For further information on natural selection and other FAQs ("frequently asked questions") about evolution, I refer the reader to the Talk.Origins website <www.talkorigins.org>.

My further comments on this chapter center around two sets of questions: (1) Is Scripture really inerrant? Is a belief in the inerrancy of Scripture shared by all Christians? (2) Is there something inherently atheistic or dehumanizing about the practice of science when it makes no petition to faith?

The Inerrancy of Scripture

Frair and Patterson state their belief in the inerrancy of the Bible and that "the primary source of revelation for the Christian is the Bible" (p. 23). I am unsure of the exact meaning they assign to *inerrant*, a word that is not part of my own church background. Does this mean there have been no typographical errors (or their handwritten equivalent), no missing pages, mistakes in translation and so on? Or does it mean that what the original author originally meant to write was somehow perfect? And perfect in what way? Perfect for readers at the time it was written, or perfect for all readers in all possible times?

However it is meant, I doubt I could agree that Scripture is inerrant. It seems uncomfortably close to bibliolatry to me. The Bible isn't God. It's a book. The most important book for our faith, yes—but still a book. It is an important source of revelation for Christians, but I don't believe that we would all assent to the emphasis placed on its authority by the authors of this chapter. For many Christians, myself included, Scripture can be inspired without being infallible, and in my own church tradition our faith is said to be Christ-centered, not Bible-centered.

I also believe that, ironically, the more we insist on the inerrant status of the Bible, the more danger there is of making our own fallible desires supreme. Language is a complex human talent, and it is so easy to hear what we want to hear from it, so tempting to take the Bible most seriously when it tells us something we would like to believe anyway. And if the words are inerrant, does that not make our desires inerrant also?

When slavery was an accepted practice, some Christians used Bible verses to justify it. When slavery was no longer culturally accepted, these same verses were no longer seen as justification, yet the words had not changed. Similarly, when it was accepted that the earth hung immobile at the center of the universe, there were Bible verses available to champion that belief. When the Copernican revolution was complete, these verses were now seen as poetical or as having been wrongly interpreted. Yet the words had not changed.

Today Bible verses are chosen to condemn homosexuality, but we hear very little condemnation of, for example, a sick person who doesn't ask to be anointed with oil by the elders of the church (Jas 5:14) or women who wear "gold ornaments or fine clothing" (1 Pet 3:3 NRSV). Why is this? Isn't it because there are more Christians who are uncomfortable, for cultural reasons, with homosexuality than there are Christians who are uncomfortable with women wearing gold jewelry?

My own denomination (Episcopalian) speaks of authority in the church as a "three-legged stool"—Scripture, tradition and reason. Certainly mistakes are still made, but there is a balance in this system: our interpretation of Scripture must be viewed in the context of what the church community has said through the ages (tradition) and what our reason tells us today.

Each Christian makes a decision of how to approach questions such as the inerrancy of Scripture, and our answers vary widely. Although my own approach differs from that of Frair and Patterson, I question neither their sincerity nor their faith, and I assume they would offer the same forbearance to me. Nevertheless, our approach to Scripture is a critical difference between our viewpoints relative to the issues addressed by this volume.

Science Without Faith

Frair and Patterson state that the Bible "is an essential part of the practice of science for a Christian" (p. 28). As a scientist I cannot agree, unless it is in the sense that the Bible is a part of my faith, and my faith is part of who I am. A person could just as well say that the Bible is an essential part of the practice of professional baseball for a Christian. True in the sense mentioned above, but the pitcher's mound is the same distance from the plate for Buddhists as it is for Methodists.

In science the rules are the same for Christians and non-Christians alike. I doubt we would really want it to be any different. With respect to the science and technique of flying an airplane, we want Christian pilots to have the same education and training every other pilot gets. We want Christian physicians to have the same understanding of human disease as every other physician. When pharmaceutical research is carried out on chimpanzees, we are willing to use those drugs, even if the theory underlying the use of chimps—inordinately expensive and difficult animals to work with—is their evolutionary closeness to humans.

We want all the modern goods and comforts technology gives us, and we don't question either the underlying science that provides these things or the religious faith of those who do the science. The Kansas Board of Education can feel free (in August 1999) to downgrade educational standards in biology because an understanding of biological evolution is not immediately necessary for the food on their tables, the heat in their homes or their water supply. Otherwise, it would have been a very different thing.

Frair and Patterson also make a number of statements concerning the anxieties scientists feel when they are confronted with a godless science. Astronomy, for example, "has produced a profound insecurity in many scientists" (p. 29) because the universe is so big, and we are such a small part of it. Geology "has driven many scientists to question the significance of a species that they believe has existed for a trivial fraction of the age of the earth" (p. 29), and biologists are "confused about the place of humankind in the animal kingdom" (p. 29).

But is this how people truly feel? I think it is important that we do not make casual assumptions about how others react to the revelations of modern science. For example, I believe that relatively few of us—scientists or nonscientists, Christians or non-Christians—are troubled by the knowledge that the earth is very, very old, and the universe is really, really big. Perhaps if a person from pre-Copernican times was transported into the twentieth century, the abrupt transition from a small, young universe to a big, old universe might be shocking. But recent generations have grown up in a world of far-away galaxies and billion-year-old rocks. Moreover, my own experience suggests that human beings have no difficulty whatsoever putting themselves at the center of the universe, regardless of what science says. Christian evolutionists—and we are legion—are particularly sensitive on this topic, having been accused all too many times of the atheistic nature of our discipline. Creationists need to spend more time asking us how *we* view the interplay between our faith and our science, and less time suggesting that we are either closet atheists or deluded.

I am not in the least bit confused about the place of humans in the animal kingdom, nor are any of the other biologists I know, although the details of our answers, of course, may vary. Frair and Patterson speak of "persistent efforts to dehumanize our race by reducing humankind to nothing more than a naked ape" (p. 51). I don't feel these sorts of statements are helpful. What efforts? Who is making these efforts? Why does a family relationship to other species on earth reduce us? Why would we be dehumanized by an evolutionary connection to apes or to starfish or to any other living thing? Is a chimpanzee less of a chimpanzee because it is related to us? Is a rose less of a rose because it is related to a petunia?

It seems arrogant to demand from God that our species arrived on earth in any particular manner. Why would it make any difference to Christians whether *Homo sapiens* is the product of a creative act sometime in the last few thousand (ten thousand or hundred thousand) years or the result of long eons of evolution? Do we choose to impose a limit on God's methods of creation? For myself, I find the idea of being part of an enormous, several billion-year family tree rather appealing.

In addition, I suggest extreme caution when claiming that "science provides no context for acting as the responsible rulers of the animal kingdom" (p. 29). This might be taken to suggest that Christians are leaders in environmental concerns, whereas non-Christian biologists are foot-draggers in this area. I believe the truth to be almost the opposite. The church *ought* to be in the forefront of the environmental movement, and I have long wished that it were so, but our record in this area is one of indifference and neglect.

We cannot assume that evolutionary biology is dehumanizing because we wish it to be so. We cannot *assume* that atheists—or agnostics, Hindus, Confucians or what have you—find no purpose or moral center to their life because we wish them not to. We must ask. Thomas Henry Huxley ("Darwin's bulldog") has been portrayed as a foe of Christianity—and there is truth to that description—but did Huxley's lack of Christian faith prevent him from finding meaning in his own life? Here is part of his reply to a clergyman friend who sought to console him on the death, in 1860, of Huxley's three-year-old son:

> As I stood behind the coffin of my little son the other day . . . the officiating minister read, as a part of his duty, the words, "If the dead not rise again, let us eat and drink, for tomorrow we die." I cannot tell you how inexpressibly they shocked me. . . . What! because I am face to face with irreparable loss, because I have given back to the source from whence it came, the cause of a great happiness, still retaining through all my life the blessings which have sprung and will spring from that cause, I am to renounce my manhood, and, howling, grovel in bestiality? Why, the very apes know better.[1]

Human beings find meaning in life through a variety of philosophies and faiths. We advance no cause by proclaiming that those who disagree with us feel something or act in some way that *they* know they do not.

---

[1]Thomas Henry Huxley, letter to Charles Kingsley, September 23, 1860, quoted in Stephen Jay Gould, *Rocks of Ages* (New York: Ballantine, 1999), p. 60.

A Qualified Agreement Response

Stephen C. Meyer

Wayne Frair and Gary Patterson make many points that I appreciate and affirm. Specifically, I appreciate their high view of the scientific enterprise and yet their caution to Christians about the need to distinguish between evidentially well-established scientific theories and the presuppositionally driven conclusions of scientists and scholars who accept a form of methodological atheism or materialism as their starting point for work in the natural sciences, social sciences and even biblical studies.

This is an important realization because "science" can have two distinct definitions. In my view (and apparently in the view of Frair and Patterson), scientists should seek the best explanation of the evidence and follow it wherever it might lead. Another view of science insists that scientists must limit themselves to strictly naturalistic or materialistic explanations no matter what the evidence might be. This view has, since Darwin's time, played an influential role in limiting scientific theorizing, not only in biology but in other fields as well. Behavioral science, for example, has insisted on strictly deterministic explanations of human action because, at least in part, its founders regarded it as their methodological duty. Others have followed suit. Physiological psychologists limit themselves to materialistic models of the mind; textual critics avoid reference to authorial intention; biblical scholars eschew textual theories that imply real prophetic foresight, miraculous events or high christology; and, of course, evolutionary biologists have categorically re-jected any theory of origins that involves intelligent design or divine action (whether expressed discretely or continually) in nature. Patterson and Frair reject such presuppositionally driven conclusions and (presumably) the method that gives rise to it. Thus they define science as "the formal study of the observable world" (p. 20) rather than, say, "the attempt to explain the observable via strictly materialistic causes." The former definition leaves open the possibility of detecting the action of personal agency or intelligence in the observable effects it leaves behind; the latter definition forecloses that possibility in advance of investigation.

Having accepted the possibility of detecting the action of intelligent agents as a methodological possibility, Frair and Patterson affirm that evidence for intelligent design exists in nature. They mention, for example, the exquisitely coordinated complexity of the DNA replication system as a salient example. They also mention a number of other scientific or archaeological discoveries that corroborate specific biblical affirmations. In particular they mention evidence from physics and cosmology for a discrete beginning of the universe and suggest that this corroborates the biblical teaching about a finite universe. Here again I agree. In this vein they close by articulating a model for the integration of science and religion that suggests the possibility of bringing our scientific and biblical understanding into progressively increasing agreement. In particular they affirm that "a proper understanding of the Bible will be consistent with all valid scientific observations of the world" (p. 47). They seem to believe, as do I, that both the natural world and the biblical text contain evidence and information we need to form a complete picture of the world. Thus they affirm the need to enter "a hermeneutical spiral" in which we may need to allow our interpretations of Scripture to be informed by scientific, historical and archaeological evidences and vice versa. They appreciate the sometimes complex and iterative nature and attempts to integrate scientific and biblical interpretation. Yet they also affirm the possibility of achieving a coherent and consistent integration of both scientific and scriptural sources of information and revelation. Indeed, they seem to affirm that to a very large degree such an integration has already, or can, be achieved. Thus their model sounds very much like my own "qualified agreement" model for integrating scientific and biblical perspectives.

Nevertheless, they call their position "Creationism: An Inerrant Bible & Effective Science." This difference in title suggests at least a difference in emphasis and raises several questions that I am hoping Frair and Patterson can answer in order to clarify how our positions may differ, especially our positions on epistemology. They do not explain, for example, whether (or how), in their view, evidence from the natural world can lend support for belief in God, creation or the accuracy of Scripture. Frair and Patterson seem, instead, to take a belief in an inerrant Bible as a kind of starting point or regulative principle for doing science. I wonder how they would justify that belief intellectually? Do they simply hold it as a brute presupposition, or do they think that reasoned arguments and evidence can be marshaled to support biblical inerrancy? If the former, on what grounds would they assert the superiority of their regulative principle over, say, the principle of "methodological naturalism" or Howard Van Till's "robust formational economy principle?" If the latter, what type of arguments for an inerrant Bible would they favor? Evidential or some other?

I ask this last question because Frair and Patterson express some diffidence about making evidential arguments for God's existence. At one point they say, "God is not the conclusion to an argument but the premise on which all theology is based" (p. 23). Yet making a case for the truth of Scripture would seem, at the very least, to require making some case for the existence of the author and central subject of Scripture, namely, God. Instead, the statement I just quoted seems to repudiate the legitimacy of apologetic arguments for God's existence. Do they also reject the legitimacy of apologetic arguments for the Bible generally? Yet Frair and Patterson also affirm various design arguments throughout their essay. Do these arguments lend any support to belief in the existence of God in their view? If, in their view, neither these arguments nor any others lend support to God's existence or to the truth of Scripture, I wonder how their position avoids subjectivism and relativism?

I ask these questions as points of clarification. Frair and Patterson seem to agree with me that biblical theism and evidence from the natural world substantially and increasingly agree. They do not articulate, as I tried to do in my essay, an understanding of how evidence can provide epistemological support for theistic and biblical faith. I would like to know what they think about this issue.

A Partnership Response

Howard J. Van Till

Regarding Broad Perspectives on Science and Theology

I find Wayne Frair and Gary Patterson's broad recommendations regarding the role of Christians in the scientific enterprise to be commendable. "We believe that scientists can be Christians," they say, "and that Christians can contribute valuable insights to the practice of science" (p. 19). I heartily concur.

I also find myself in agreement with them on the need for a spirit of open and self-critical inquiry in the practice of both theology and the sciences. "Both scientific and theological activities," they note, "must be open to thorough examination and discussion" (p. 20). Furthermore, "Any scientist who wishes to work in a particular area has an obligation to be in intellectual touch with the appropriate working community" (p. 27). Clearly this is excellent advice.

What happens when scientific inquiry is carried out in this spirit? According to Frair and Patterson, scientific theories are likely to be improved, but sometimes at the price of introducing ideas that take us into radically new conceptual territory. "The price of improved science is often a radical departure from the comfortable world of unaided human observations and intuitive common sense notions of physical reality" (p. 22).

General relativity, for instance, is considered to be an improvement over Newtonian gravitational theory, but it demands the employment of a conceptual vocabulary with which very few persons are familiar. I suggest that the same disparity between well-informed theorizing and commonly held notions is equally prevalent in the arena of cosmic history. Scientific theorizing on the formation of galaxies or on the formational history of life forms requires a familiarity with empirical data and theoretical concepts that few people possess, hence the need to pay attention to the judgments of professional scientists who do have the requisite basis for theory evaluation.

Regarding Biblical Interpretation
In the arena of biblical interpretation I find several of the general principles stated by Frair and Patterson to be sound. They rightly note, for instance, that the Bible contains a diversity of literary styles and that it "is not a flat text that reads like a textbook exposition" (p. 27). Given this literary diversity and given the close relationship of any text to its cultural setting, Frair and Patterson are offering valuable advice when they note that "establishing the cultural, social and historical context of a particular biblical text is essential for a proper understanding. . . . The use of defective hermeneutical protocols will not advance the cause of Christ" (pp. 27-28).

Furthermore, say Frair and Patterson, "The understanding of the Bible has changed from the founding of the church in the first century to the present" (p. 31). "However," they continue, "at any given time the best hermeneutics uses the best knowledge base and philosophical framework available. . . . Christians can only benefit from sound scholarship that produces a true understanding of science and history. . . . The Bible cannot be interpreted properly apart from the valid tools of scholarly analysis" (p. 31). Well said.

However, in the context of their candid recognition of the diversity of meanings that have been derived by people of faith from a text that is both highly varied in literary style and framed in a conceptual vocabulary drawn from cultural, social and historical contexts radically different from ours, I find Frair and Patterson's next statement highly problematic. "The basic premise of our analysis," they say, "is that the Bible is an inerrant revelation from God" (p. 31).

This familiar statement, frequently repeated by persons of good intention, must, however, be seen as a humanly crafted proposition that is open to critical scrutiny. It is my conviction that this proposition, often used as a litmus test for identifying "true" Christians from others, can be either impossible or misleading when applied uncritically to issues relevant to modern natural science. How, for instance, can any biblical statement that employs the ancient Near-Eastern concept of a three-storied universe be considered inerrant in the light of our current knowledge about the spatial structure of the creation? Christians must, I would argue, become far more realistic regarding the character of the Bible. The approach favored by Frair and Patterson is ordinarily called *concordism*—an enterprise whose goal is to demonstrate a concord (agreement) between the ancient biblical text and modern empirical science. However, employing humanly crafted propositions that place impossible demands on the biblical text will, no matter how pious the intent, have negative consequences, as the remainder of this response will demonstrate.

Regarding the Character of the Creation and Its Formational History

As one example of how preconceptions about the character and appropriate use of the biblical text can play a negative role in scientific theorizing, consider Frair and Patterson's reflections on the way in which the first life forms may have come to be assembled. In particular, note how quickly they move from a proper recognition that our current scientific understanding is incomplete to a speculative conjecture that the creation was not equipped by God with the requisite capabilities to accomplish what science seeks to understand.

"Life requires highly concentrated solutions of molecules," say Frair and Patterson, "but at the present time no one has been able to demonstrate how this could have occurred spontaneously. The current popular notion that chemistry leads inevitably to life is based on nothing more than unsupported conjecture. . . . Given the difficulty modern chemists have in reproducing the chemicals of life, it requires remarkable faith to believe that they arose spontaneously under the hostile conditions that are believed to have existed on earth during the suggested time period!" (pp. 38-39).

Has a commitment to biblical inerrancy and the accompanying concept of episodic creationism led these authors to hold low views regarding the formational capabilities of the creation? It would appear so to me. Why wouldn't the formation of the requisite molecules and molecular systems take place without need for episodes of form-imposing divine intervention? Did God intentionally withhold certain key formational capabilities so as to preclude that remarkable accomplishment? And why do Frair and Patterson consistently use the word "spontaneously" instead of something like "as the outcome of the creation using its God-given formational capabilities"?

A similar question about word choice arises in their employment of a comparison commonly found in literature that favors episodic creationism and biblical inerrancy. "A common analogy that fully applies to the present subject [of the formation of first life forms] is that it would be just as likely for a tornado ripping through a junkyard to produce a fully functioning 747 jet as it would be for random processes to produce all the interior structures of a cell!" (p. 41). Upon reflecting on this assertion, several comments come to mind: (1) Their analogy "fully applies" only if one holds to the concept of a creation from which key formational capabilities have been withheld. (2) The exercise of God-given formational capabilities that might well have led to the actualization of the first living forms is here reduced to the phrase, "random processes." (3) I see no reason to presume that God could not have chosen to employ such processes to explore a vast array of fruitful possibilities that constitute the robust "being" given by God to the creation. If we Christians hold dear the idea that every creaturely capability is to be celebrated as a "gift of being" from the Creator, then why expect certain key formational capabilities to be absent? Why hold to a low view of the creation's giftedness? Has the concept of textual inerrancy or the strategy of concordism functioned as a barrier to a higher view?

Additional examples of problematic word choices could be noted. For instance, "While it is simple to conceive how a molecule of water could be formed in the outer reaches of a star," say Frair and Patterson, "it is much more difficult to imagine how a cell could be formed by spontaneous processes" (p. 40). "Spontaneous processes"? How about "remarkable processes made possible by God's generously given formational capabilities"? "Simple"? Only for persons familiar with the scientific discoveries of the last century! Surely we must expect our understanding of life, including the formation of the first life forms, to grow considerably in the next century. I think it extremely unwise for Christians to depend on the incompleteness of present-day scientific understanding as a means of preserving a small piece of territory to be occupied by biblical inerrancy and episodic creationism.

In another setting, Frair and Patterson rightfully recognize that God's action in the universe is not limited to a few extraordinary occasions. "Rather than occasionally intruding on the universe, God is constantly at work, and the Bible helps us to recognize God's activity" (pp. 23-24). I agree, and I suggest that a reading of Psalm 104 would serve as a fitting reminder that the everyday actions of the creaturely world provide us with an inexhaustible reservoir of vivid examples of God's "gifts of being" functioning fruitfully in the ordinary workings of the creation. What we often call "ordinary" is truly awesome!

Regarding the Case for Creation
Frair and Patterson conclude their chapter with what they choose to call "a case for creation." They see their case as being especially strong in the arena of life. "It is our conviction that a compelling case can be made for the creation of life—the very complex structure and highly regulated functions of biological organisms have all the appearance of being created" (p. 48).

In a fundamental sense I could agree with this statement, *but only if the particular meanings of the words* creation *and* created *were not confined to the restricted meanings assigned by episodic creationism.* With Frair and Patterson, I believe the universe to be a creation that has been given its being by God. I also believe that this universe gives abundant evidence of its being the outcome of thoughtful conceptualization. I see this in the character of atoms, in the periodic table of the elements, in the panoply of molecules that form as the outcome of chemical interactions, in the simplest of life forms and in the diverse array of complex organisms that now inhabit the surface of planet Earth. But in no way do I believe that God could have accomplished this *only* by means of occasional episodes of form-imposing intervention. In fact, I believe that God has gifted the creation with a robust formational economy so that God's intentions for the appearance of such structures and organisms would be effected in the creation's formational history.

As I have often indicated in my writing, I think that one of the factors that has contributed to the widespread Christian prejudice against the concept of biotic evolution is the prevalence of irresponsible rhetoric that presents various tenets of an atheistic worldview as if they were legitimate scientific conclusions. Against that background I was especially pleased when Frair and Patterson wrote, in the context of reflections on the earth sciences, "Christians should be wary of attempts to use the current scientific consensus on some issues as an argument in favor of atheism, but the misuse of science should not be employed as an excuse to reject sound scientific observations and carefully reasoned conclusions that dominate the actual work in this field" (p. 47).

I find that to be excellent advice that deserves to be applied more generally. For example, the historical sciences (portions of cosmology, astronomy, geology and biology) have made great progress in reconstructing the formational histories of both inanimate structures and life forms. One of the presuppositions that have contributed to this success is what I call the *robust formational economy principle* (see pp. 216-20). Some preachers of naturalism have tried to claim ownership of that principle, but we Christians have, I believe, both the right and the responsibility to expose that as a transparently false claim (see pp. 217-25). That being the case, we may freely consider the evidence and argumentation that leads the vast majority of natural scientists (including most Christians trained in the sciences) to the conclusion of biotic evolution.

Toward the end of their chapter Frair and Patterson say, "It is our conviction that every new discovery in the life sciences will only increase our appreciation of the Creator of life" (p. 50). I concur, and I will close these remarks with my own version of this fitting sentiment: *Every time the sciences discover one more of the creation's formational capabilities, I grow more confident that the creation satisfies the robust formational economy principle, and I celebrate the Creator's unfathomable creativity (in conceptualizing that rich menu of capabilities) and the Creator's unlimited generosity (in giving the creation such fullness of being).*

2 Independence
Mutual Humility in the Relationship Between Science & Christian Theology

Jean Pond

The noted endocrinologist, John Cortelyou, president of DePaul University in Chicago, was elected secretary of a newly founded organization for Roman Catholic scientists. He promptly set about disbanding the group. Cortelyou, whose specialty is the study of endocrine glands in amphibian animals, explained his action thus: "There are no Catholic frogs."[1]

After making a telescope for himself in 1609, Galileo Galilei saw spots on the sun and on the moons orbiting the planet Jupiter. These observations presented various problems for Aristotelian cosmology, which held that the earth was stationary at the center of the universe, and the heavens were perfect. The sunspots demonstrated that the sun rotated on its axis and was imperfect. The moons of Jupiter suggested that a planet could be orbited by moons while it orbited the sun. If Jupiter, why not the earth? As a result of his observations Galileo became a strong supporter of the heliocentric astronomy of Nicolaus Copernicus.

In the early 1500s Copernicus had proposed that the earth, like all other planets, is in orbit around the sun. But the Church, basing its teachings on

---

[1]Henry Margenau and David Bergamini, eds., *The Scientist* (New York: Time, 1964), p. 15.

Aristotle's cosmology and the earth-centered astronomy of Ptolemy, had proclaimed the opposite. Common sense was on the side of the Church (Does the earth *look* like it's moving? Can you feel it?), as well as Holy Scripture:

> You set the earth on its foundations,
>   so that it shall never be shaken. (Ps 104:5)

> "Sun, stand still at Gibeon,
>   and Moon, in the valley of Aijalon."
> And the sun stood still, and the moon stopped,
>   until the nation took vengeance on their enemies. (Josh 10:12-13)

The politics of the situation between Galileo and the Church, and the motivations of the various players in it, were complicated. But the consequences to Galileo were quite straightforward. In 1633 he was summoned before the Inquisition in Rome, forced to recant his heliocentric teachings and placed under house arrest for the remainder of his life.

Two centuries later, British citizen Charles Darwin was in no danger from the Roman Inquisition. But with his theory of the evolution (via natural selection) of all species from a common ancestor, he was also working in a sensitive area. Not all Christians rejected Darwin's work, but many found its implications, including the idea of a common ancestry for human beings and other animals, to be anathema.

It has been argued in two recent biographies that Darwin's numerous and protracted illnesses were due at least in part to the stress of finding his science in conflict with his society.[2] He was, as Ronald Clark puts it, "an unhappy dynamiter."[3] But Darwin's problems went beyond illness and stress. In his *Autobiography* he writes of a gradual loss of faith in his later years.[4] Although the death of a beloved daughter in childhood probably contributed to this loss, Darwin's science seems to have played its part. He apparently felt that there was inherent conflict between science and faith,

---

[2]Ronald W. Clark, *The Survival of Charles Darwin* (New York: Random House, 1984); Adrian Desmond and James Moore, *Darwin* (New York: Warner Books, 1991).
[3]Clark, *Survival*, p. 61.
[4]Nora Barlow, ed., *The Autobiography of Charles Darwin* (New York: W. W. Norton, 1969), pp. 85-96.

and the more credible one of these became, the less credible must be the other.

This conflict also distressed Emma, Darwin's wife. After her death in 1896 (fourteen years after Charles's) two letters to him were found among her papers, expressing concern over his lack of faith in God: "May not the habit in scientific pursuits of believing nothing till it is proved, influence your mind too much in other things which cannot be proved in the same way, and which if true are likely to be above our comprehension."[5] Both letters have comments added by Charles Darwin. "God bless you. C.D. 1861," reads one; the other has this note: "When I am dead, know that many times, I have kissed and cryed over this. C.D."[6]

Our philosophies have consequences to real people. In his book *Genesis 1 Through the Ages*, theologian Stanley Jaki tells of Abbé Michonneau, a priest ministering to the poor of Paris:

> According to [Abbé Michonneau] the apparent conflict between science and the six-day creation story was much more effective in promoting atheism among the poor and the relatively uneducated than were the social injustices that cut in their flesh and blood.[7]

A few years ago this story might have seemed overstated to me. What would half-starved Parisians care about science? But our family recently spent a year in a poor, rural area of Africa. As my husband and I (volunteers at a church-sponsored high school) struggled to teach our students biology, we discovered that some of them had been told that the theory of evolution was anti-Christian. They could hardly understand how we could be Christian and evolutionists at the same time, and they rejected the idea of becoming biologists themselves. These students *needed* an education; they needed the jobs an education might help them find. It was one way out of a poverty so deep as to be beyond the imagination of most Americans. But our philosophies have consequences to real people.

Americans today live in a society that is remarkably and increasingly tolerant of variations in personal philosophy. (I claim this without finding it

[5]Ibid., p. 236.
[6]Ibid., p. 237.
[7]Stanley L. Jaki, *Genesis 1 Through the Ages* (London: Thomas More, 1992), p. x.

always to my liking.) One of the effects of this tolerance is that most of us—including scientists—have little reason to fear serious pressure from the church. Nevertheless, a perceived conflict between science and faith continues to exist for many individuals. Our battlefields are the letter and editorial pages of our local newspaper, school board meetings and textbook selection committees. We may not argue with the church as an institution, but we argue with each other. Some of these arguments have proceeded far enough to end up in courts of law.[8]

Can we do better than this?

Can we do better than Darwin, the sickly agnostic, or Galileo under house arrest, on his way to becoming a three-hundred-and-some-year excuse for people to disdain Christianity? Is there a way to avoid skirmishes between science and Christian theology? Must many Christians view science with distrust, sending their children off to colleges and universities with instructions to avoid—as far as possible—entire fields of study?

Is there a way to avoid, too, the arrogant response of some scientists to the power of their own disciplines? Biologist William Provine has written:

> The implications of modern science . . . are clearly inconsistent with most religious traditions. . . . A thoughtful attorney from San Antonio, Tex., wrote recently to ask, "Is there an intellectually honest Christian evolutionist position? . . . Or do we simply have to check our brains at the church house door?" The answer is, you indeed have to check your brains.[9]

Can we do better than this?

Avoiding Conflict Between Science and Christian Theology

> For in much wisdom is much vexation,
>   and those who increase knowledge increase sorrow. (Eccles 1:18)

If a disagreeable conflict continues, one way to escape it, of course, would be for Christians to shun scientific and technical pursuits altogether.

---

[8]See, for example, the legal wrangles described in Ronald L. Numbers, *The Creationists* (New York: Alfred A. Knopf, 1992), pp. 243-51.

[9]William Provine, "Scientists Face It! Science and Religion are Incompatible," *The Scientist* 2 (1988): 10.

We could take the Bible and the traditions of the church for our only authority, our answer for all questions, and ignore the rest.

There is an attractiveness to the return to being tentmakers in an Internet world. And there are Christian groups (the Amish, for example) who have taken this road to some extent. But most of us have not. Would we prefer a world without Christian physicians, Christian geneticists or Christian nuclear physicists? Would we prefer to be without voice when there are ethical questions regarding the use of science and technology?

An alternative road to avoiding conflict would be to attempt to demonstrate that science and Christian theology (when both are correctly undertaken and interpreted) are in essential agreement. Rather than science and faith battling each other, to the detriment of each, they offer mutual strength. This is the position taken in at least one other chapter of the present work, to which I leave its explanation and defense.

A third way to avoid conflict between science and theology—and the way that I suggest is the most useful and appropriate—is to maintain an *independence* between these two very different and very human pursuits. Stephen Jay Gould has written, "Science and religion are not in conflict, for their teachings occupy distinctly different domains."[10] Gould calls this the NOMA principle, NOMA referring to "non-overlapping magisteria":

> Each subject has a legitimate magisterium, or domain of teaching authority—and these magisteria do not overlap. . . . The net of science covers the empirical universe; what it is made of (fact) and why does it work this way (theory). The net of religion extends over questions of moral meaning and value.[11]

Or in more concrete terms, *the right tool for the right job.*

Independence Is an Appropriate Relationship Between Science and Christian Theology

There has been a considerable amount written concerning the differences between science and religion. Gould mentions some of these differences in

---

[10]Stephen Jay Gould, "Nonoverlapping Magisteria," *Natural History* 106 (March 1997): 16. This article lays the groundwork for Gould's recent book *Rocks of Ages: Science and Religion in the Fullness of Life* (New York: Ballantine, 1999).

[11]Ibid., p. 19.

his article about the NOMA principle, as mentioned above. His springboard for this article was a 1996 statement issued by Pope John Paul II, "Truth Cannot Contradict Truth." This statement confirmed that evolutionary biology does not contradict anything in Catholic doctrine, a conclusion based in part on the contrasting methods used in science and theology:

> Consideration of the method used in the various branches of knowledge makes it possible to reconcile two points of view which would seem irreconcilable. The sciences of observation describe and measure the multiple manifestations of life with increasing precision and correlate them with the time line. . . . But the experience of metaphysical knowledge, of self-awareness and self-reflection, of moral conscience, freedom, or again of aesthetic and religious experience, falls within the competence of philosophical analysis and reflection, while theology brings out its ultimate meaning according to the Creator's plans.[12]

A necessary separation between science and religion was also strongly argued by Protestant theologian Karl Barth (1886-1968). Barth said that the proper subject matter of science—the natural world—is clearly distinct from the subject matter of theology—the revelation of God in Christ. The methods of the two fields are also different, according to Barth. Science proceeds by human initiative and reason, whereas theology is wholly dependent on God's initiative in reaching out to us.

More support for the idea that science and theology represent different spheres of inquiry came from existentialists.[13] The existentialist movement stressed the detached objectivity of scientific research, as opposed to the subjective and personal nature of theological inquiry. The supposed de-

---

[12]John Paul II, "Truth Cannot Contradict Truth," address to the Pontifical Academy of Sciences, October 22, 1996; printed in the October 30 issue of *L'Osservatore Romano* (English edition), but more easily available on the Internet at <www.newadvent.org/docs/jp02tc.htm>.

[13]For a brief overview of the contributions of Barth and the existentialists, see Ian G. Barbour, "Ways of Relating Science and Religion, II: Independence," in *Religion and Science: Historical and Contemporary Issues* (San Francisco: HarperCollins, 1997), pp. 84-89; see also Michael Peterson, William Hasker, Bruce Reichenbach and David Basinger, "Religion and Science: Compatible or Incompatible?" in *Reason and Religious Belief: An Introduction to the Philosophy of Religion* (New York: Oxford University Press, 1991), pp. 196-218.

tached objectivity of scientists has come under recent attack,[14] and I suspect few scientists today would claim perfect objectivity all of the time. Nevertheless, detached objectivity remains a valid goal for scientists and an important distinction between science and theology. It has been my experience in science laboratories that this goal is approached more closely and more often than contemporary criticisms would have you believe.

Writing more recently than Barth and the existentialists, theologian Hans Küng has commented extensively on the necessity of maintaining a boundary between science and theology:

> Mathematically oriented science, then, has its complete justification, its autonomy and inherent laws, which no theologian or churchman may dispute by appealing to a higher authority (God, Bible, Church, Pope). Against any sort of patronizing by theology and Church, it must be emphasized that a demarcation between mathematical-scientific and metaphysical-theological statements is right and necessary.[15]

Although Küng here warns against the rejection of science via appeal to a higher religious authority, he actually seems most concerned about the opposite, that is, a rejection of faith via appeal to science: "As against any sort of patronizing by mathematics and natural science, it must be observed that there is no mathematical-scientific criterion in the light of which metaphysical-theological statements can be described as senseless."[16] Küng feels that alienation between science and Christian theology was a disaster that contributed to the development of modern atheism. This disaster could have been averted, he argues, if both science and theology had remained within the limits of their respective authority. Science had to leave God out of science, as was appropriate, but science could not declare God absent from reality as a whole.

Further Thoughts on the Nature of Knowledge in Science and Theology

Much of what has been written on the relationship between science and theology is the product of philosophers and theologians rather than scien-

---

[14]See, for example, Harry M. Collins and Trevor Pinch, *The Golem: What Everyone Should Know About Science* (New York: Cambridge University Press, 1993).
[15]Hans Küng, *Does God Exist?* (Garden City, N.J.: Doubleday, 1980), p. 121.
[16]Ibid.

tists themselves. I think it is understandable (and essential) that science, as an immensely powerful component of modern society, should be the focus of so much outside interest.

Nevertheless, this philosophizing *about* science often feels oddly off the mark. There seems to be an emphasis on pinning down how science operates in theory. As a consequence, less time is taken in acknowledging the very individual and varied ways it operates in fact.

Ernst Mayr writes:

> Although philosophers of science often state that their methodological rules are merely descriptive and not prescriptive, many of them seem to consider it their task to determine what scientists *should* be doing. Scientists usually pay no attention to this normative advice but rather choose that approach which (they hope) will lead most quickly to results; these approaches may differ from case to case.[17]

Mayr, one of the major figures in twentieth-century biology, later comments, "I do not know of a single biologist whose theorizing was much affected by the norms proposed by philosophers of science."[18]

What do scientists themselves think about how their enterprise compares to that of Christian theology? I propose several areas of practical difference, outlined below. I do not claim to speak for all scientists in these remarks or even all scientists within my field, which is (broadly) biology. But I have tried to restrict my comments to areas in which I believe my opinions are reasonably mainstream.

Having a great respect for the *discipline* part of academic disciplines, I also do not claim expertise in Christian theology, despite being a Christian. Lack of expertise in biology has not stopped some theologians and philosophers from critiques on, say, the theory of evolution. But I can only apologize in advance for the misconceptions I undoubtedly harbor concerning how theologians go about their business.

☐ *In science, new data arrive daily; in contrast, the primary data available to theologians are relatively fixed.* In his autobiography Charles Darwin wrote of his

---

[17]Ernst Mayr, *This Is Biology: The Science of the Living World* (Cambridge, Mass.: Belknap, 1997), p. 36.
[18]Ibid., pp. 46-47.

strong reluctance to give up the Christian faith: "I can remember often . . . inventing day-dreams of old letters between distinguished Romans and manuscripts being discovered at Pompeii or elsewhere which confirmed in the most striking manner all that was written in the Gospels." [19]

There are, one assumes, many discoveries in archeology yet to be made. Some of these discoveries will have relevance to our understanding of the Bible.[20] We can also hope that the Dead Sea Scrolls will not be the last major addition to our store of ancient biblical texts. But Darwin's day-dreams seem likely to remain unfulfilled. Theologians continue to write, but the amount of primary material they have to write about remains about the same. The ratio of exegesis to original text climbs ever higher.

There is nothing *wrong* with this. If nothing else, new translations from the biblical Hebrew and Greek must be made periodically as modern languages change. And the meaning of the Bible must be restated for human beings in new situations:

> The history of Christian theology is always the record of a continuous conversation, carried on within the church and between the church and the world in which it lives. . . . It is the effort of [the community of faith] to understand itself and to make clear the nature of its faith—in relation to the thought and life of earlier generations, in relation to new insights into the meaning of the gospel, and in relation to the perspectives of the world to which the community proclaims the gospel." [21]

The Bible is not less valid because it is an old and relatively stable text. But the situation in the sciences is very different. New scientific data arrive daily. A primary driving force behind the revision of scientific theories is new data, not new human beings. Old science is not always wrong science, but in a given field it is generally less complete or less detailed or simply more muddled than the new.

DNA serves as a recent example of the continuing explosion of scientific

---

[19]Barlow, *Autobiography*, p. 86.

[20]For a recent example of an archeological discovery relevant to biblical interpretation, see Amy Dockser Marcus, "As Debate Simmers, Walls Fall at Jericho, and Ahab's a Hero," *Wall Street Journal*, December 31, 1997, p. A1.

[21]John Dillenberger and Claude Welch, *Protestant Christianity Interpreted Through Its Development* (New York: Charles Scribner's Sons, 1954), p. 179.

information. The structure and function of the DNA molecule—the double helix—were poorly understood (at best) prior to 1953 and the breakthrough paper by James Watson and Francis Crick.[22] In the ensuing forty-five years we have progressed from our first hazy image of what DNA looks like, to being able to read the information coded in the base sequences of DNA, to being able to manipulate DNA and even synthesize pieces of it. Our explanations of how DNA operates have not yet kept pace with the new things we learn about it every day. For DNA, exegesis is in its infancy.

□ *Scientific knowledge is provisional.*

In the august halls of the Institute for Advanced Study at Princeton, one day in the late 1940s, Dr. Walter Stewart, an economist on the staff, stood and watched a number of young graduate students in physics as they came bursting out of a seminar. "How did it go?" [he asked them.] "Wonderful!" came the reply. "Everything we knew about physics last week isn't true!"[23]

There is an obvious consequence to all these new data, and another way in which knowledge in science is very different from that in theology. Scientific knowledge is always subject to change, in ways both major and minor.

Things are rarely as extreme as in the example above, of course. But any field of science has its examples of theories turned upside down. In biology classes of thirty years ago, for example, students were taught that there was a strictly one-way flow of genetic information within the cell. DNA directed the synthesis of the molecule RNA, which in turn directed the synthesis of cell proteins. This idea was given an imposing name: The Central Dogma of Molecular Biology.

Dogma suffered a serious blow when the enzyme called *reverse transcriptase* was discovered around 1970. Reverse transcriptase reverses the information flow within the cell, allowing RNA to direct the synthesis of DNA. The idea that there might be reverse transcription occurring within cells was initially strongly resisted, even derided. But the discovery of this

---

[22]J. D. Watson and F. H. C. Crick, "A Structure for Deoxyribose Nucleic Acid," *Nature* 171 (April 1953): 737-38.

[23]Margenau and Bergamini, *Scientist,* p. 10.

very unexpected enzyme—now a part of the dogma itself—has led to major revisions in our understanding of viruses and the evolution of DNA.

Can theology claim anything similar? Are our Christian dogmas truly subject to this type of revision?

The Struggle for Consensus in Science and Theology

The fabric of science. Imagine that you are a biologist who wants to write a textbook containing all the knowledge that has accumulated so far in biology. DNA, diagrams of bones, cell structure, the enzymes of photosynthesis—this book would have it all. But this textbook is intended to represent your field as a whole to everyone on the planet, so it can only contain information agreed upon by, say, 95 percent of all biologists. On any given occasion, what percentage of the total knowledge in biology would your book contain?

Scientific knowledge is always provisional and subject to change. But let us not make our point too fine. In practice, there is an enormous amount of information in each scientific field that is agreed upon by just about everybody.

In any given subject science tends to arrive at a point of consensus, a point at which little more needs to be said. An example in point: the molecule hemoglobin carries oxygen within red blood cells. Hemoglobin does more than that, and oxygen is carried in other ways, but this function of the molecule is established. If there was further dispute about the oxygen-carrying function of hemoglobin, participants would be expected to bring more data—and significantly *new,* breakthrough data—to the table.

The provisional nature of scientific knowledge and a strong consensus seem to be antithetical notions. How can there be an established body of information if every part of it is subject to change? Perhaps this can be better understood if a scientific theory is thought of as the intricate design on a large piece of fabric. Thousands of different colored strands of the fabric—representing the bits of data, logic and conjecture contributing to the theory—make up the design. A single strand, or many, can be frayed, broken or even removed without major disruption in the appearance of the fabric. Why? Because of all the other strands still in place, still interwoven with one another.

In molecular biology, as mentioned above, the discovery of reverse transcription came as a surprise. The thread representing a supposed one-way flow of genetic information within cells was broken, and a major change in theory was the result. But in another sense the discovery did not matter much. Most of what we knew about cellular activities was still true (in a provisional, scientific sense, of course). Textbooks were eventually revised, and biology went on.

In some cases (if we can place a final burden on this analogy) the fabric may become tattered beyond repair, the pattern lost. Science then takes up the threads that are left and starts to weave.[24]

Consensus is sometimes a long time arriving in science, and consensus can be wrong. Consider Aristotle and the earth-centered universe: the geocentric cosmos survived, in error, for almost two thousand years. But on the whole, as time passes, science arrives at an ever clearer and more detailed description of what the natural world looks like and how it operates. This description is, for the most part, mutually agreed upon by participants in the scientific enterprise.

Some commentators have claimed that consensus in science is artificial or political.[25] Scientists agree to agree merely to keep their position in some power structure. It should be no surprise to hear that scientists make mistakes or even that some have engaged in outright fraud. But to make too much of this is to misrepresent the professional lives of working scientists as a whole. *Scientific* consensus is built on a foundation of data, logic, experimental reproducibility and heuristic or explanatory power. Differing opinions are ultimately arbitrated by the data. Consensus is part of the practical power of science. Science tends toward *what works in the physical world,* and *what works* can be very useful indeed.

Consensus in Christianity is strongest at the core. In the first centuries of the church there were several councils that ruled on major theological disputes. The Council of Nicaea in A.D. 325, for example, condemned Arianism. The Council of Chalcedon (A.D. 451) dealt with monophysitism; the contention—argued for by the Byzantine monk Eutychus—that Jesus has a single and solely divine nature. Creeds were written and consensus

---

[24]The idea of scientific theories as fabric is not original with me. See N. David Mermin, "What's Wrong with This Sustaining Myth?" *Physics Today* 49 (March 1996): 11-13.
[25]Collins and Pinch, *Golem.*

reached in which variant ideas were ruled heresy.

But where did all the Christian denominations come from? And why do we still disagree about so many things? The Episcopal cleric Urban T. Holmes wrote the following about councils and unity in the church: "What constitutes a church council? . . . An ecumenical council is representative of the whole church. Such a council in our view has not been possible since 1054, when the church of the East finally broke with the church in the West."[26]

All Christians believe the Bible contains truth revealed by God. There are a number of central truths to which we firmly adhere. However, despite consensus at the core of our beliefs we remain disparate in our individual theologies. Historically and among contemporary Christians various points of theology have been argued vigorously without achieving consensus. Schools of interpretation may gain favor among certain groups. New insights into the ancient texts may inform our interpretations. But without the arbitration of new revelation, can peripheral points be resolved?

In my denomination—the Episcopal Church—there have been ongoing arguments in the last decade centered over two topics: (1) the ordination of women to the priesthood, and (2) the response of the church to issues of human sexuality. The discussions on these two subjects have seemed endless. I suspect many readers will be familiar enough with similar controversies in their own denominations to need little elaboration here. Everyone involved in the arguments has theological and biblical interpretation to support their points of view. These issues do not threaten the core of Christian belief. Nevertheless, the result has been a threatened split in the Episcopal church.

Data-driven consensus is characteristic of science. What about recent controversies in science? There has been an ongoing argument in AIDS research during the last decade too. It has been suggested by some—notably virologist Peter Duesberg and Nobel Laureate Kary Mullis (chemistry, 1993)—that the human immunodeficiency virus (HIV) is not the true cause of AIDS. This suggestion was strongly resisted from the beginning by most workers in the field.

---

[26]Urban T. Holmes III, *What Is Anglicanism?* (Wilton, Conn.: Morehouse-Barlow, 1982), p. 15.

When Duesberg first presented his criticisms of the HIV-causes-AIDS theory, there were reasons to take him seriously. Prior to the 1980s nobody knew that HIV even existed. It is a tricky virus, and AIDS is a complicated disease. The original theories on how the virus initiated infection and maintained its existence within the body were less than satisfactory. The debate became somewhat rancorous, however, with comments that might be considered less than objective on the one side ("It's the virus, stupid.") and accusations of government censorship and cover-up on the other.[27]

But new data continued to accumulate, even as scientists were arguing, along with better theories of how the virus and immune system interact.[28] The current consensus is strongly in favor of HIV as the cause of AIDS, although Duesberg, if his web site is any indication, remains unreconciled.[29] Is it possible that this growing consensus might be incorrect? New evidence can be actively sought, and if we are unsure today, we will be less unsure tomorrow.

But what does the Episcopal Church do about the ordination of women or its response to same-sex couples who want a blessing on their union? What happens when every theologian has been polled, every conceivable Bible passage consulted, and we still do not agree? It could be argued here that science itself can provide the new data for theology. The proposed genetic basis for homosexuality is a case in point. But do we all agree that our theology will change if homosexuality is shown to be genetically determined? And I am unclear about what science could contribute to the debate over the ordination of women.

We have now come full circle. Controversies in science can be illuminated and consensus reached because there is always the possibility, indeed the inevitability, of new evidence. In theology, new data is less likely to arrive, and we must instead depend on the continued interpretation of the old. Science tends to come to consensus *because of*, not despite, new

---

[27]For a fascinating look at the conspiracy theorist at work, see the July 1, 1996, letter to Duesberg from Joel A. Schwartz, available through Duesberg's website <www.duesberg.com/bribepd.html>.

[28]See the articles about David Ho (*Time*'s Man of the Year) in the January 6, 1997, issue of *Time* for a short and readable account of some of the recent advances in AIDS research.

[29]Duesberg's website is found at <www.duesberg.com>.

data; but the fruits of theology include schism.

Achieving and Maintaining the Independence of Science and Theology

Science and theology are different ways of acquiring different kinds of truths about the world. Science and theology differ in their areas of inquiry and in the methods they use. Stephen Gould has written that science and religion have a common goal: "Our shared struggle for wisdom in all its various guises."[30] This is a sentiment with which I agree. But within that common goal the individual goals of science and theology differ. Science seeks an understanding of the physical or natural world, whereas theology seeks the fullest possible knowledge of God's actions in human history and God's purpose for our own lives.

So independence between science and Christian theology is appropriate. Is it then possible?

"Theology is the study of nothing": the misuse of science. For independence to be maintained—the NOMA principle observed—there are two primary requirements. First of all, people must not use the admitted strength and power of science when it operates within its own realm to attempt to reject the very existence of other realms of truth. Science must not deny what lies outside of science. Notice that my sentence above reads "*people* must not . . ." rather than "*scientists* must not . . ." I am far from convinced that scientists are the primary offenders in overstepping this particular boundary. Gould writes:

> Most scientists show no hostility to religion. Why should we, since our subject doesn't intersect the concerns of theology? . . . Unless at least half my colleagues are inconsistent dunces, there can be—on the most raw and direct empirical grounds—no conflict between science and religion.[31]

On a more personal level, I am a scientist, an evolutionist, a great admirer of Charles Darwin and a Christian. *I'm* not using science to deny the existence of God.

So who is? There is certainly a small group of prominent scientists who

---

[30]Stephen Jay Gould, "Darwinism Defined: The Difference Between Fact and Theory," *Discover* 8 (January 1987): 70.
[31]Ibid., p. 70.

are vocal proponents of scientific materialism. Biologist Richard Dawkins is perhaps the best-known example. In a 1997 letter to the editor of *BioEssays* (a journal in molecular, cellular and developmental biology), Dawkins writes:

> de Pomerai's case against Peter Atkins and me is that we don't know enough "theology" to criticise belief in God. This is not the first time I have encountered this superficially plausible yet deeply foolish argument, and it needs an answer. It presupposes that "theology" is a subject at all. de Pomerai thinks it is. I don't. . . . If God is non-existent, theology is the study of nothing. You cannot be ignorant of nothing.[32]

In the same letter Dawkins describes "Do miracles such as the Virgin Birth occur?" as a "strictly scientific" question.

This is the scientific materialist position: there is no truth other than scientific truth; there is no world other than the physical world. Another letter in the same issue of *BioEssays* is even more direct on this point: "Organisms consist of molecules which obey the laws of physics and chemistry. . . . [This] rules out a non-material soul and an after-life."[33]

Carl Sagan was criticized for taking a scientific materialist position, especially regarding his statement "The Cosmos is all that is or ever was or ever will be." It may be so, but I always felt that particular statement sounded more like a simple working definition in cosmology. Consider what Sagan writes immediately following: "Our feeblest contemplations of the Cosmos stir us. . . . We know we are approaching the greatest of mysteries."[34]

But why should we care anyway? William Provine was quoted earlier as an example of a scientist who sees inevitable conflict between science and religion. In the same article he contends that a person who claims that science and religion are compatible is likely to be someone who "believes things demonstrably unscientific."[35] To which I can only add, you are absolutely right, and by the way, thanks for noticing.

Statements by Dawkins, Provine and others can certainly be taken as

---

[32]Richard Dawkins, letter to the editor in *BioEssays* 19 (August 1997): 743.

[33]Robin Holliday, letter to the editor in ibid.

[34]Carl Sagan, *Cosmos* (New York: Random House, 1980), p. 4.

[35]Provine, "Scientists, Face It!" p. 10.

ammunition by nonscientists who, for whatever reason, want to argue against a belief in God. But who is really allowing these arguments to be taken seriously? Prominent scientists can have strong opinions on many things, besides religion, outside their fields. These opinions are not always popular with the establishment of the day. Linus Pauling and Carl Sagan, for example, were both known as political liberals with pacifist leanings. Pauling, who received the Nobel Peace prize in 1962, fought long against the testing of nuclear weapons. The State Department refused him a passport at one point, and in 1960 he was called before the Internal Security Committee of the United States Senate to explain his antiwar activities.[36]

If you read Sagan's *Cosmos*—which was on the *New York Times* best-seller list for seventy weeks—you will find a few things indicating that its author was not fond of organized religion. You will find a great deal more about the need for nuclear disarmament: "The global balance of terror, pioneered by the United States and the Soviet Union, holds hostage the citizens of the Earth."[37]

Both Pauling and Sagan were respected in their scientific fields (Pauling won his first Nobel Prize, in 1954, for chemistry), and both used scientific data to bolster political causes. Those who agree with Pauling or Sagan can use their views, their celebrity status and their reputations for high intelligence in support of a political agenda. But you do not hear much about chemistry or astronomy being *inherently* pacifistic fields. People seem to be able to recognize that different scientists can hold differing political views.

I suggest that it is (some) Christians themselves who are tempting science to overstep its NOMA boundary with respect to theology. They do this by making claims that science—usually the theory of evolution—is *inherently* antitheistic.

Evil evolutionary atheists: the misuse of Scripture. The second requirement for the independence of science and Christian theology is this: believers (or mischievous nonbelievers, for that matter) must not make blanket claims about the supposed religious implications of scientific theories. In his book *A History of the Warfare of Science with Theology in Christendom,* pub-

---

[36]"Linus Pauling," in *Encyclopedia of World Biography,* ed. P. K Byers and S. M. Bourgoin, 2nd ed. (Detroit, Mich.: Gale Research, 1998): 150-52.
[37]Sagan, *Cosmos,* p. 326.

lished in 1896, Andrew Dickson White (the first president of Cornell University) summarized some of the responses of nineteenth-century theologians to Darwin. White quotes one cleric as saying that Darwinism is "an attempt to dethrone God," and there were many others to sound the same warning:

> If the Darwinian theory is true, Genesis is a lie, the whole framework of the book of life falls to pieces, and the revelation of God to man, as we Christians know it, is a delusion and a snare. . . .
>
> If this hypothesis be true, then is the Bible an unbearable fiction; . . . then have Christians for nearly two thousand years been duped by a monstrous lie. . . . Darwin requires us to disbelieve the authoritative word of the Creator.[38]

White's comment on this last author was that he had "plunged into an exceedingly dangerous line of argument."[39] But this type of response has not been restricted to Christians of the nineteenth century. Henry Morris, a well-known young-earth creationist, has been quite straightforward in his feelings about the theological implications of evolution:

> The fruit of evolution's tree is always evil, whereas creationism is the tree of good fruit . . . evolutionary philosophy [is] the basis of every non-biblical religion and . . . the root of every harmful philosophy and practice in the modern world.
>
> The Evolution Model, *by its very nature,* is an atheistic model.[40]

Pope John Paul II, as we saw above, does not agree. And many Protestant denominations have not supported the idea of conflict between the theory of evolution and Christianity. But as time goes on, the mainstream churches seem to be less and less representative of American religion. A brief look at the shelves of my local public library, for example, produced

---

[38]Andrew Dickson White, "The Final Effort of Theology," in *Darwin,* ed. Philip Appleman, 2nd ed. (1896; reprint, New York: W. W. Norton, 1979), p. 363.

[39]Ibid.

[40]Henry M. Morris, *Biblical Creationism* (Grand Rapids, Mich.: Baker, 1993), pp. 272-73; Henry M. Morris and Gary E. Parker, *What Is Creation Science?* rev. ed. (El Cajon, Calif.: Master Books, 1987), p. x (italics added).

The Evolution Conspiracy. The authors, avowedly Christian, are no less direct in their appraisal of evolution than is Henry Morris:

> The theory of evolution is one of Satan's most lethal weapons. . . .
> Evolutionism contests God, His creative power, His unique plan and purpose for man, His time span (the design of time and the length of His days), His morality, and His judgments.[41]

I agree with Andrew Dickson White that this is all a very dangerous business. If Christians will persist in trying to fashion science (or at least evolution) into a weapon, why should we be surprised when it gets used as one?

Interpreting the Bible

The issue of Scriptural interpretation is a key issue in any understanding of the relationship between science and theology. Conflict arises primarily when passages such as the first chapters of Genesis are interpreted in a descriptively literal sense. Some Christian groups interpret the Bible in this way; others do not. For the former, conflict between science and theology becomes almost inevitable. There is no point trying to be diplomatic or less than clear on this point. The book of the Bible most commonly used in making scientific assertions is Genesis. If the NOMA principle is to be observed, the first chapter in Genesis cannot be used to claim creation in six twenty-four-hour days, or six eons or anything of the kind. Genesis 2:7 reads:

> Then the LORD God formed man from the dust of the ground, and breathed into his nostrils the breath of life; and the man became a living being.

This should not be taken as a scientific description of the origin of the human species. Nor is Genesis 1:1 pertinent to the big bang theory in physics.

How *should* we read the Bible? Catholic theologian Thomas Merton has said:

> We must not therefore open the Bible with any set determination to

---

[41]Caryl Matrisciana and Roger Oakland, *The Evolution Conspiracy* (Eugene, Ore.: Harvest House, 1991), p. 22, 41.

reduce it to the limits of a preconceived pattern of our own. . . . All attempts to narrow the Bible down until it fits conveniently into the slots prepared for it by our prejudice will end with our misunderstanding the Bible and even falsifying its truth.[42]

The Bible should not be interpreted as a scientific document. Can I prove this? Plainly, I cannot. It simply has never seemed reasonable to me that the Bible should be used in this way, nor helpful in promoting my spiritual growth. The first few chapters of Genesis have always seemed (to me) to be primarily concerned with the establishment of two things:

1. The universe was created by God, as was everything in it, including human beings.

2. Human beings, through their own choice, became separated from God, with the consequences of this sin manifest in the life of every individual.

In the support of these assertions Genesis has always been utterly convincing to me. On the other hand, neither of these two items seems to require any particular view—in a scientific sense—of *when* the universe was created, *how* the universe was created, or *when and how* human beings were created. Genesis speaks to the meaning of human life and our position as creatures of God, rather than to the specifics of how this creation came about. The position on biblical interpretation that I am describing is nothing new: it is certainly not the invention of twentieth-century theologians. In 1638, for example, René Descartes wrote: "To want to draw from Sacred Scripture the knowledge of truths which belong solely to the human sciences and have no bearing on salvation is to use Scripture for a purpose for which God did not intend it and consequently to abuse it."[43] And here is Galileo, writing in 1615 to the Grand Duchess Christiana of Tuscany:

> I should judge the authority of the Bible was designed to persuade men of those articles and propositions which, surpassing all human reasoning, could not be made credible by science. . . . But I do not feel obliged to believe that the same God who has endowed us with senses, reason,

---

[42]Thomas Merton, *Opening the Bible* (Collegeville, Minn.: Liturgical Press, 1986), p. 69.
[43]René Descartes, quoted in Küng, *Does God Exist?* p. 10.

and intellect has intended to forgo their use and by some other means to give us the knowledge which we can attain by them.[44]

Nor is this position on biblical interpretation an arbitrary or idiosyncratic one. If I contended that the Qur'an cannot be read as a scientific document, that would be an arbitrary claim. I have never read the Qur'an. But I do read the Bible daily, and my understanding of how Scripture is to be interpreted stands well within the tradition of my denomination, the Episcopal Church. Urban T. Holmes wrote this about the Anglican understanding of authority in the church:

> Our authority is the association of Scripture, tradition and reason. . . .
> Scripture for the Anglican is a fundamental source of authority for the church; but apart from reason it is dangerous. It becomes the mirror for the misdirected person to project his or her own opinions and give them the authority of God. The sin of schism is the result. . . . The Scripture must also be read in the awareness that everyone embodies his or her past and community, that is, their tradition.[45]

Holmes is talking here about a pitfall that every Christian faces in interpreting the Bible: the temptation to use Scripture as personal ammunition. The Anglican tradition seeks to lessen this temptation by providing a fixed cycle of Bible readings:

> The Bible must be read intelligently and as whole. This is why in the Anglican Communion we do not allow ourselves to cherish our favorite book, dismissing those that do not appeal to us, and we reject efforts to pick and choose texts in our sermons that support our own interests. Instead, we read publicly during several years in the Eucharist and Daily Offices . . . the major percentage of the entire Bible.[46]

In his comments on reading the Bible, Holmes goes on to describe several steps that are necessary in understanding Scripture. The first step is to try to establish what the words of the Bible meant when they

---

[44]Stillman Drake, ed. and trans., *Discoveries and Opinions of Galileo* (Garden City, N.Y.: Doubleday Anchor, 1957), pp. 181-83.

[45]Holmes, *What Is Anglicanism?* pp. 11, 13-14.

[46]Ibid., p. 21.

were written: "It is neither desirable nor possible for us to approach Holy Writ with an empty head, but we need to avoid as best we can reading into the words objects of reference which are alien to the period in which they were written."[47] Holmes uses three examples here: prohibition (of alcoholic drinks), the ordination of women to the priesthood, and the supposed superiority of the capitalist economic system. Scripture cannot be used in arguments over these issues, which are modern and outside the consideration of the culture in which the words were written. It is essential to see biblical authors as people existing within a particular time and culture. We should also remember that as readers of Scripture we too live within a certain time and culture, and we must allow our own interpretations to be questioned and challenged in dialogue. "The exploration of the Bible should evoke questions whose answers evoke even more questions. This happens as we share our insights into Holy Writ and allow our interpretation to be challenged by others."[48] In other words, our understanding of Scripture should be a dynamic one and open to change.

What about denominations other than Anglican? Raised a Methodist, I have no memory of being told that conflict existed between Christianity and, say, the theory of evolution. Genesis was not taught as having scientific relevance.

For Catholics, there is the statement "Truth Cannot Contradict Truth" by John Paul II.[49] In addition, the National Conference of Catholic Bishops has prepared a pamphlet titled *Science and the Catholic Church*. In it we find this:

> Much of the tension [between science and religion] comes from "overreaching," trying to extend a body of knowledge or a method beyond its proper bounds. Religious resistance to evolutionary theory, for example, arose in part from a failure to recognize Scripture's limitations as a commentary on nature.[50]

---

[47]Ibid., p. 22.
[48]Ibid., p. 23.
[49]See full reference in note 12, above.
[50]Quote taken from "Science and the Catholic Church," a pamphlet prepared by the National Conference of Catholic Bishops, Committee on Science and Human Values (Washington, D.C.: United States Catholic Conference, 1995), publication no. 085-0.

And from the *Encyclopedia of the Lutheran Church:*

> It is both helpful and important for both disciplines—science and theology—to keep within their area of competence; it is likewise important that the Christian keep in mind that the Word of God is just that and not a textbook on science.[51]

Dissenting voices. The position on biblical interpretation outlined above is well-supported in many Christian groups. But it is not, of course, a matter of universal agreement. In his acclaimed study *The Creationists,* Ronald L. Numbers comments on the increasing strength of creationism in a number of American denominations. He notes that although young-earth creationism is often not distinguished from old-earth creationism in opinion polls, a 1991 Gallup poll found 47 percent of Americans professing belief in "a recent special creation."[52]

The Institute for Creation Research (ICR) is the best-known Christian association for young-earth creationism in the United States. The statement "ICR Tenets of Creationism" includes the following:

> All things in the universe were created and made by God in the six literal days of the creation week described in Genesis 1:1—2:3, and confirmed by Exodus 20:8-11. The creation record is factual, historical, and perspicuous; thus all theories of origins or development which involve evolution in any form are false.[53]

Another document at the ICR site on the Internet is "The Bible Is a Textbook of Science" by Henry Morris. Morris does not mean quite what the title seems to imply: "The Bible is not a scientific textbook in the sense of giving detailed technical descriptions and mathematical formulations of natural phenomena."[54]

But he does believe that there are "numerous portions of Scripture

---

[51]Karl T. Schmidt, "Science and Christianity," in *The Encyclopedia of the Lutheran Church,* ed. Julius Bodensieck (Minneapolis: Augsburg, 1965), 3:2144.

[52]Numbers, *Creationists,* p. 300.

[53]"ICR Tenets of Creationism," Institute for Creation Research, n.d. <www.icr.org/abouticr/tenets.htm>.

[54]Henry M. Morris, "The Bible Is a Textbook of Science," *Bibliotheca Sacra,* October-December 1964, Institute for Creation Research <www.icr.org/bible/tbiatos.htm>.

which *do* deal with natural phenomena and historical events."[55] And in a recent book Morris has written that the "Bible taught clearly and explicitly that all things were made by God in a six-day week of natural days."[56]

Old-earth creationist Hugh Ross lists a number of "biblical statements of cosmological significance" in his book *The Fingerprint of God.* Ross makes the following assertion: "The Bible is the only religious text that teaches a cosmology in full agreement with the latest astrophysical discoveries."[57] Is the reader persuaded one way or the other? No? The underlying problem remains. The unifying element of a Christian interpretation of the Bible is that Christians will not agree on how to interpret the Bible. This is not meant to imply that there is nothing fundamental to Christian belief, that is, that there is nothing you must be in accord with in order to be a Christian. The Nicene Creed is my own starting point, and for a further description I would refer you to *Mere Christianity* by C. S. Lewis.[58] But a particular view on the scientific pertinence of the Bible is not one of those matters essential to being a Christian. You may dispute even this last statement, of course. But you are then faced with a choice: either change your mind or deny that I am Christian. For anyone choosing the latter, there is nothing further to discuss.

But let us say that we *do* agree that a Christian may avoid reading scientific statements into the Bible. What might be the consequences of maintaining the independence of science and Christian theology? Would the benefits outweigh any costs?

Living with Independence: Further Observations on Science and Christianity

☐ *Nonbifurcated people.* Christians who maintain an independence between science and faith are sometimes accused of being "bifurcated" people. That is, our lives are compartmentalized. The religion compartment operates on Sunday—in church—but on Monday the science compartment takes over as work resumes in the laboratory. I've never understood why a job in sci-

[55]Ibid.
[56]Morris, *Biblical Creationism*, p. 13.
[57]Hugh Ross, *The Fingerprint of God,* 2nd ed. (Orange, Calif.: Promise, 1991), pp. 180, 179.
[58]C. S. Lewis, *Mere Christianity* (New York: Macmillan, 1960).

ence should be much different than a job in, say, major league baseball. We operate according to the commonly accepted rules of science just as baseball players have a set of rules in baseball. Science and faith come together in individual people, who experience life as a whole. Stephen Gould writes that

the two magisteria [of science and religion] bump right up against each other, interdigitating in wondrously complex ways along their joint border. Many of our deepest questions call upon aspects of both for different parts of a full answer—and the sorting of legitimate domains can become quite complex and difficult.[59]

I like the physical image that *interdigitating* suggests. Clasp your hands together, fingers and thumbs entwined. You can make a very strong grip that way, but the fingers are still separate entities.

In areas outside biblical interpretation it is human reason that tells us that science and faith remain separate. Imagine that your two-year-old child has a life-threatening bacterial infection. Do you rely on antibiotics or do you rely on prayer?[60] Perhaps you have taken your child to a Christian physician who prescribes a standard antibiotic but who also offers a prayer for the child's health. The child recovers. Was it the antibiotic or was it the prayer?

We may give ourselves a comforting answer: God worked through the antibiotic. And that answer is, I believe, ultimately the truth. God is the source of good in the world. But it is not the scientific truth, nor do we—whatever we claim for Genesis—mistake it for such. Because if the child's illness had worsened, and there was evidence of resistance by this strain of bacteria to the first drug, the physician would try another antibiotic. Neither parents nor doctors rely on God to work through antibiotics that bacteria are resistant to anymore than they would rely on God to heal an infection using sugar pills. What we are really counting on, *at the level of the antibiotic,* is science.

This is not a denial of miracles. Miracles are an activity of God beyond

---

[59]Gould, "Nonoverlapping Magisteria," p. 20.
[60]This example is used to make a point relevant to a substantial percentage of Christians. It is in no way intended to disparage those groups who emphasize reliance on prayer.

the understanding or realm of science. We may believe they occur—I do, anyway—but we do not depend on them. If they could be depended on they would not be miracles.

☐ *Science is a moving target.* Physicist Erwin Schrödinger has written:

> [Immanuel] Kant's attitude toward science was incredibly naïve, as you will agree if you turn the leaves of his *Metaphysical Foundations of Science*. . . . He accepted physical science in the form it had reached during his lifetime (1724-1804) as something more or less final and he busied himself to account for its statements philosophically. This happening to a great genius ought to be a warning to philosophers ever after.[61]

Scientific theories are subject to change. Sometimes the changes are major. So there is always a problem in conflating scriptural interpretation with a scientific theory. What is scientific bedrock today can be quicksand tomorrow. C. S. Lewis warned:

> We must be very cautious of snatching at any scientific theory which, for the moment, seems to be in our favour. We may *mention* such things; but we must mention them lightly and without claiming that they are more than "interesting." Sentences beginning "Science has now proved" should be avoided. If we try to base our apologetic on some recent development in science, we shall usually find that just as we have put the finishing touches to our argument science has changed its mind and quietly withdrawn the theory we have been using as our foundation stone.[62]

The church found this out in the years following Galileo. Various verses of the Bible had been interpreted as scientifically relevant and in support of an earth-centered cosmology. When the cosmology changed, so did interpretation. How often do we want to be in the position of putting theology secondary to science? This is not a game of rock, paper, scissors, where rock won this time, but paper's turn may be next. In issues of science, science wins. In Galileo's case

---

[61]Erwin Schrödinger, *What Is Life?/Mind and Matter* (Cambridge, UK: Cambridge University Press, 1967), p. 158.
[62]C. S. Lewis, *God in the Dock*, ed. Walter Hooper (Grand Rapids, Mich.: Eerdmans, 1970), p. 92.

the Church lost, not because scientific and secular enterprises became more powerful in ensuing years, nor because the Catholic hierarchy lost influence, nor indeed for any reason requiring sophisticated historical analysis.
The Church lost because the earth rotates around the sun.[63]

Stanley Jaki has made a study of the problems that various people—from the time of the Jewish sages and the church fathers through to the present day—have encountered in the interpretation of the first chapter of Genesis. Jaki says his story is a dismal one. He describes the great intellects of the church as, one after another, they go through mental contortions trying to fit the verses of Genesis 1 to whatever happened to be the science of the time.[64]

Currently (apart from young-earth creationists), the primary use of Scripture in support of science, or vice versa, is with reference to the big bang theory in physics. This theory says that the observed universe came into existence through the rapid expansion of all known matter and energy from a single point of infinite density. This expansion is thought to have started some ten to twenty billion years ago with "the big bang." The theory also implies that time itself has a starting point. Genesis 1:1 is generally quoted as relevant to big bang physics, and sometimes verses from the New Testament are added:

In the beginning God created the heavens and the earth. (Gen 1:1 NIV)

Who hath saved us, and called us with an holy calling, not according to our works, but according to his own purpose and grace, which was given us in Christ Jesus before the world began. (2 Tim 1:9 KJV)

In hope of eternal life, which God, that cannot lie, promised before the world began. (Tit 1:2 KJV)

Genesis 1:1 is used because it suggests creation *ex nihilo* ("out of nothing") at a specific time (but see Jaki, who says that exegetical opinion has not been unanimous on that point).[65] The phrase "before the world began" from Titus and 2 Timothy is also suggested to be in accord with big bang,

---

[63]Jean Pond, "Catholic Frogs," *Faculty Dialogue,* fall 1992, p. 84.
[64]Jaki, *Genesis 1.*
[65]Ibid., pp. 2-6.

since the theory gives a defined beginning point to the universe, "before" which there could be only God.[66] I should note that I needed to use the King James Version for the two New Testament verses. The Revised Standard Version translates the phrase "before the world began" as "ages ago" in each case, which does not have quite the same big bang ring and which may point out the difficulties of making fine exegetical points in a different language a few thousand years removed from the original.

English *is* a notoriously unruly language, capable of endless nuance. It is all too easy to read into words the things you wish to hear. An acquaintance of mine—a member of the Episcopal clergy—was upset with a passage in the "new" (1979) Book of Common Prayer. This book is used in the direction of services (e.g., morning prayer, evening prayer, the Eucharist) in the Episcopal church.

The offending passage was a prayer said before communion in praise of God:

> At your command all things came to be: the vast expanse of interstellar space, galaxies, suns, the planets in their courses, and this fragile earth, our island home. By your will they were created and have their being.

> From the primal elements you brought forth the human race, and blessed us with memory, reason, and skill.[67]

My acquaintance was disturbed by this prayer *because it was pro-evolution.* Would this also be the reader's conclusion?

☐ *"I fear the Greeks even when they bear gifts."*

> Logic demands that if I assume life is inexplicable and turn this into proof for the existence of God, then I must allow the use of explicability as a criterion for his absence.... This is how the vitalist banishes the Creator of the universe from our everyday world into distant nooks and crannies.[68]

---

[66]Ross, *Fingerprint of God*, p. 180.

[67]*The Book of Common Prayer According to the Use of the Episcopal Church* (New York: Oxford University Press, 1979), p. 370. The passage is part of eucharistic prayer C of rite two.

[68]Hoimar von Ditfurth, *The Origins of Life: Evolution as Creation* (San Francisco: Harper & Row, 1982), pp. 105-6.

Scientific data is equal-opportunity data. Once inside the arena of theology or philosophy it can be used by anyone. As a young undergraduate at Cambridge University, Charles Darwin had studied and been much impressed by the work of William Paley, the author of *Natural Theology; or, Evidences of the Existence and Attributes of the Deity, collected from the Appearances of Nature* (first published in 1802). As the title suggests, Paley's arguments focused on deducing the existence of God from evidences of design in nature. In making this argument Paley had described his world as a happy one, minimizing the existence of suffering and pain: "I believe the cases of bites which produce death in large animals (of stings I think there are none) to be very few."[69]

After a five year voyage around the world on HMS Beagle and another twenty years of study in biology, Darwin could no longer agree. He was particularly disturbed by the example of the parasitic Ichneumon wasps: "I cannot persuade myself that a beneficent and omnipotent God would have designedly created the Ichneumonidae with the express intention of their feeding within the living bodies of Caterpillars."[70]

If nature's beauty is grounds for the existence of God, what does its ugliness reveal? You can get around this puzzle, of course, by assuming that the ugly bits are a consequence of the Fall. But the result (beauty, God; ugliness, the Fall), is unsatisfying in a *scientific sense*.

Similarly, if good design is evidence for a creator, what is bad design? The martyrs to back pain among us might ask, with Stephen Gould: "Why does our body, from the bones of our back to the musculature of our belly, display the vestiges of an arrangement better suited for quadrupedal life?"[71]

Should we conclude that Adam was four-footed before the Fall?

Another case illustrating the equal-opportunity nature of science is the use of big bang cosmology as evidence supporting the existence of God. It is becoming popular to believe that it does so. But if you allow the argument in one direction, you must be prepared for argument in the other. In

---

[69]William Paley, quoted in Sir Gavin de Beer, "Biology Before the *Beagle*," in *Charles Darwin: A Scientific Biography* (New York: 1964), and reprinted in Philip Appleman, ed., *Darwin*, 2nd ed. (New York: W. W. Norton, 1979), p. 9.

[70]From a letter Darwin wrote to Asa Gray, quoted in Desmond and Moore, *Darwin*, p. 479.

[71]Gould, "Darwinism Defined," p. 68.

the book *Theism, Atheism, and Big Bang Cosmology,* philosophers William Lane Craig and Quentin Smith engage in a debate on this very point. Both agree that "empirical evidence warrants the belief that the universe began to exist with the Big Bang about 15 billion years ago."[72] Craig uses big bang cosmology in support of the existence of a personal Creator of the universe. Smith argues the *opposite:*

> If the arguments in this paper are sound, then God does not exist if Big Bang cosmology, or some relevantly similar theory, is true. If this cosmology is true, our universe exists without cause and without explanation.[73]

I will let Stanley Jaki state the conclusion:

> To take any verse of Genesis 1 (or of the entire Bible for that matter) for a scientific guideline invites the logic of consistency expressed in the phrase about the gander, the goose, and the sauce.[74]

☐ *Supernatural explanations* in science *are not intellectually satisfying.*

Sherlock Holmes: Well, I see a bit of some strange paste in this tin. And there was something oddly familiar about that portrait of Hugo Baskerville. But—we have no case—it is all surmise and conjecture. The best inference, my dear Watson, is that Sir Charles was killed by a gigantic hound from Hell.

Dr. Watson: I beg your pardon?
(with apologies to Sir Arthur Conan Doyle)

Doing research on a difficult problem in science is sometimes described as being like a detective in a murder mystery. At first, everything is confused. There might be a bit of evidence here, a shred of a clue there. But nothing fits together to make a coherent explanation of what has happened. Good mystery writers will throw in false clues, a red herring or two—the more deviously plausible, the better for the story.

---

[72]William Lane Craig and Quentin Smith, *Theism, Atheism, and Big Bang Cosmology* (New York: Oxford University Press, 1993), p. vi.
[73]Ibid., p. 216.
[74]Jaki, *Genesis 1,* p. 301.

Sir Arthur Conan Doyle was particularly adept—in his Sherlock Holmes stories—at variations on the locked-room mystery. The victim is found in some situation (such as a room locked from the inside) where it seems impossible that a crime could have occurred. The clues first appear hopelessly inadequate for even Holmes to solve the case. In *The Hound of the Baskervilles,* for example, one of the characters suggests that the death of Sir Charles Baskerville may be a problem that the detective cannot handle:

"There is a realm in which the most acute and most experienced of detectives is helpless."

"You mean that the thing is supernatural?"

"I did not positively say so."

"No, but you evidently think it."[75]

This character—Dr. Mortimer—believes that Sir Charles may have been run to his death by "the curse of the Baskervilles"—a very large and quite supernatural dog. In the end, of course, the real murderer is caught, and Holmes provides Dr. Watson with a logical, rational explanation for every relevant detail of the story. How surprised Watson would be if Holmes had settled for Mortimer's explanation! And how disappointed the reader!

Explanations involving God are not satisfactory explanations *in science,* whether you are talking about how worms wriggle or how life originated on earth. This is not because it is impossible that they might be the *only* true explanations. I have already stated that as a Christian I believe God created the universe and everything in it. It is just the details of *how* this happened that I question scientifically. It is certainly possible that the *only* true explanation for the origin of life on earth is that "God did it." It is possible that there will *never* be a natural (as opposed to supernatural) theory to explain, for example, the first cells. "God did it" is a straightforward answer and has the virtue of simplicity. But it is no more intellectually satisfying to most scientists *in a scientific context* than the demon hound theory was to Sherlock Holmes.

---

[75]Arthur Conan Doyle, "The Hound of the Baskervilles," in *The Complete Sherlock Holmes* (Garden City, N.Y.: Doubleday, 1930), 2:680-81.

☐ *God from a machine.* This is also not to say that explanations involving God are intellectually unsatisfying *per se.* Is there a purpose for our lives? *Why* does the universe exist? What is our moral responsibility to our neighbors? For Christians, God has a place in the answer to each of these questions because we accept the reality of a supernatural realm. But in *science* invoking a supernatural force is the equivalent of cheating in sport, that is, the equivalent of introducing a factor that—regardless of relative training, effort, or skill—will always allow one person or one team to win. In literature, this cheating is referred to as *deus ex machina*—God from a machine. The *deus ex machina* is an unexpected and contrived solution to a difficult problem of the plot.

In ancient Greece it was expected that some plays would end with one of the gods tidying up loose ends. Plot difficulties can always be solved in this way, but it is not considered satisfying in a *literary* sense when the device is overused. Nor are playwrights considered atheists if they finish their stories without recourse to supernatural intervention. Consider also a real-life murder investigation. In a perplexing case is it not always *possible* that the real solution is a supernatural one?—God struck the victim dead. And yet the public would be very unhappy with the detective who closed a case using this hypothesis as a rationale. We do not call it materialistic philosophy when murder cases are left open in the absence of material evidence: we call it good police practice.

☐ *The cat is always right.* Hoimar von Ditfurth writes: "To this day science is by definition the attempt to see how far man and nature can be explained without recourse to miracles."[76] This is not a statement of a materialist philosophy. This is an explanation of the rules of the game. The rules are well understood. The game has been a highly successful one in the past and continues successful today. Playing the game according to the rules does not make one an atheist. Science is fun, a job, the road to fame, interesting. It is powerful, provides endless ethical problems to think about, disciplines the mind. Science fascinates young children. It can provide moments of awe. It is one of the things human beings do while shuffling around on earth.

Science is never completely under the control of scientists. We may wander off with our theories for a while, but nature always fights back. The

---

[76]Von Ditfurth, *The Origins of Life,* p. 177.

physical world is an uncontrolled vision of God. It can (we believe) be understood by our reason, but it is not controlled by our reason.

David Hicks, a member of the biology department of Whitworth College, used to teach a laboratory class in the dissection of preserved cats. As is common in dissections, the diagrams in the textbook often did not match the reality of the inside of the animal. A student, confused, asked which was correct: the diagram or the cat? "Ah," said Dr. Hicks, "the cat is always right."

Independence and Origins

Finite or infinite? I turn now to the question of origins: the origin of the universe, the earth and life on earth. What does the principle of keeping independence between science and Christian theology imply for these issues in particular? For the origin of the universe the current consensus in cosmology and physics is that the big bang theory accounts best for the observational data we now have and is supported by excellent and straightforward evidence, including the (approximately) 2.7 degree Kelvin cosmic background radiation. The age of the universe, although still under discussion, seems to be within the ten to twenty billion year range.

Such an ancient universe is rejected by young-earth creationists on biblical grounds. On the other hand, old-earth creationists and others, as discussed earlier, feel that it is supported biblically and, in fact, that the big bang is evidence for the existence of God.

For the adherent to NOMA, of course, the Bible neither supports nor refutes the big bang, or vice versa. We are happy to accept the cosmological knowledge that the big bang offers, but we recognize that (as a scientific theory) it is subject to revision. We may find, personally, that the big bang fits well (or does not fit well) with our overall worldview, including our idea of what is aesthetically pleasing in nature. If we are Christians, we do not worry about it too much one way or the other.

I think that an individual's response to big bang cosmology (as to the earlier, competing steady-state cosmology) tends to be primarily an emotional one. It has been suggested, with good evidence, that British astronomer Fred Hoyle championed steady-state theories in part to avoid the supposed theistic implications of a big-bang universe.[77] Others have noted

---

[77]Craig and Smith, *Theism,* pp. 43-47.

that the big bang just *feels* wrong to them. In a 1967 book review for *Scientific American*, cosmologist Dennis Sciama wrote:

> I must add that for me the loss of the steady-state theory has been a cause of great sadness. The steady-state theory has a sweep and beauty that for some unaccountable reason the architect of the universe appears to have overlooked. The universe in fact is a botched job, but I suppose we shall have to make the best of it.[78]

There is no theological ground to be gained by making the universe finite as opposed to infinite. Each has its mysteries, and each seems inexplicable in some ultimate sense. We may dig scientifically into questions of how the universe exists but science cannot tell us *why*.

Planet earth and the life on it. Current consensus in physics and geology says that the earth is about four billion years old. Life, in the form of one-celled organisms, seems to have begun on earth about three and a half billion years ago. The theory of evolution, which has been around in one form or another from the time of the ancient Greeks, tells us that the living things on earth, past and present, are related. That is, we are all part of creation's three and a half billion year old family tree.

Evolutionary ideas were never particularly convincing to scientists until Charles Darwin published *The Origin of Species* in 1859. Darwin's great contribution was to provide a mechanism by which evolution could have occurred. The shorthand term biologists use for this mechanism is *natural selection*. In the years since 1859 other mechanisms (such as endosymbiosis) have been added to evolutionary theory as a whole. Advances in molecular biology, itself a young science, have proved highly pertinent, and the field of evolution is currently in a state of creative ferment.

This creative ferment has been mistaken by some for weakness. If we return to the analogy of a pattern on fabric, individual threads of evolutionary theory have been strengthened or weakened, broken or added, but the overall picture remains the same. There is no "proof" of evolution in the sense that all possible relevant questions now have satisfactory answers. Writing about the Galileo affair, Owen Gingerich points out that "science as we have come to use it relies very little on proof. Science is primarily

---

[78]Dennis Sciama, "Book Review," *Scientific American* 217 (September 1967): 293.

looking for a self-consistent description of nature that hangs together in a convincing way. . . . Science works by coherence, not by proof." [79] "Nothing in biology makes sense except in light of evolution," said geneticist Theodosius Dobzhansky, [80] and the theory (imperfect as it may be) brings a profoundly satisfying coherence to the field.

Is the idea of the common descent of all life on earth contrary to Scripture? According to some, the words of Genesis indicate that it must be: "God made the wild animals of the earth of every kind, and the cattle of every kind, and everything that creeps upon the ground of every kind. And God saw that it was good" (Gen 1:25). According to others, these words were never intended to be descriptive of a particular method of creation. Again it is a question of interpretive style, with the NOMA principle coming down firmly on the side of *not* restricting verses such as Genesis 1:25 to any scientific sense. Disagreements over the manner in which different animal and plant species arrived on earth have tended to move away from "is too, is not" theology into debates about the scientific validity of the theory of evolution. It would be fruitless to argue the scientific specifics here, and I can only remind the reader that biology, like theology, is a *discipline*.

Beyond the first cell. That evolution has occurred—that organisms are connected by common descent—seems clear to most biologists, Christian and non-Christian, even while the importance of the various mechanisms involved is being debated. But what about the emergence of that first cell? Various ideas have been proposed to explain—scientifically—how this might have happened. None of them seems complete or particularly convincing to me. This is a cause for great rejoicing, as I contemplate how many fascinating things we have yet to learn.

Nevertheless, it has been argued that it is *impossible* to explain the origin of the first cells without recourse to supernatural intervention. For example, it is contended that there is *no* mechanistic way to account for the complexity of DNA sequences in even the simplest cell. Perhaps it is so. But any statement of impossibility seems premature, given our current level of understanding with regard to DNA and with regard to conditions on the

[79]Owen Gingerich, "How Galileo Changed the Rules of Science," *Sky and Telescope* 85 (March 1993): 36.

[80]Theodosius Dobzhansky, quoted in Jan Sapp, *Evolution by Association: A History of Symbiosis* (New York: Oxford University Press, 1994), p. 187.

pre-biotic earth. Less than sixty years ago biologists were still arguing over whether DNA or protein was the molecule carrying genetic information. We got our first idea of DNA structure only forty-five years ago. It is difficult to predict what may come next—or when.

The most important knowledge in science is the knowledge that we don't know we don't know. I am reluctant to believe—in fact, I would be amazed to learn—that the physical universe has now run out of major surprises. But in addition, to insist on the *impossibility* of a purely scientific solution to the origins of the first cell bothers me as a Christian. There are two ways to account for the origins of the first cell: it happened in a "natural" way, open to human theory and investigation, or in a supernatural way, obscured to human science. I can imagine that either may be true, but the only *scientific* possibility is the former. Why limit God to one choice? Other Christians have been troubled on this same point. In 1982 the 67th General Convention of the Episcopal Church passed a resolution urging the rejection of "Creationism" on the grounds (in part) that it imposes limits on God:

> "Creationism and "Creation-science" . . . specify certain methods and timing of the creative acts, and impose limits on these acts which are neither scriptural nor accepted by many Christians. . . .
>
> Resolved, that the 67th General Convention affirm the glorious ability of God to create in any manner, whether men understand it or not.[81]

Conclusions

Reasons to believe. From the time of Galileo science has challenged our interpretations of the Bible. For some Christians science threatens a way of looking at Scripture that makes sense to them and is fulfilling. Christian evolutionists, of which there are many, recognize that the theory of evolution has been profoundly disturbing to some people. Scientific materialists, whether scientists themselves or not, add to the discord with claims that things that cannot be studied scientifically cannot exist.

---

[81]The full text of this resolution is available on the "Voices for Evolution" website: <www.aaas.org/SPP/DSPP/DBSR/Voices/Voicetoc.htm> (see part three, "Religious Organizations"). Similar statements from other denominations are available at this same site.

If we maintain an independence between science and theology, if we allow each the proper authority within its own field, many of these problems are avoided. Gould calls this a position of mutual humility:

> NOMA represents a principled position on moral and intellectual grounds, not a mere diplomatic stance. NOMA also cuts both ways. If religion can no longer dictate the nature of factual conclusions properly under the magisterium of science, then scientists cannot claim higher insight into moral truth from any superior knowledge of the world's empirical constitution. This mutual humility has important practical consequences in a world of such diverse passions.[82]

With the independence of science and theology, science can make no claims to represent the sum of reality.

To ignore the evidences of science—to deny the fruitfulness and power of the big bang theory in physics or evolution in biology—is to make too little of the authority of science within its own domain. Historically this has not been a successful endeavor, and when the church has tried it, the church has been forced to retreat. The Christian's relationship with God does not grant him or her the authority to make pronouncements regarding the veracity of scientific theories.

To try to *combine* science and theology—to fit science into a pretty package and tie a religious ribbon around it—is to ask for a different kind of trouble. H. L. Mencken (early-twentieth-century American journalist and critic) had an appropriately irreverent description of the scientist: "[A scientist] is not the liberator releasing slaves, the good Samaritan lifting up the fallen, but a dog sniffing tremendously at an infinite series of rat holes."[83] Do not mix science up with the search for ultimate answers about the meaning of life when it has its nose down a rat hole. Christians should not feel the need to shore up their faith with science. Only a fool despises Christians for being imperfect. But imperfect as we are, we do not need to be inactive. While science may challenge our *interpretation* of Scripture, it cannot invalidate our faith. If Christian lives are transformed—if we are

[82]Gould, "Nonoverlapping Magisteria," pp. 61-62.
[83]H. L. Mencken, quoted in René Dubos, *Reason Awake: Science for Man* (New York: Columbia University Press, 1970), p. 31.

welcoming strangers and dealing charitably with our neighbors—if we are feeding the hungry, clothing the poor, visiting the sick and imprisoned— then there will be enough reasons to believe. Thomas Merton writes that we go to Scripture with questions about the meaning of life, but the Bible asks back, When do you intend to start living?[84]

---

[84]Merton, *Opening the Bible*, p. 30.

A Creationist Response

Wayne Frair & Gary D. Patterson

We commend the promotion of mutual humility in the relationship between science and Christian theology by Jean Pond. One of the best principles of Christian living is expressed in Philippians 2:3: "Do nothing out of selfish ambition or vain conceit, but in humility consider others as better than yourselves" (NIV). As Christians we should take the lead in seeking true peace.

Pond's opening paragraph raises the important question of the relevance of someone's personal background in the practice of science. One of the most hallowed assumptions of most scientists is that, in the long run, the data and conclusions reached by the practice of science are universal and do not depend on when or where they were obtained. We share this scientific faith, but we also recognize the uncertain path that usually leads to the recognition of truly general principles. As scientists we should more openly acknowledge the provisional nature of most scientific conclusions. One of the greatest freedoms of healthy science is the right to be wrong. If we are forced to defend our current errors rather than to consider new data and better arguments, we abandon the path that leads to truth.

While the philosophy of Plato was highly appreciated by Christian theologians in the patristic period, the systems of Aristotle held sway in the scholastic era. Since neither of these philosophies is derived from the Bible, we should learn from the history of the Copernicans that a commitment by Christian theologians to a particular non-Christian worldview will lead to conflict when the reigning consensus changes. Unless there is some degree of independence between Christian theology and science, our faith will depend on the latest scientific reports and hastily concocted explanations. If, on the other hand, our interpretation of the Bible is completely independent of external knowledge, the result tends to be some form of rigid dogma rather than a living faith. The extent to which current scientific thinking should be incorporated in the interpretation of the Bible is not a settled question, but the two limiting cases do not commend themselves.

One of the most characteristic aspects of the practice of science is to see the connections between different observations. There is an obvious commonality among all living organisms, which has only been reinforced by modern scientific investigations. A Christian theological response to these studies is that all creatures have a common Creator. Since this conclusion is based on biblical revelation, it does not depend on the details of biology. One scientific response is that all living organisms are related by a common ancestry. A common fallacy is the proposition that acceptance of the common ancestry theory requires rejection of the common Creator doctrine. This rigid coupling assertion is promoted by both militant atheists, who believe that the scientific evidence is so strong that atheism is assured, and by militant theists. As Christians we can rest assured that God is the Creator and patiently consider the scientific observations of past and present living organisms. As scientists we can search for the connections between the observations in terms of physical mechanisms that can be demonstrated in the laboratory or the field. In the words of one of the other authors of this book, science should not be held hostage by either militant group.

Francis Schaeffer stressed the importance of consistency between Christian doctrine and daily living. It does matter what we teach. We share Pond's concern for the personal consequences of public actions. While the actions of militant atheists have often fanned the flames of controversy, this is no excuse for Christians to cease to behave like Christ or to mistake the antireligious opinions of atheists for the sober conclusions of legitimate science. As Christians who are also scientists, we can help to educate our brethren about scientific issues that impact our Christian faith. As scientists who are also Christians, we can demonstrate that the study of God's creation does not require any loss of commitment to our faith. The fate of Darwin is not the inevitable consequence of becoming a scientist.

Stephen Jay Gould is a popular writer with a large following. The article cited by Pond from *Natural History* is generally gracious and has much to recommend it. Gould affirms his commitment to a respectful discourse with constant input from both religion and science toward a common goal of wisdom. While openly acknowledging his own agnosticism, he recognizes that science alone is not sufficient to guide humankind. He appears to believe in the ability of *Homo sapiens* to create moral meaning by talking with one another. However, his generous spirit does not extend to people (Christians) who doubt evolution. He denies that they are sincere or that they have good will. Marginalization is an equal opportunity vice.

We share Pond's position that the methods of science and the methods of Christian theology are different, and that an appreciation of these differences must be taken into account in any discussion that requires input from both disciplines. The humility that acknowledges the limitations of science and the fallibility of Christian theology make possible a fruitful discourse, rather than a struggle for supremacy that demeans both human activities. The attempt of scientists to explain one observation in terms of other observations means that the methods of science cannot answer all questions of relevance to humankind. Nor should Christian theologians denigrate the methods of science as godless when only observable phenomena are considered.

We agree that the Bible must be interpreted afresh by every generation. The interpretation of a stable text depends on the creation of conceptual tools. The hard work of hermeneutics is worth the effort, and we have faith that unnecessary conflict will be reduced by careful exegesis. The role of presuppositions in the interpretation of the Bible or DNA still needs to be acknowledged. If the Bible is believed to be a meaningless collection of human inventions, the connections between various passages will be missed because they are not expected to be there. If DNA is expected to be nothing but the current product of a random process, the purpose of many of the sequences will be missed because the existence of "junk" DNA is predicted by that model. We believe that the new frontier of DNA analysis will yield exciting new discoveries as we learn to interpret the "text" better.

One appropriate time period to consider for Christian theology is the first century. Substantial new data was being revealed, and the response of the Christian community is recorded in the New Testament. One of our problems today is that we discount the value of those revelations and either insist on reoccurrences or deny the reality of the originals. The New Testament presents the Holy Spirit as the great consensus builder in the Christian church. We must acknowledge our sin in presenting a divided church to the world when the power to do otherwise exists.

As scientists who are humans and Christians, we join Pond in reiterating the limited domain of scientific inquiry. We thoroughly enjoy the practice of science, but there is much more to life than is envisaged by the evolution of a point in phase space. We also concur with Pond's exposure of the fallacy of extending the meaning of science beyond the range of its data. For example, Social Darwinism was an attempt to use the prestige of biological Darwinism to promote genocide. We also share Pond's concern that the Bible be allowed to speak in its own voice and that modern concepts and questions should not be imposed on the text. The most fundamental questions of humankind have not changed, and the Bible is just as relevant today as ever for these issues.

We agree that both science and Christian theology are important inputs to our ongoing lives and that we must integrate them in practice as we seek wisdom. The appearance of cruelty in the biological world is a good example of the failure to distinguish scientific from theological concepts. Accusing a wasp of cruelty is a projection of our own moral notions onto a morally neutral cycle of life. Without the moral compass provided by the Bible, we tend to distort both our practice of science and our theological reasoning. Without the clarifying observations of the external world, we tend to misinterpret the biblical text.

We commend Pond's repeated insistence that the field of human discourse is larger than the restricted domains of science or Christian theology and that parochial views are a hindrance to wisdom. Respect for the discipline of science is not disrespect for the supernatural realm. We agree that in matters of science, clear observations are to be trusted over any conjecture, whatever its source. The explosion in our ability to observe the biological world also leads us to be excited about the future prospects of the discipline of biology. The humility promoted by this chapter will be a liberating influence on the conceptual frameworks adopted to produce coherence in the explanation of the observations.

It is interesting to recount a visit of Harvard professor Owen Gingerich to Pittsburgh. While at Carnegie Mellon University he delivered a lecture sponsored by the Templeton Foundation on the history of the Galileo affair. As part of his visit the history and philosophy of science faculty at the University of Pittsburgh invited him to give a lunch talk on a subject of his choice. He chose to address the question, "Dare a scientist believe in design?" The talk was repeatedly interrupted by members of the biology faculty who tried to prevent him from introducing evidence or arguments that were most coherently explained by the existence of an intrinsic design in the structure of the universe. Apparently the concept of design was felt to be so threatening to these scientists that only an inappropriate emotional response was possible. Owen Gingerich is a very humble man, and he was gracious throughout this ordeal. His Christian grace triumphed over the boorish behavior of a parochial group of biologists.

We believe that the time has come when questions of design in biology should not be confused with attempts to impose theological presuppositions on science. Biology neither proves nor disproves the existence of God, and biologists should be free to employ those conceptual frameworks that bring the greatest coherence to the observations. More than one framework may be necessary to account for the full range of data. Restricting discussion to one nineteenth-century idea seems to compromise the creativity necessary to reach the next level of description. We share Jean Pond's excitement as new ideas create the intellectual ferment needed to bring light to a very complicated subject. The study of the many mechanisms used by cells to conserve the information contained in DNA has revealed a complex interdependent set of molecules that test and repair the native DNA constantly. On the other hand, the molecular basis of the incredible number of substances that the human body can recognize as foreign and against which it can mount an allergic response requires a truly combinatorial generation of DNA molecules in a short time period. A full spectrum of mechanisms will be necessary to explain the full range of even the present data. Attempts to impose philosophical atheism or any form of supernaturalism on biology will not help to identify new mechanisms or to create the truly coherent frameworks needed to explain the complex phenomena of physical life.

We join Pond in concluding that the Christian life is more than a philosophical debate. We observe the transformations of other humans and interpret them as the activity of God in the world. We experience the interactions with other Christians and interpret their actions toward us as evidence of the reality of Jesus Christ in their lives. We experience the activity of the Holy Spirit bearing witness with our spirit that we are children of God, and we conclude that Jesus Christ is real to us. We express the love of God to others in practical ways, and the cycle of Christian life continues.

A Qualified Agreement Response
Stephen C. Meyer

Jean Pond defends the "independence" of science and Christianity. Following Stephen Jay Gould she insists that "the teachings" of science and Christianity "occupy distinctly different domains," or what Gould calls "non-overlapping magisteria" (or NOMA).[1] Pond insists, quoting Gould, that "science covers the empirical universe; what it is made of (fact) and why it works this way (theory)," while "religion extends over questions of moral meaning and value" (p. 71). In her view, scientific discoveries and theories (properly understood) cannot have any larger religious or metaphysical implications (whether favorable or unfavorable to Christian belief). According to Pond scientific theories and religious doctrines have different interests altogether, indeed even when they seem to address the same topic such as the origin of the universe or the origin of life. Pond argues that those who think otherwise either misappropriate science or misinterpret the Bible (or both). Thus Pond insists that the teachings of science can neither support nor contradict the teachings of Christianity (or vice versa). As she puts it aphoristically, "There are no Catholic frogs."

While admittedly science and biblical Christianity do often address many different subjects (and while, clearly, there are no Catholic frogs!), it does not follow that science and Christianity *never* make claims about the

---

[1]Stephen Jay Gould, *Rocks of Ages: Science and Religion in the Fullness of Life* (New York: Ballantine, 1999), p. 5.

same subject in clearly comparable propositional language. Pond, following Gould, however, attempts to define the factual/empirical world as the *exclusive* province of science and to limit the interest of religion to matters of morality and meaning. If this were true, the case for "independence" would hardly need defending. Unfortunately, the relationship between science and religion is not quite as simple as Pond and Gould make it out to be.

In the first place, Christianity in particular does not simply address questions of morality and meaning as Gould's NOMA principle asserts, but it also makes factual claims about history, human nature and, it would seem, the origin of the natural world. The historic creeds of the church, as well as the Bible itself, make this abundantly clear. Consider, for example, the Apostles' Creed: "I believe in God the Father Almighty, Maker of heaven and earth: And in Jesus Christ his only Son, our Lord; Who was conceived by the Holy Spirit, born of the Virgin Mary, suffered under Pontius Pilate, was crucified, dead, and buried; the third day He rose again from the dead." Note that this creed contains a series of affirmations about real actions and events, most of which allegedly occurred in space, time and history. The Bible too makes specific factual claims, chiefly about the history of the Jewish people, the life of Jesus and the early church, but also about other factual matters including the nature and origin of the natural world (see below). Luke's Gospel, for example, indicates that Jesus of Nazareth began his public ministry during the reign of Tiberius Caesar, when Pontius Pilate was governor of Judea, Herod was tetrarch of Galilee, and Lysanius was tetrarch of Abilene (Lk 3:1-2). The Gospels insist that Jesus was tried before Pilate when Caiaphas served as the Jewish high priest, and that during this trial one of Jesus' disciples, a fisherman named Peter, denied knowing Jesus three times. These are specific factual claims. Though certainly the narrative that encompasses these events does have larger moral and theological meaning, it does not *just* include statements about morality and meaning.[2]

---

[2]Instead, it includes specific claims about events that the Bible writers claim to have observed empirically within space and time, and that consequently invite either empirical refutation or corroboration by archaeological and other historical evidence. As 1 John 1:1 says, "That . . . which we have heard, which we have seen with our eyes, which we have looked at and our hands have touched—this we proclaim" (NIV).

The Bible, taken at face value, also seems to affirm that God created and designed the natural world (Gen 1:1; Job 38—41; Ps 104:24; Is 42:5; Jn 1:3; Rev 4:11), that the universe and time itself began as a result of his initial creative act (Gen 1:1; 2 Tim 1:9; Tit 1:2), and that God formed the physical universe in such a way that his power and wisdom are "clearly seen, being understood from what has been made" (Rom 1:20 NIV; cf. Ps 19:1-4). The Bible also assumes that humans have the freedom to choose between alternative courses of action (Gal 6:7-8; 2 Pet 3:5) but nevertheless also have a proclivity to selfish (sinful) behavior (Rom 3). Thus the Bible appears to make claims not only about events in human history but also about human nature, the origin of the natural world and the kind of evidence that should remain in it as a result of God's creation and design.

In the second place, science does not just address questions about the material composition of the natural world or questions about why (or how) the world operates as it does, as Gould and Pond claim. Instead, science also addresses many of the same kinds of questions that religious belief systems (including Christianity) address; admittedly though, such questions are not the focus of most scientific research.[3] Nevertheless, historical scientists, for example, address questions about what happened in the past (as Gould himself acknowledges in other writings)[4] or about what happened in the past *to cause* certain entities to originate.[5] Thus neo-Darwinian and chemical evolutionary theories make claims, (as does the Bible, see below) about the causes by which life arose and the cause of the appearance of design in the living world. Similarly, social scientists ask questions about

---

[3]The majority of scientific research focuses on more ideologically neutral questions about how the natural world works or what it is made of. But scientists, acting in their capacity as scientists, also ask questions with larger metaphysical and religious implications—questions that various religions also address.

[4]Stephen Jay Gould, "Evolution as Fact and Theory" and "Genesis and Geology," in *Science and Creationism*, ed. Ashley Montagu (New York: Oxford University Press, 1984), pp. 117-25, 126-35; and his "The Senseless Signs of History," in *The Panda's Thumb* (New York: W. W. Norton, 1980), pp. 27-34.

[5]Gould notes that historical scientists use observation of present-day evidences to reconstruct historical events or causes. In his words, historical scientists proceed by "inferring history from its results" (Stephen Jay Gould, "Evolution and the Triumph of Homology: Or, Why History Matters," *American Scientist* 74 [1986]: 61). See also Stephen C. Meyer, "Of Clues and Causes: A Methodological Interpretation of Origin of Life Studies" (Ph.D. dissertation, Cambridge University, 1990).

the causes of human behavior and about the nature of human nature itself. Thus some schools of psychological thought have characterized humans not as free moral agents (as the Bible appears to do) but as creatures completely determined in their behavior by either environmental, genetic or physiological factors.[6] Some biologists (sociobiologists and neurophysiologists) have even addressed questions about the nature and origin of human morality[7] and the nature and cause of religious belief.[8]

It certainly appears that biblical Christianity has something to say about these questions.[9] Nevertheless, those committed to the NOMA principle

---

[6]B. F. Skinner argued that human behavior is entirely determined by environmental factors. He states, "A person does not act on the world, the world acts on him" (B. F. Skinner, *Beyond Freedom and Dignity* [New York: Alfred A. Knopf, 1971], p. 211). Michael Ruse and sociobiologist E. O. Wilson argue that science teaches that genes determine our behavior: "Our starting point is with science. Two propositions appear to have been established beyond any reasonable doubt. First, the social behaviour of animals is firmly under the control of the genes, and has been shaped into forms that give reproductive advantages. Secondly, humans are animals" (Michael Ruse and E. O. Wilson, "The Evolution of Ethics," in *Religion and the Natural Sciences: The Range of Engagement*, ed. J. E. Huchingson [Orlando, Fla.: Harcourt Brace 1993], pp. 308-9).

[7]Michael Ruse and E. O. Wilson explain the origin of human morality as the result of natural selection: "As evolutionists we see that no [ethical] justification of the traditional kind [of morality] is possible. Morality, or more strictly our belief in morality, is merely an adaptation put in place to further our reproductive ends. Hence the basis of ethics does not lie in God's will. . . . Ethics is illusory inasmuch as it persuades us that it has an objective reference. This is the crux of the biological position"(Ruse and Wilson, "Evolution of Ethics," p. 310).

[8]J. L. Saver and J. Rabin argue that certain physiological structures in the brain give rise (or predispose some) to religious experience (see J. L. Saver and J. Rabin, "The Neural Substrates of Religious Experience," *Journal of Neuro-Psychiatry & Clinical Neuroscience* 9, no. 3 [1997]: 498-510). Further, some sociologists explain religious experience (such as speaking in tongues) as a product of certain kinds of group dynamics. Earlier Sigmund Freud explained all religious experience as the result of a psychological projection of a human wish for a strong father figure (see Sigmund Freud, *The Future of an Illusion*, trans. W. D. Robson-Scott [New York: Doubleday, 1957]). On the other hand, the Bible claims that legitimate religious experience results from the activity of the Holy Spirit (Acts 2). Thus both social and biological theories and the Bible give causal explanations of the same phenomenon, again contradicting NOMA.

[9]Most religious belief systems provide answers to certain fundamental questions, questions about the origin of the natural world, the nature of human nature and the nature and origin of morality. When particular scientific fields address these same questions, they intersect with the metaphysical concerns of religious belief systems. Indeed, science and Christianity in particular appear (at least) to make claims about some of the same subjects in clear propositional language.

insist, as Jean Pond does, that science and Christian belief never really address the same subject, no matter how much they appear to do so. Thus they reject not only the existence of conflict between Christian theism and apparently materialistic theories but also the apparent agreement between Christian theism and theories that seem to support aspects of a Christian or theistic worldview (such as the big bang theory, the contemporary design hypothesis or dualist theories of mind-brain interaction).[10]

Nevertheless, to justify claims of complete independence and religious neutrality, NOMA advocates must subtract empirical content from either biblical affirmations, scientific theories or both.[11] Consider, for example, Pond's account of the relationship of Darwinian evolutionary theory and biblical teaching. Pond seeks to show that Darwinism does not contradict biblical teaching and thus does not constitute an exception to the NOMA principle. Even so, she never really states that the Bible and Darwinism are talking about two different (nonoverlapping) subjects—a tough sell, since both clearly do discuss the origin of new life forms on earth. Instead she suggests that the Bible does not teach anything specific enough about origins to either affirm or contradict Darwinian theory. To justify this claim she quotes one short passage from Genesis (1:25) that tells that God created every kind of animal. She then avers that "these words were never intended to be descriptive of a particular method of creation" (p. 101). Perhaps so. But curiously, she justifies this claim not by analyzing the meaning of the text in its original context or by any other independent hermeneutical criterion but by citing the very NOMA principle she is apparently seeking (or at least needs) to defend. She argues in the very next sentence: "Again it is a question of interpretive style, *with the NOMA principle* coming

---

[10]Neurophysiologists such as Sir John Eccles and Wilder Penfield have provided evidence for a dualist view of human nature in which mental states can and do cause brain states and behavior without themselves being completely determined by environmental, genetic or physiological factors. See, for example, Wilder Penfield, *The Mystery of Mind* (Princeton, N.J.: Princeton University Press, 1975), p. 113.

[11]Many cosmologists have noted that both the Bible and the big bang theory (and general relativity) affirm that the universe (and time itself) had a beginning. Pond notes this apparent convergence as well but then summarily dismisses the biblical affirmations as insignificant. She doesn't justify this on hermeneutical or scientific grounds but instead asserts, "For the adherent to NOMA, of course, the Bible neither supports nor refutes the big bang, or vice versa" (p. 99).

down firmly on the side of not restricting verses such as Genesis 1:25 to any scientific sense" (p. 101, emphasis added). But this statement reveals an obvious circularity. By this point in her essay Pond has clearly explained what the NOMA principle entails: NOMA denies the factual or scientific importance of all biblical statements. The real question is (or should be): Are biblical statements devoid of factual and scientific content as NOMA insists? To invoke NOMA to assure us of this only begs the question.

To sustain her claims about the religious neutrality of contemporary evolutionary biology, Pond offers, at least for the purposes of her analysis of Darwinism's relationship to Christian teaching, an inaccurately minimalist definition of contemporary Darwinism: (1) descent with modification (2) from a common ancestor. She then asks, "Is the idea of the common descent of all life on earth contrary to Scripture?" (p. 101). Bible scholars and biologists can of course debate this question. But in so doing they should not overlook, as Pond does, that Darwinism makes other claims that have far more obvious metaphysical implications. Darwinism not only claims that things have changed or that modern organisms have evolved from a common ancestor (a scientifically dubitable proposition, by the way),[12] but

---

[12]Fossil evidence from around the world shows a "biological big bang" near the beginning of the Cambrian Period (530 million years ago) when at least twenty-five new, separate and major groups of organisms, or phyla (including all the basic body plans of modern animals), emerged suddenly without clear precursors (see R. S. Boardman, A. H. Cheetman and A. J. Rowell, eds., *Fossil Invertebrates* [Blackwell Scientific, 1987], p. 18; Pat Wilmer, *Invertebrate Relationships: Patterns in Animal Evolution* [Cambridge: Cambridge University Press, 1990], pp. 62-70; J. Y. Chen and Guiqing Zhou, "Biology of the Chengjiang Fauna," in *The Cambrian Explosion and the Fossil Record*, ed. J. Y. Chen, Y. N. Chang and H. V. Iten [Taichung, Taiwan: Division of Collection and Research, National Museum of Natural Study, 1997], pp. 11-106; J. W. Valentine, D. Jablonski, and D. H. Erwin, "Fossils, Molecules, and Embryos: New Perspectives on the Cambrian Explosion," *Development* 126 [March 1999]: 851-59; Simon Conway Morris, *The Crucible of Creation: The Burgess Shale the Rise of Animals* [New York: Oxford University Press, 1998]). Though many of the authors who document the Cambrian explosion have not publicly challenged the doctrine of common descent, the paleontological data taken at face value do not support the existence of a single common ancestor for all the animal forms but instead suggest multiple separate origins for the major groups of animals. For discussions of other scientific evidence that has challenging implications for common descent, see Paul A. Nelson, *On Common Descent*, Evolutionary Monographs (Chicago: University of Chicago, forthcoming); Jeffrey C. Schwartz, "Homeobox Genes, Fossils, and the Origin of Species," *The Anatomical Record* (New Anat.) 257 (1999): 15-31; A. D. Bradshaw, "Genostasis and the Limits to Evolution," *B Phil. Trans. Royal Society* 333 (1991):

it also claims that organisms have arisen as the result of purely naturalistic mechanisms (such as natural selection acting on random variation) and that these mechanisms suffice to explain the "appearance" of design in complex organisms. Indeed Darwin himself formulated natural selection as a kind of "designer substitute"[13]—a purely naturalistic mechanism that could accomplish what intelligent humans do in the selective breeding of animals. Evolutionary biologist Ernst Mayr observes, "The real core of Darwinism . . . is the theory of natural selection. This theory is so important for the Darwinian because it permits the explanation of adaptation, the 'design' of the natural theologian, by natural means, instead of by divine intervention."[14] And Francisco Ayala, evolutionary biologist and 1994 president of the American Association for the Advancement of Science, explains:

> It was Darwin's greatest accomplishment to show that the directive organization of living beings can be explained as the result of a natural process, natural selection, without any need to resort to a Creator or other external agent. . . . [Darwin's] mechanism, natural selection, excluded God as the explanation accounting for the obvious design of organisms.[15]

In short, Darwinism acknowledges evidence of apparent, but not actual, design in biology. For this reason the propositional content (and implications) of neo-Darwinism stands in clear contradiction to not just Genesis literalism but to almost any kind of theistic or Christian understanding of creation. Biblical Christianity, based on almost any reasonable, nonquestion-begging hermeneutic, affirms at minimum that God designed the natural

---

289-305; Brian Hall, "Bauplane, Phylotypic Stages, and Constraint: Why There Are So Few Types of Animals," *Evolutionary Biology* 29 (1996): 215-61; Kazuo Kawano, "How Far Can the Neo-Darwinism Be Extended? A Consideration from the History of Higher Taxa in Coleoptera," *Rivista di Biologia/Biology Forum* 91 (1998): 31-56; Jonathan Wells and Paul Nelson, "Homology: A Concept in Crisis," *Origins & Design* 18, no. 2 (1997): 12-19.

[13]Darwin saw that natural forces would accomplish the work of a human breeder and thus that blind nature could come to mimic, over time, the action of a selecting intelligence—a designer.

[14]Ernst Mayr, foreword to *Darwinism Defended,* by Michael Ruse (New York: Addison-Wesley, 1982), pp. xi-xii.

[15]Francisco Ayala, *Creative Evolution?!* ed. John H. Campbell and J. William Schoff (Boston: Jones & Bartlett, 1994), pp. 4-5.

world (including life) and that the natural world should evidence not just apparent design but God's wisdom in "what has been made" (Rom 1:20).

By stating that the words of Genesis "were never intended to be descriptive of a particular method of creation" (p. 101), Pond implies that God somehow used an evolutionary process to create life. And of course he may well have done that. But contemporary neo-Darwinism does not envision a God-guided process of evolutionary change. As the late evolutionary biologist George Gaylord Simpson (Gould's predecessor at Harvard) explains in his classic *The Meaning of Evolution*, neo-Darwinism teaches that "man is the result of a *purposeless* and natural process that did not have him in mind."[16] Yet to say that God guides an inherently unguided natural process, or that God designed a natural mechanism as a substitute for his design, is clearly contradictory. Thus to demonstrate the absence of conflict between modern evolutionary theory and biblical teaching, Pond overlooks or subtracts some of Darwinism's key propositional commitments, namely, its affirmation of the creative sufficiency of natural selection (and other similarly unguided naturalistic mechanisms) and its denial of actual, as opposed to apparent, design in biology.

Lest readers entertain any doubts about whether Pond has employed a truncated definition of Darwinian theory, it may prove instructive to see how Gould himself reacts to attempts to synthesize Darwinism with Christian notions of creation. Gould, who insists that Darwin formulated "an evolutionary theory based on chance variation and natural selection; . . . a rigidly materialistic (and basically atheistic) version of evolution,"[17] categorically rejects the theistic evolutionary idea (proposed by Arthur Peacocke) that God "is creating all the time" through the Darwinian evolutionary process. Gould's intemperate response to Peacocke: "What am I to conclude from such fuzziness?—Has the factuality of an old-fashioned God been proven because Darwin used developmental language. . . . [I]s Mr. Peacocke's God retooling himself in the spiffy language of modern science?"[18] should alert Christians to the perils of accepting peace between science and religion on Gould's terms. As Gould's response shows, his NOMA

---

[16]George Gaylord Simpson, *The Meaning of Evolution* (Cambridge, Mass.: Harvard University Press, 1967), p. 345 (emphasis added).

[17]Stephen Jay Gould, *Ever Since Darwin* (New York: W. W. Norton, 1977), p. 33.

[18]Gould, *Rocks of Ages*, p. 217.

scheme brooks no place for divine intrusions into the factual world of space and time. According to the NOMA, *all* factual claims about God's action in the world, whether continual, episodic or singular, are "out of line" because they let "the magisterium of religion dictate a conclusion within the magisterium of science."[19]

Consider finally what conceding NOMA's intellectual compartmentalism would mean for the orthodox creeds of the church and the biblical affirmations on which they are based. If we take NOMA seriously, then biblical narratives cannot be treated as actual accounts of real historical events since historical events are facts. In *Rocks of Ages*, for example, Gould discusses John's account of the appearance of Jesus to doubting Thomas after the resurrection. Gould characterizes this account as a "moral tale."[20] His NOMA principle does not permit him to do otherwise. The accounts of the appearances of Jesus, like the accounts of the resurrection itself, come from a religious document, and religion, for Gould, must confine its claims to matters of "moral and meaning value." Accordingly, Gould deftly offers his readers an interpretation of the "moral" of the doubting Thomas story without ever considering whether it could possibly have really happened.

Thus we see that advocates of NOMA keep science and religion from encroaching on their respective domains (as Gould defines them) *only* by subtracting specific empirical content from either scientific theories or religious texts. The writer of John's Gospel specifically insists that the events he records really happened—a claim he certifies by attesting that he himself witnessed the events he records (Jn 21:24). Nevertheless, NOMA precludes this possibility by definition. Thus Gould redefines a decidedly historical claim as "a moral tale" without providing any independent evidence or hermeneutical analysis to support his dehistoricized interpretation.

Nevertheless, the God affirmed in the orthodox creeds of the church and revealed by Jewish and Christian Scripture has not seen fit to confine his activity to the nonfactual domain that NOMA has left to religion. Indeed biblical Christianity (again, given any reasonable and nonquestion-begging hermeneutic) claims that Jesus of Nazareth lived in Palestine, died

---

[19]Stephen Jay Gould, "Nonoverlapping Magisteria," *Natural History* (March 1997): 22.
[20]Gould, *Rocks of Ages*, p. 14.

by crucifixion, and was buried and resurrected during Pilate's governorship of Judea. Yet to stay within the bounds that Gould has defined for religion, Christians must desist from making all such claims, for such claims involve matters of fact. The church, however, by its historic creeds has long insisted that the affirmation of these and other factual claims constitute a necessary part of orthodox Christian confession. The NOMA principle consistently applied, therefore, requires subtracting content not just from science or literalistic fundamentalism but from basic orthodox Christianity.

I know Jean Pond well enough to know that she *is* an orthodox Christian. I do not question *her* orthodoxy. But I do wonder how she can reconcile her religious beliefs with her apparently unqualified endorsement of Stephen Gould's view of the relationship between science and religion. Perhaps on this matter she can enlighten us.

A Partnership Response

Howard J. Van Till

On the Meaning of "Independence"

Some years ago I wrote a book entitled *The Fourth Day: What the Bible and the Heavens Are Telling Us About the Creation*. One of my strategies in that work was to note the diversity of questions that we ask about the world of which we are a part and to identify the several categories into which those questions could be placed. A related concern was to direct these questions to appropriate sources for answers. My conclusion at that time was that some categories of questions could best be addressed to the Scriptures and to biblically informed theology but that other categories of questions needed to be addressed to the universe itself and to be investigated by the means and methods of the empirical sciences. Biblically informed theology and empirically informed science each had something to contribute to the larger enterprise of human curiosity, but each had its own distinct domain of expertise. I called this a relationship of "categorical complementarity."

In spite of my efforts to the contrary, many readers took this distinguishing of scientific and theological concerns from one another as a call for compartmentalization—for keeping science and theology in isolated compartments. I was often accused of denying my own heritage, known for its insistence on the integration of faith and learning. My "categorical complementarity" guidelines were taken by some critics as a declaration that science and theology had no bearing on one another, no way of interacting and nothing to gain from each other. I have some fear that Jean Pond's call for the "independence" of science and theology may be subjected to the same set of criticisms. If so, would the charges be warranted? Is Pond's call for the independence of theology and science equivalent to a declaration that they are unrelated? I think not, but it may be the case that portions of Pond's chapter are vulnerable to that reading.

On Motivation

After recounting some historical episodes of dissipative conflict between empirically informed science and biblically informed theology, Pond asks, "Is there a way to avoid skirmishes between science and Christian theology?" (p. 70). In other words, is it necessary that Christian theology and the sciences be engaged in endless battle?

Not at all, says Pond, and she offers three ways for Christians to avoid the perpetuation of this fruitless conflict: (1) Christians could simply avoid the scientific enterprise altogether; (2) Christians could work toward demonstrating that science and theology are in agreement on matters of common interest; or (3) Christians could seek to "maintain an *independence* between these two very different and very human pursuits" (p. 71). Pond favors the third of these alternatives, an approach she describes as being similar to Stephen J. Gould's NOMA principle of "nonoverlapping magisteria." "Or in more concrete terms," says Pond, "*the right tool for the right job*" (p. 71).

In many ways I find this to be good advice. Pond is quite correct, I believe, to note that past failures to "choose the right tool for the right job" have led to no end of unnecessary skirmishes between science and theology. I would suggest, however, that the motivation for Pond's recommendation could be far more substantive than merely as a means of avoiding conflict. I think she has a right to recommend it as a superior means of moving in the direction of greater understanding.

On the Differences Between Science and Theology

A few years ago a local theologian led a "theology review" class in our church. I was quite disturbed, however, by his description of the theological enterprise. As he described it, theology seemed more like a museum piece than a dynamic enterprise. When I made a comment to that effect and asked where there might be opportunity in theology for growth or for learning or for the incorporation of new information, I was promptly informed that I was trying to make theology "just like science." He was, in fact, quite correct in his assessment of my vision for a dynamic and progressive theology.

Against that background I find Pond's comments on the differences between science and theology to be noteworthy. *"In science,"* notes Pond, *"new data arrive daily; in contrast, the primary data available to theologians are relatively fixed.* ... Theologians continue to write, but the amount of primary material they have to write about remains about the same. The ratio of exegesis to original text climbs ever higher" (pp. 74-75).

Pond sees this as the basis for the contrast between the attainment of consensus in science but fragmentation in theology. "Controversies in science can be illuminated and consensus reached because there is always the possibility, indeed the inevitability, of new evidence. In theology, new data is less likely to arrive, and we must instead depend on the continued interpretation of the old. Science tends to come to consensus *because of*, not despite, new data, but the fruits of theology includes schism" (pp. 80-81).

But Pond's judgments seem to be based on the presumption that Christian theology is necessarily limited to little more than the biblical text for its primary material. This is a common view of theology, but perhaps it needs to be replaced by a vision that opens the window of theological concern to an unlimited universe of relevant "data." Why not view the whole of human experience as the data of theology? Why limit the theological enterprise to a study of those few experiences recorded in the text of the ancient Hebrew and early Christian communities? Perhaps the prevailing differences between science and theology are an artifact of theology's choice to be content with a small selection of old data. Pond's contrasting of science and theology does apply to some traditional concepts of the theological enterprise, but rather than being resigned to those traditions perhaps we ought to be stimulated to develop a new vision for an enterprise grown stale. Perhaps one of the bitter fruits of historical "independence" is a static theology that has cut itself off from the stimulation that the sciences could provide.

The Fruits of Independence

Pond rightly calls attention to a number of factors that have contributed to the present state of conflict between science and theology—factors that would be eliminated, she says, by adopting her independence model. The first is what I would call triumphalist scientism. "People must not use the admitted strength and power of science when it operates within its own realm to attempt to reject the very existence of other realms of truth. Science must not deny what lies outside of science" (p. 81). The rhetorical excesses of Richard Dawkins, Carl Sagan and William Provine are cited as examples of what would be eliminated by the adoption of Pond's independence model. I agree that the elimination of this genre of naturalistic preaching would be a great improvement over the present situation.

But Pond is equally critical of another type of preaching that has contributed to the conflict now prevalent. The message that she is concerned to eliminate, whether preached by believers or "mischievous nonbelievers," is the claim "that science—usually the theory of evolution—is *inherently* antitheistic" (p. 83). Those of us who have spent our lifetimes in theologically conservative communities know this message well. It is, no matter how ill-founded and misleading, a familiar theme in contemporary Christian preaching and publishing. Go to your local Christian bookstore. Look at the books in the "Christianity and Science" section. I fear you will find it to be dominated by books preaching this distortion. I wholeheartedly join Pond in calling for a cessation of this rhetoric. As Pond says, "If Christians . . . persist in trying to fashion science (or at least evolution) into a weapon, why should we be surprised when it gets used as one?" (p. 85).

A third unnecessary conflict that Pond wishes to eliminate proceeds from the familiar attempt to read the early chapters of Genesis in a "descriptively literal" fashion. Drawing on the resources of several Christian denominations, Pond rightly demonstrates that no matter how popular this literalism may be, it is not universally recommended by Christian leadership. Neither does it lead to consensus among Christians. "The unifying element of a Christian interpretation of the Bible is that Christians will not agree on how to interpret the Bible" (p. 90). Although this statement is obviously true, it seems not to stop the flood of claims that the Bible categorically rules out the possibility of biological evolution.

Another common strategy that Pond wishes to discourage is the practice of plugging in divine action wherever a person finds today's scientific understanding of some particular phenomenon to be incomplete. It is obvious to all that our scientific understanding of the way things work is incomplete. When this involves a phenomenon that we can observe at the present time, our usual practice is to keep on investigating until a satisfactory scientific account is developed. Most Christians would, I presume, take that to be good scientific strategy.

But note what happens when the phenomenon in question is something that happened *in the past* and is related to the *formational history of life on earth*. Now a new strategy seems all too tempting to some Christians. Is science not now able to give a full account of exactly how some particular species or biotic system came to be formed? Well then God must have done it. God must have imposed a new form on the raw materials at hand. Extraordinary divine action is brought in as a means of solving a difficult scientific problem.

With Pond I find these moves to be intellectually unsatisfying. They are just too easy, too contrived. It might be compared to playing a game of chess with a person who, when in danger of being checkmated, would declare, "Sorry, but my king can move to any square at any time." In this spirit Pond says, "Explanations involving God [as an occasional intervener] are not satisfactory explanations *in science*, whether you are talking how worms wriggle or how life originated on earth" (p. 97). In this circumstance "invoking a supernatural force is the equivalent of cheating in sport. . . . In literature this cheating is referred to as *deus ex machina*—God from a machine. The *deus ex machina* is an unexpected and contrived solution to a difficult problem of the plot" (p. 98). What should a Christian scientist do when confronted with a scientific puzzle that resists easy solution? Posit a divine "special effect"? No, Pond and I would agree, one should do better science.

Once Again, on the Meaning of "Independence"
I began this response by expressing a concern that Pond's call for the "independence" of science and theology might be misunderstood as a call for the isolation of these two enterprises. If I have read her chapter correctly, she is not calling for the radical compartmentalization of science and theology into noninteracting endeavors but for the maintaining of a

distinction of their differing competencies. By so doing, each can be respected both for what kinds of questions it is capable of answering and for those on which it must remain respectfully silent. Furthermore, this mutual respect for differing competencies opens the door for their being mutually informative enterprises and joint contributors to a more comprehensive enterprise. Perhaps what Pond here calls "independence" is not very far removed from what I have called a "partnership in theorizing." Football players and referees may operate independently of one another, with distinctly differing competencies and proximate goals, but they are nonetheless partners in the larger enterprise of giving the spectators what they came to see—a game played both well and in accordance with the rules.

3 Qualified Agreement
Modern Science & the Return of the "God Hypothesis"

Stephen C. Meyer

And thus much concerning God;
to discourse of Whom from the appearances of things,
does certainly belong to Natural Philosophy.
SIR ISAAC NEWTON

Part 1: Introduction

Alfred North Whitehead said that "when we consider what religion is for mankind and what science is, it is no exaggeration to say that the future course of history depends upon the decision of this generation as to the relations between them."[1] Whitehead spoke early in the twentieth century at a time when most elite intellectuals believed that science contradicted classical theism with its traditional belief in a divine creation, the uniqueness of humanity and the immortality of the soul. For many intellectuals a scientifically informed worldview was a materialistic worldview in which entities such as God, free will, mind, soul or purpose could play no objective role. Scientific materialism denied evidence of any intelligent design in nature and any ultimate purpose to human existence. As Whitehead's contemporary Bertrand Russell put it, "Man is the product of causes which had

---

[1]Alfred North Whitehead, *Science and the Modern World* (New York: Macmillan, 1926), p. 260.

no prevision of the end they were achieving" and that predestine him "to extinction in the vast death of the solar system."[2]

It is not hard to see why many intellectuals held this opinion. Over the previous two hundred years Western science and philosophy had witnessed a profound shift away from its earlier Judeo-Christian orientation. Starting in the Enlightenment many philosophers began to deny the validity of the classical proofs for God's existence from nature. Philosophers such as David Hume and Immanuel Kant raised powerful objections to the design argument and the cosmological argument, the two most formidable theistic arguments of this kind.

Further, despite the now well-documented influence of Judeo-Christian thinking on the rise of modern science from the time of Ockham to Newton,[3] much of science took a decidedly materialistic turn. In astronomy the French mathematician Laplace offered an ingenious theory known as the nebular hypothesis to account for the origin of the solar system as the outcome of purely natural gravitational forces. In geology Charles Lyell explained the origin of the earth's most dramatic topographical features— mountain ranges and canyons—as the result of slow, gradual and completely naturalistic processes of change. In cosmology a belief in the infinity of space and time obviated any need to consider the question of the ultimate origin of matter. Perhaps most significantly, Darwin's evolutionary theory sought to show that the blind process of natural selection acting on random variations could and did account for the origin of new forms of life without any divine intervention or guidance. According to Darwin living organisms only *appeared* to be designed by an intelligent creator; nature itself was the real creator.[4] As Francisco Ayala has explained, "The func-

---

[2]Bertrand Russell, quoted in James B. Conant, *Modern Science and Modern Man* (New York: Doubleday/Anchor, 1953), pp. 139-40.

[3]R. Hooykaas, *Religion and the Rise of Modern Science* (Grand Rapids, Mich.: Eerdmans, 1972); P. E. Hodgson, review of S. L. Jaki's *Science and Creation* in *Nature* 251 (October 1974): 747; A. N. Whitehead, *Science and the Modern World* (New York: Free Press, 1967), pp. 3-4, 12-13; Loren Eisley, *Darwin's Century: Evolution and the Men Who Discovered It* (Garden City, N.Y.: Anchor, 1961), p. 62; Herbert Butterfield, *The Origins of Modern Science 1300-1800* (New York: Free Press, 1957), pp. 16-17, 19; M. B. Foster, *Mind* 43, no. 172 (1934): 446; C. F. von Weizsacker, *The Relevance of Science* (New York: Harper & Row, 1964) p. 163; Nancy R. Pearcy and Charles B. Thaxton, *The Soul of Science* (Wheaton, Ill.: Crossway, 1994), pp. 17-42, 43-56.

[4]Charles Darwin, *The Origin of Species* (London: Penguin, 1985).

tional design of organisms and their features would . . . seem to argue for the existence of a designer. It was Darwin's greatest accomplishment to show that the directive organization of living beings can be explained as the result of a natural process, natural selection, without any need to resort to a Creator or other external agent."[5]

These theories taken jointly suggested that the whole history of the universe could be told as a seamless, or nearly seamless, unfolding of the potentiality of *matter and energy*. Science seemed to support a materialistic or naturalistic worldview, not a theistic one. Science no longer needed to invoke a preexistent mind to shape matter in order to explain the evidence of nature. Matter had always existed and could—in effect—arrange itself without a preexistent designer or Creator. Thus by the close of the nineteenth century both the logical and evidential basis of theistic arguments from nature had seemingly evaporated.

The demise of theistic arguments from nature and the corresponding rise of a scientifically based materialistic worldview fostered a profound shift in the way thinking people conceptualized the relationship between science and Christian faith. Many scientists, philosophers and even theologians during the twentieth century began to perceive science and Christianity as standing in conflict with one another. Others, however, denied that science contradicts Christian belief. Nevertheless, they have typically done so by portraying science and religion as such totally distinct enterprises that their teachings do not intersect in significant ways. Two such models, independence (or compartmentalism) and complementarity (or "partnership," to use Van Till's term),[6] are discussed in the introduction to

---

[5]Francisco J. Ayala, "Darwin's Revolution," in *Creative Evolution?!* ed. John H. Campbell and J. William Schopf (Boston: Jones & Bartlett, 1994), p. 4.

[6]Michael Peterson provides a helpful threefold typology of perceived relationships between science and religion in *Reason and Religious Belief* (Oxford: Oxford University Press, 1989), pp. 196-216. Peterson discusses the conflict, compartmentalism and complementarity models of science and religion interaction. He does not, however, consider the possibility that scientific evidence might support theistic belief, though that remains a logical possibility. I have, therefore, proposed (and am defending here) a fourth model called "qualified agreement" or "epistemic support." See Stephen C. Meyer, "The Demarcation of Science and Religion," in *The History of Science and Religion in the Western Tradition: An Encyclopedia*, ed. Gary Ferngren, Edward Larson and Darrel W. Amundsen (New York: Garland, 2000), pp. 17-23; William A. Dembski and Stephen C. Meyer, "Fruitful Interchange or Polite Chit-Chat? The Dialogue Between

this book. Both these models assume the religious and metaphysical neutrality of scientific knowledge.[7] Thus, some have seen the witness of science as hostile to theistic and Christian faith, while others have attempted to cast it as entirely neutral. Few, however, have thought—in contrast to the founders of early modern science such Kepler, Boyle and Newton—that the testimony of nature (i.e, science) actually supports important tenets of a theistic or Christian worldview.

This essay will reassert this classical view and argue that scientific evidence does provide epistemological support (but not proof) for the theistic worldview affirmed by biblical Christianity (see Acts 17; Rom 1; Col 1, for example). It will develop a model of the relationship between science and Christianity that I call "qualified agreement" or "mutual epistemic support." This model maintains that, when correctly interpreted, scientific evidence and biblical teaching can and do support each other. Though advocates of qualified agreement acknowledge (with independence and complementarity advocates) that much scientific research and theorizing *does* address metaphysically and religiously neutral topics, we do not agree that *all* scientific theories have this character. Instead, the qualified agreement model, like the conflict model, asserts that some scientific theories do have larger metaphysical implications. Nevertheless, unlike the conflict model, qualified agreement denies that the best or most truthful theories ultimately contradict a theistic or Christian worldview. Instead, it views theological and scientific truth as issuing from the same transcendent and rational source, namely, God. Advocates of qualified agreement anticipate therefore that these two domains of knowledge when rightly understood and interpreted will come increasingly into agreement as advances in science and theology eliminate real points of conflict that sometimes have existed.

Because many of the founders of early modern science held this view (though with a less-nuanced justification, perhaps), we might also refer to

[7]Donald M. MacKay, *The Clockwork Image* (Downers Grove, Ill.: InterVarsity Press, 1974), pp. 51-55; Howard Van Till, *The Fourth Day* (Grand Rapids, Mich.: Eerdmans, 1986), pp. 208-15; Howard Van Till, Davis Young and Clarence Menninga, *Science Held Hostage* (Downers Grove, Ill.: InterVarsity Press, 1988), pp. 39-43, 127-68. See also Oskar Gruenwald, "Science and Religion: The Missing Link," *Journal of Interdisciplinary Studies* 6 (1994): 1-23, for a different interpretation of complementarity that affirms methodological autonomy of science and religion but conjoins their findings.

this model as the "classical" formulation of the relationship between science and religion. Indeed, from the late Middle Ages through the scientific revolution (roughly 1250-1750) scientists often affirmed the agreement between "the book of nature" and "the book of scripture," both of which were understood to be mutually reinforcing revelations of the same God.

I will reformulate this view by showing that contemporary scientific evidence from cosmology, physics and biology now supports a theistic worldview. I will also provide a more refined notion of epistemological support. Many thinkers, both theistic and naturalistic, have assumed that science supports a Christian or theistic worldview only if it can provide the basis for a deductively certain proof of God's existence. I will show how evidence from the natural sciences can and does provide epistemological support for Christian theism even if it does not make possible such a deductively certain proof. I will first, however, examine how the demise of theistic arguments from nature helped undermine the classical view of the relationship between science and Christian faith.

Part 2: The Rise and Fall of Theistic Arguments

Two types of arguments from nature for God's existence have proven especially effective in the history of Western thought: design and cosmological arguments. The classical design argument begins by noting certain highly ordered or complex features within nature, such as the configuration of planets or the architecture of the vertebrate eye. It then proceeds to argue that such features could not have arisen without the activity of a preexistent intelligence (which has typically been equated with God). The cosmological argument starts from the existence and causal regularity of the universe and seeks to deduce a necessary being—that is, God—as the first cause or sufficient reason for the universe's existence.[8] Perhaps the most empirically contingent version of the argument, the *kalam* cosmological argument, asserts that the universe had a temporal beginning—a proposition that medieval philosophers typically sought to justify by showing the logical or mathematical absurdity of an infinite regress of cause and effect. The argument then concluded that the beginning of the physical universe must

---

[8]William Lane Craig, *Reasonable Faith* (Wheaton, Ill.: Crossway, 1994), pp. 79-83.

have resulted from an uncaused first cause (God) that exists independently of the universe.[9] Throughout Western history many philosophers and scientists formulated various empirically based theistic arguments. Consequently, many also viewed science and theistic belief as mutually reinforcing. Yet many important versions of these arguments came into disrepute by the end of the nineteenth century, chiefly due to developments within science.

2.1. Classical Design Arguments

A survey of Western thought reveals theistic design arguments in the writings of Christian and non-Christian writers alike. Among non-Christians, design arguments are found in the work of Greek philosophers such as Plato, Roman philosophers such as Cicero and Jewish theologians such as Maimonides.[10] The Roman philosopher Cicero formulated a sophisticated version of the design argument[11] that anticipated by almost two thousand years the later work of William Paley.

Design arguments are also found in the writings of early Christian theologians including Basil the Great, Gregory of Nazianzus, Theophilus of Antioch, Minucius Felix and Augustine. During the latter Middle Ages thinkers such as Roger Bacon, Robert Grosseteste, Duns Scotus, William of Ockham and Thomas Aquinas formulated their ideas about science in the context of an explicitly Christian philosophy of nature that either presupposed or provided arguments for the existence of a transcendent Designer and Creator.

Support for the design hypothesis did not abate during the period of the

---

[9]William Lane Craig, *The Cosmological Argument from Plato to Leibniz* (London: Macmillan, 1980), pp. x, xi, 48-126, 158-204, 282-95; Craig, *Reasonable Faith*, pp. 79-80; Richard Swinburne, *The Existence of God* (Oxford: Clarendon, 1979), pp. 116-32.

[10]Plato, *The Laws*, trans. A. E. Taylor (London: Dent, 1969), p. 279; Cicero, *De Natura Deorum*, trans. H. Rackham (Cambridge, Mass.: Harvard University Press, 1933), pp. 217-19.

[11]In his *De Natura Deorum* Cicero (45 B.C.) writes, "When we see something moved by machinery, like an orrery or clock . . . we do not doubt that these contrivances are the work of reason; when therefore we behold the whole compass of heaven moving with revolutions of marvelous velocity and executing with perfect regularity the annual changes of the seasons with absolute safety and security for all things, how can we doubt that all this is effected not merely by reason, but by a reason that is transcendent and divine?" (ibid.)

scientific revolution (1500-1700).[12] Many of the founders of early modern science assumed that the natural world was intelligible precisely because they also assumed that it had been designed by a rational mind. In addition, many individual scientists—Johannes Kepler (1571-1630) in astronomy,[13] John Ray (1627-1705) in biology,[14] Robert Boyle (1627-1691) in chemistry[15]—made specific design arguments based upon discoveries in their respective fields. This tradition attained an almost majestic rhetorical quality in the writing of Isaac Newton (1642-1727). In the general scholium to the *Principia*, Newton suggested that the stability of the planetary system depended not only upon the regular action of universal gravitation but also upon the very precise initial positioning of the planets and comets in relation to the sun. As he explained:

> Though these bodies may, indeed, persevere in their orbits by the mere laws of gravity, yet they could by no means have at first derived the regular position of the orbits themselves from those laws. . . . [Thus] this most beautiful system of the sun, planets, and comets, could only proceed from the counsel and dominion of an intelligent and powerful being.[16]

Or as he wrote in the *Opticks:*

> How came the Bodies of Animals to be contrived with so much Art, and for what ends were their several parts? Was the Eye contrived without

---

[12]Neal Gillespie, "Natural History, Natural Theology, and Social Order: John Ray and the Newtonian Ideology," *History of Biology* 20, pt. 1 (1987): 1-49.

[13]See, e.g., chapter two of Johannes Kepler, *Mysterium Cosmographicum (The Secret of the Universe)* (New York: Abaris, 1981), pp. 93-101; and his *Harmonies of the World* bk. 5 (Amherst, N.Y.: Prometheus, 1995), pp. 170, 240-45. That Kepler believed that the work of God is evident in nature can been seen by his statement in the *Harmonies of the World* that God "by the light of nature promote[s] in us the desire of the light of grace, that by its means [God] mayest transport us into the light of glory" (Kepler, *Mysterium Cosmographicum*, p. 240). See also Morris Kline, *Mathematics: The Loss of Certainty* [New York: Oxford University Press, 1980], p. 39).

[14]John Ray, *The Wisdom of God Manifest in the Works of Creation,* 3rd ed. (London: Printed for Smith and Walford, at the Prince's Arms in St. Paul's Church-yard, 1701).

[15]Robert Boyle, *Selected Philosophical Papers of Robert Boyle,* ed. M. A. Stewart (New York: Macmillan, 1979), pp. 172-74.

[16]Isaac Newton, *Mathematical Principles of Natural Philosophy* (Berkeley: University of California Press, 1960), pp. 543-44.

Skill in Opticks, and the Ear without Knowledge of Sounds? . . . And these things being rightly dispatch'd, does it not appear from phaenomena that there is a Being incorporeal, living, intelligent, omnipresent[?][17]

For Newton and other like-minded early modern scientists, observable evidences in nature testified to an unobservable and intelligent Designer whom they identified with the God of the Judeo-Christian Bible.

2.2. The Demise of the Design Argument

With the advent of the Enlightenment both Judeo-Christian belief and the design argument came under attack. For example, the skeptical empiricist philosopher David Hume (1711-1776) rejected the existence of God and the validity of the design argument.[18] Hume maintained in his *Dialogues Concerning Natural Religion* (1779) that the design argument depended upon a flawed analogy with human artifacts. He admitted that biological organisms have certain similarities to complex human artifacts. Eyes and pocket watches both depend on the functional integration of many separate and specifically configured parts. Nevertheless, he argued, biological organisms also differ from human artifacts—they reproduce themselves, for example—and the advocates of the design argument fail to take these dissimilarities into account. Since experience teaches that organisms always come from other organisms, Hume argued that analogical argument really ought to suggest that organisms ultimately come from some primeval organism, not a transcendent mind or spirit. Hume also argued that arguments about the design of the universe as a whole depend on a flawed induction. Inductive reasoning, Hume argued, depends on repeated experience. Since the universe as a whole belongs to a class of one, we can make no inferences about the causes of universes in general or, therefore, about our universe in particular.

Despite these objections, Hume's categorical rejection of the design argument did not prove decisive with either theistic or secular philosophers. Thinkers as diverse as the Scottish Presbyterian Thomas Reid (1710-1796)

---

[17]Isaac Newton, *The Opticks, Book Three, Part One, Query 28* (New York: Dover, 1952), pp. 369-70.
[18]See David Hume, *Dialogues Concerning Natural Religion* (Buffalo, N.Y.: Prometheus, 1989), pp. 61-66.

and the Enlightenment deist Thomas Paine continued to affirm the validity of the design argument because of the order they perceived in nature.[19] Even Immanuel Kant (1724-1804), who rejected the design argument as a proof of the transcendent and omnipotent God of Judeo-Christian theology, still accepted the conclusion that it could establish the reality of a powerful and intelligent author of the world. In his words, "physical-theological argument can indeed lead us to the point of admiring the greatness, wisdom, power, etc., of the Author of the world, but can take us no further."[20] Kant sought to limit the scope of the design argument but did not reject it wholesale.

In any case, science-based design arguments continued into the early nineteenth century, especially in biology. William Paley's (1743-1805) *Natural Theology*, published in 1803 (several years after Hume's criticism of the design argument), is the most notable example. Paley's work cataloged a host of biological systems that suggested the work of a superintending intelligence. He argued that the astonishing complexity and superb adaptation of means to ends in such systems could not originate strictly through the blind forces of nature anymore than could a complex pocket watch.

Paley also responded directly to Hume's claim that the design inference rested upon a faulty analogy. A watch that could reproduce itself, he argued, would constitute an even more marvelous effect than one that could not.[21] Thus, for Paley the differences between artifacts and organisms that Hume cited only seemed to strengthen the conclusion of the design argument. And indeed, despite the widespread currency of Hume's objections, many scientists continued to find Paley's watch-to-watchmaker reasoning compelling well into nineteenth century.

Thus it was not ultimately the arguments of the philosophers that destroyed the popularity of the design argument but the emergence of increasingly powerful materialistic explanations of apparent design, particularly Charles Darwin's theory of evolution by natural selection. Darwin argued in 1859 that living organisms only appeared to be designed. Darwin proposed a specific mechanism, natural selection acting on random varia-

---

[19]Thomas Paine, *The Life and Works of Thomas Paine*, vol. 8: *The Age of Reason* (New Rochelle, N.Y.: Thomas Paine National Historical Association, 1925), p. 6.

[20]Immanuel Kant, *Critique of Pure Reason*, trans. Norman Kemp Smith (London: Macmillan, 1963), p. 523.

[21]William Paley, *Natural Theology* (Boston: Gould & Lincoln, 1852; reprint), pp. 8-9.

tions, that could explain the adaptation of organisms to their environment without actually invoking an intelligent or directing agency.

As noted earlier, this trend was reinforced by the emergence of other fully naturalistic origins scenarios in astronomy, cosmology and geology. It was also reinforced by an emerging positivistic tradition in science that increasingly sought to exclude appeals to supernatural or intelligent causes from science *by definition*.[22] Natural theologians such as Robert Chambers, Richard Owen and Asa Gray, writing just prior to Darwin, tended to oblige this convention by locating design in the workings of natural law rather than in the complex structure or functions of natural objects. While this move certainly made the natural-theology tradition more acceptable to shifting methodological canons in science, it also gradually emptied it of any distinctive empirical content, leaving it vulnerable to charges of subjectivity and vacuousness. By locating design more in natural law and less in complex contrivances that could be understood by direct analogy to human creativity, later British natural theologians ultimately made their research program indistinguishable from the positivistic and fully naturalistic science of the Darwinians.[23] As a result, the notion of design, to the extent it maintained any intellectual currency, soon became relegated to a matter of subjective belief. The idea that a mind superintended the workings of nature was still believable, but the assertion that nature and its laws existed on their own was just as believable. Thus by the end of the nineteenth century, natural theologians could no longer point to any specific artifact of nature that required intelligence as a necessary explanation. Intelligent design became undetectable except "through the eyes of faith."

2.3. The Demise of the Cosmological Argument

The demise of the cosmological argument also began with Enlightenment philosophers. Kant, for example, challenged the medieval arguments about the need for a first cause of the universe. To many medievals the principle of causality and the existence of the material universe implied the existence of a necessary first cause—a cause that they equated with God. Kant

---

[22]For a discussion of this methodological shift, see Neil Gillespie, *Charles Darwin and the Problem of Creation* (Chicago: University of Chicago Press, 1979), pp. 41-66, 82-108.

[23]William A. Dembski, "Demise of British Natural Theology," *Philosophia Christi*, series 2, vol. 1, no. 1 (1999): 17-43.

denied that the universe needed a necessary first cause. He argued that there could be an unbroken line of effects and causes going back infinitely in time, thus eliminating the need for a temporally transcendent or divine first cause. Kant accepted the possibility that the universe itself might be eternal and self-existent.[24]

Kant's skepticism about the cosmological argument, and the *kalam* version of it in particular, was reinforced by the science of his day. Though Newton supported the design argument, one aspect of his physics—the postulation of infinite time and space—helped to undermine the classical *kalam* cosmological argument.[25]

Though Newton's infinite universe[26] had scientific problems even in its

---

[24]Kant, *Critique*, pp. 511-12.

[25]The *kalam* cosmological argument attempts to argue for the existence of God as a necessary first cause for the origin of a finite universe. The *kalam* argument is not the only version of the cosmological argument, however. Thomas Aquinas argued for God as a necessary first cause of the universe, not in a temporal sense but in an ontological sense (Craig, *Reasonable Faith*, p. 80-83). Gottfried Leibniz championed another version of the cosmological argument in which he postulated God as the only "sufficient reason" for the contingent causal structure of the universe as a whole. These versions of the argument were not predicated on a finite universe. Though they remained in philosophical currency well after the repudiation of the *kalam* argument during the Enlightenment, they had less popular appeal due in part to their philosophical complexity. In any case, the demise of the *kalam* argument had a tremendously negative effect on both popular and scholarly perceptions of the relationship between science and religion. Moreover, its resuscitation as the result of scientific discoveries in the twentieth century has provided considerable epistemic support for a theistic worldview, whatever the status of the Thomistic and Leibnizian versions of the cosmological argument then and now.

[26]According to Newton's theory of universal gravitation, all bodies attract one another with a force proportional to the product of their masses and inversely proportional to the square of the distance between them. His theory implied that *all* bodies of matter in the universe attract one another. Yet this created a puzzle. According to Newton's theory, every star should gravitate toward the center of the universe until the whole universe collapses in on itself. Thus the universe must either be collapsing or expanding (to offset its tendency to collapse). Either way, it could not be static.

To avoid abandoning either his theory of gravity or the notion of a static universe, Newton proposed that "the matter was eavenly diffused through an infinite space" so that "it would never convene into one mass" (Isaac Newton, *The Correspondence of Isaac Newton*, ed. Herbert W. Turnbull et al., 7 vols. [Cambridge: Cambridge University Press, 1959-1977], 3:234). Newton thought that if there were an infinite number of stars scattered evenly throughout an infinite space, then every star would attract every other star with equal force in all directions simultaneously. Thus the stars would remain forever suspended in a tension of balanced gravitational attraction (see Stephen Hawking, *A* own day, naturalistically minded physicists following Newton found his infinite-and-static universe paradigm philosophically agreeable.[27] Some philosophical naturalists rallied to support the infinite-static model proposed by Newton specifically because it eliminated the need to explain the beginning of time and space. By the end of the nineteenth century this view had become deeply entrenched in the scientific community and provided a powerful reason for rejecting the *kalam* cosmological argument, which depended upon the premise of a finite universe.

2.4. Consequences of the Demise of Theistic Arguments

The demise of these two theistic arguments and the emergence of a fully materialistic account of the origin of the natural world—from the infinite past to the dawn of human life on earth—had a profound effect on the perception of the relationship between science and theistic belief.

Philosophical materialists regarded the emergence a comprehensive materialistic account of natural history as epistemic support for their worldview. Consequently, they perceived science and theism as standing in opposition. If theism asserts the reality of a purposive creation, and if science could account for the origin of living organisms, for example, by reference to wholly undirected material processes, then one of these two views must be incorrect. For this reason the demise of the design and cosmological arguments during the late nineteenth and early twentieth centuries contributed to the rise of the "conflict" model of the relationship between science and religion.

The Darwinian denial of actual design figured centrally in this intellectual shift. Most historians of science now regard as extremely simplistic the attempts by nineteenth century historians such as William Draper and Andrew Dickson White to cast the whole history of science as a battle between science and Christianity.[28] Yet many twentieth-century scientists

Brief History of Time: From the Big Bang to Black Holes [New York: Bantam, 1988], p. 5). Newton also found the infinite universe appealing for theological reasons. Newton thought of space and time as a "Divine Sensorium," a medium in which God perceived his creation. Since God was infinite, space and time had to be as well.

[27]George Smoot and Keay Davidson, *Wrinkles in Time* (New York: William Morrow, 1993), p. 27.

[28]John William Draper, *History of the Conflict Between Religion and Science* (New York: D. Appleton, 1875); and Andrew Dickson White, *A History of the Warfare of Science with Theology in Christendom*, abridged ed. (1896; reprint, New York: Dover, 1960).

and philosophers have held to the conflict model on other grounds. Many conflict advocates cite neo-Darwinism (with its fully naturalistic selection/mutation mechanism for the creation of new biological structure) and other similarly materialistic accounts of origins as the principal and irreconcilable locus of this conflict. Francisco Ayala, Daniel Dennet, William Provine, Douglas Futuyma, Richard Dawkins and the late G. G. Simpson, for example, all agree that neo-Darwinism (taken as a realistic portrayal of the history of life) denies, contra biblical theism, any discernible evidence of divine purpose, guidance, direction or design.[29] Neo-Darwinism teaches, as Simpson once put it, "that man is the result of a purposeless and natural process that did not have him in mind."[30]

Of course, even granting the truth of neo-Darwinism, many evolutionary biologists admit that science cannot categorically exclude the possibility that some kind of deity still might exist. Nor can they deny the possibility of a divine designer who so masks his creative activity in apparently natural processes as to escape scientific detection. Yet for most scientific materialists such an undetectable entity hardly seems worthy of consideration. While the existence of an undetectable designer has remained a logical possibility, the vast majority of Darwinian biologists have rejected this idea as an unnecessary and unparsimonious explanation for the appearance of design in nature. At the very least Darwinism makes "theological explanations" of life "superfluous," as Douglas Futuyma argues.[31] If, however, theism insists that God's qualities "have been clearly seen . . . from what has been made" (Rom 1:20) as the apostle Paul averred, then conflict most certainly exists since, as noted, Darwinism explicitly denies anything more than the appearance of design in nature.

Advocates of independence (or compartmentalism) and complementarity developed their models to defend theistic belief against the aggressive philosophical materialism of many conflict theorists. Even so, advocates of

---

[29]Ayala, "Darwin's Revolution," pp. 4-5; Daniel C. Dennett, *Darwin's Dangerous Idea: Evolution and the Meanings of Life* (New York: Simon & Schuster, 1995); William Provine, "Evolution and the Foundation of Ethics," *MBL Science* 3, no. 1 (1988): 25-29; Douglas Futuyma, *Evolutionary Biology* (Sunderland, Mass.: Sinauer, 1986); Richard Dawkins, *The Blind Watchmaker* (London: Longman, 1986); George Gaylord Simpson, *The Meaning of Evolution* (Cambridge, Mass.: Harvard University Press, 1967).

[30]Simpson, *Meaning*, pp. 344-45.

[31]Futuyma, *Evolutionary Biology*, p. 3.

these models have generally conceded the failure of science-based theistic arguments. Instead, advocates of independence and complementarity (or "partnership" in Van Till's lexicon) have insisted upon the strict metaphysical and religious neutrality of even the most apparently materialistic origins theories.[32] They have argued that such origins theories do not necessarily contradict theological accounts of creation since God may have used Darwinian or other similarly materialistic processes to create the world. On this view, statements about the purposelessness of evolution do not represent scientific statements per se but "Evolutionism"—an "extrascientific" or "pseudoscientific" apologetic for philosophical materialism. Even so, advocates of independence and complementarity generally have agreed with staunch Darwinists on one point. Both deny that evidence of intelligent design (as opposed to merely apparent design) is scientifically detectable in the living world.

Clearly, the very existence of the independence and complementarity perspectives shows that the demise of the theistic arguments did not eliminate theistic belief, even among scientists. It did, however, radically change the terms of engagement between science and religion. Unlike the early modern scientists such as Kepler, Boyle and Newton, who saw evidence of design in nature as support for their belief in a personal and transcendent God, much of the scientific establishment during the twentieth century would deny that such evidence exists. Thus, since the demise of theistic arguments in the late nineteenth century, scientists have either asserted that science contradicts Christian or theistic belief or they have denied that science has any religious or metaphysical implications whatsoever. Either way, scientists and philosophers have for the most part denied that the testimony of nature lends any support to a theistic worldview.

Part 3: The Return of the God Hypothesis

During the twentieth century a quiet but remarkable shift has occurred in science. Evidence from cosmology, physics and biology now tells a very different story than did the science of the late nineteenth century. Evidence

[32]MacKay, *The Clockwork Image*, pp. 51-55; Howard Van Till, *The Fourth Day* (Grand Rapids, Mich.: Eerdmans, 1986), pp. 208-15; Howard Van Till, Davis Young and Clarence Menninga, *Science Held Hostage* (Downers Grove, Ill.: InterVarsity Press, 1988) pp. 39-43, 127-68.

from cosmology now supports a finite universe, not an infinite one, while evidence from physics and biology has reopened the question of design.

3.1. The Big Bang and General Relativity

In 1915-1916 Albert Einstein shocked the scientific world with his theory of general relativity.[33] Though Einstein's theory challenged Newton's theory of gravity in many important respects, it also implied (as did Newton's) that the universe could not be static but instead was simultaneously expanding and decelerating. According to relativity theory, massive bodies alter the curvature of space so as to draw nearby objects to them. Einstein's conception of gravity implied that all material bodies would congeal unless the effects of gravitation were continually counteracted by the expansion of space itself.[34] Einstein's theory implied an expanding, not a static, universe.

Einstein disliked this idea in part for philosophical reasons. An actively expanding universe implied a beginning to the expansion and thus to the universe.[35] Relativity theory suggested a universe of finite duration racing outward from an initial beginning in the distant past. For Einstein, however, a definite beginning to the universe seemed so counterintuitive that he introduced an arbitrary factor in his theory to eliminate the implication. He postulated a repulsive force, expressed by his "cosmological constant,"[36]

---

[33]Albert Einstein, "Die Feldgleichungen der Gravitation," *Sitzungsberichte der Koniglich Preussischen Akademie der Wissenschaften,* November 25, 1915, pp. 844-47 (the following reference includes this reference); Einstein, "Die Grundlage der allgemeinen Relativitatstheorie," *Annalen der Physik* 49 (1916): 769-822; the English translation is in H. A. Lorentz et al., *The Principle of Relativity,* with notes by A. Sommerfield and trans. W. Perrett and G. B. Jeffrey (London: Methuen, 1923), pp. 109-64; Eric Chaisson and Steve McMillan, *Astronomy Today* (Englewood Cliffs, N.J.: Prentice-Hall, 1993), p. 604-5.

[34]Arthur S. Eddington, "On the Instability of Einstein's Spherical World," *Monthly Notices of the Royal Astronomical Society* 90 (1930): 668-78.

[35]As the Russian physicist Alexander Friedmann showed in 1922, general relativity implied that, in the words of Stephen Hawking, "at some time in the past (between ten- and twenty-thousand-million years ago) the distance between neighboring galaxies must have been zero" (Hawking, *Brief History,* p. 46; see also Alexander Friedmann, "Uber die Krummung des Raumes," *Zeitschrift Fur Physik* 10 [1922]: 377-86).

[36]Recent measurements showing that the universe may be accelerating in its expansion have resuscitated discussions of the cosmological constant. These measurements seem to require some kind of repulsive force in opposition to gravitation in order to explain the acceleration. These data do not provide any new support for a static or temporarily infinite universe, however. Quite the reverse, they suggest instead a repulsive force now strong enough to accelerate the expansion and to prevent any subsequent con-

of precisely the magnitude necessary to counteract the expansion that his theory implied.[37] By thus seeking to preserve a static universe Einstein, like Newton, inadvertently concealed an important cosmological reality implicit in his theory of gravitation.

Yet the heavens would soon talk back. In the 1920s and 1930s astronomer Edwin Hubble made a series of observations that shocked even Einstein. While working at the Mt. Wilson Observatory in Southern California, Hubble discovered that our Milky Way galaxy is but one of many galaxies spread throughout the universe. More importantly, he discovered that the galaxies beyond the Milky Way are rapidly receding from ours. Hubble noticed that the light from these distant galaxies was shifted toward the red end of the electromagnetic spectrum. This "red shift" suggested recessional movement, for the same reason—the so-called Doppler effect—that a train whistle drops in pitch as a train moves away from a stationary observer. Hubble also discovered that the rate at which these other galaxies retreat from ours is directly related to their distance from us—just as if the universe were undergoing a spherical expansion in all directions from a singular explosive beginning—from a "big bang."[38]

During the remainder of the twentieth century, physicists and cosmologists formulated many alternatives to the new big bang cosmology, most of which restored the idea of an infinite universe. Some of these cosmological models were formulated for explicitly philosophical reasons. For example, in the late 1940s Fred Hoyle, Thomas Gold and Hermann Bondi proposed the "steady state" model specifically to explain galactic recession without invoking the objectionable notion of a beginning. According to their theory, as the universe expands, new matter is generated spontaneously in the space between expanding galaxies. On this

traction from occurring. Indeed, if these results hold up, they will provide additional disconfirmation of another infinite universe cosmology, the oscillating universe model (see below). See P. J. E. Peebles, "Evolution of the Cosmological Constant," *Nature* 398 (1999): 25-26; John Noble Wilford, "Cosmologists Ponder 'Missing Energy' of Universe," *New York Times*, May 5, 1998, F1.

[37]Albert Einstein, "Kosmologische Betrachtungen zur allgemeinen Relativitatstheorie," *Sitzungsberichte der Koniglich Preussischen Akademie der Wissenschaften*, Febuary 8, 1917, pp. 142-52.

[38]Edwin Hubble, "A Relation Between Distance and Radial Velocity Among Extra-Galactic Nebulae," *Proceedings of the National Academy of Sciences* 15 (1929): 168-73.

view our galaxy is composed of matter that spontaneously popped into existence between other galaxies, which in turn came out of the empty space between other galaxies and so on.[39] Thus the steady state theory denied the need to postulate a singular beginning and reaffirmed a universe without beginning or end.

By the mid-1960s, however, Hoyle's theory had run aground as the result of a discovery made at the Bell Telephone Laboratories in New Jersey. According to the steady state model the density of the universe must always remain constant, hence, the creation of new matter as the universe expands. Yet in 1965 two Bell Lab researchers, Arno Penzias and Robert Wilson, found what physicists believed to be the radiation left over from the universe's initial hot, high-density state. The discovery of this "cosmic background radiation," at roughly 2.7 degrees Kelvin, proved decisive.[40] Physicist George Gamow had predicted its existence as a consequence of the big bang model.[41] Advocates of the steady state theory acknowledged that given their model such radiation should not exist. The steady state theory also implied that galaxies should have radically different ages, but advances in observational astronomy have revealed that galactic ages cluster narrowly in the "middle-age" range. By the 1970s even Bondi, Gold and Hoyle had abandoned their theory.[42]

Following the demise of the steady state model, the "oscillating universe" model arose as an alternative to a finite universe. Advocates of this model envisioned a universe that would expand, gradually decelerate, shrink back under the force of its own gravitation and then by some unknown mechanism reinitiate its expansion on and on ad infinitum. But as physicist Alan Guth showed in 1983, our knowledge of entropy suggests that the energy available to do work would decrease with each successive

---

[39]Hermann Bondi and Thomas Gold, "The Steady-State Theory of the Expanding Universe," *Monthly Notices of the Royal Astronomical Society* 108, no. 3 (1948): 252-70; Fred Hoyle, "A New Model for the Expanding Universe," *Monthly Notices of the Royal Astronomical Society* 108, no. 5 (1948): 372-82.

[40]Arno Penzias and Robert Wilson, "A Measurement of Excess Antenna Temperature at 4080 Mc/s," *Astrophysical Journal* 142, no. 1 (1965): 419-21.

[41]George Gamow, "Expanding Universe and the Origin of the Elements," *Physical Review* 70, nos. 7 and 8 (1946): 572-73.

[42]Helge Kragh, "The Steady State Theory," in *Cosmology: Historical, Literary, Philosophical, Religious, and Scientific Perspectives,* ed. Norriss S. Hetherington (New York: Garland, 1993) pp. 391-406, especially p. 403.

cycle.[43] Thus presumably the universe would have reached a nullifying equilibrium long ago if it had indeed existed for an infinite amount of time. Further, recent measurements suggest that the universe has only a fraction—roughly one-fifth—of the mass required to create a gravitational contraction in the first place.[44]

Prior to the formulation of the oscillating universe theory, three astrophysicists, Stephen Hawking, George Ellis and Roger Penrose, published a series of papers that explicated the implications of Einstein's theory of general relativity for space and time as well as matter and energy.[45] Previously, physicists like Friedmann had shown that the density of the universe would approach an infinite value as one extrapolated the state of the universe back in time. In a series of papers written between 1966 and 1970, Hawking and his colleagues showed that as one extrapolated back in time the curvature of space also approached infinity. But an infinitely curved space corresponds to a radius (within a sphere for example) of zero and thus to no spatial volume. Further, since in general relativity space and time are inextricably linked, the absence of space implies the absence of time. Moreover, neither matter nor energy can exist in the absence of space. Thus Hawking's result suggested that general relativity implies that the universe sprang into existence a finite time ago from literally nothing, at least nothing physical. In brief, general relativity implies an absolute beginning of time, "before" which neither time and space nor matter and energy would have existed.

The space-time theorem of general relativity was, of course, conditional. It stated that if general relativity obtains for the universe, then space and time themselves must have originated in the same initial explosion that created matter and energy. In a series of experiments beginning just two years after Einstein published his results and continuing on to

---

[43]Alan Guth and Marc Sher, "The Impossibility of a Bouncing Universe," *Nature* 302 (1983): 505-7.

[44]James Peebles, *Principles of Physical Cosmology* (Princeton, N.J.: Princeton University Press, 1993) pp. 475-83; Peter Coles and George Ellis, "The Case for an Open Universe," *Nature* 370 (1994): 609-13; Kathy Sawyer, "Hubble Finding: Expansion of Universe May Never End," *Seattle Times*, January 14, 1992, p. A5; P. J. E. Peebles, "The Mean Mass Density of the Universe," *Nature* 321 (1986): 27-32; Hugh Ross, *The Creator and the Cosmos* (Colorado Springs, Colo.: NavPress, 1993), p. 58.

[45]Stephen Hawking and Roger Penrose, "The Singularities of Gravitational Collapse and Cosmology," *Proceedings of the Royal Society of London*, series A, 314 (1970): 529-48.

the present, the probable error of general relativity (as estimated quantitatively) has shrunk from 10 to 1 to .05 percent, to a confirmation out to the fifth decimal place. Increasingly accurate tests conducted by NASA have continued to shrink the probable error associated with the theory.[46] Thus general relativity now stands as one of the best-confirmed theories of modern science. Yet its philosophical implications and those of the big bang theory are staggering. Taken jointly, general relativity and the big bang theory provide a scientific description of what Christian theologians have long described in doctrinal terms as *creatio ex nihilo*—creation out of nothing. These theories place a heavy demand on any proposed causal explanation of the universe since the cause of the universe must transcend time, space, matter and energy.

3.2. Anthropic "Fine-Tuning"

While evidences from cosmology now point to a transcendent cause for the origin of the universe, new evidences from physics suggest an intelligent cause for the origin of its fundamental architecture. Since the 1960s physicists have discovered that the existence of life in the universe depends upon a highly improbable balance of physical factors.[47] The constants of physics, the initial conditions of the universe and many other of its contingent features appear delicately balanced to allow for the possibility of life. Even very slight alterations in the values of many independent factors such as the expansion rate of the universe or the precise strength of gravitational or electromagnetic attraction, would render life impossible. Physicists now refer to these factors as "anthropic coincidences" and to the fortunate convergence of all these coincidences as the "fine-tuning of the universe." Many have noted that this fine-tuning strongly suggests design by a preexistent intelligence. As physicist Paul Davies has put it, "The impression of design is overwhelming."[48]

To see why, consider the following illustration. Imagine a cosmic

---

[46]Hugh Ross, *The Creator and the Cosmos*, pp. 66-67; R. F. C. Vessot et al., "Test of Relativistic Gravitation with a Space-Borne Hydrogen Maser," *Physical Review Letters* 45, no. 26 (1980): 2081-84.

[47]See Karl Giberson, "The Anthropic Priniciple," *Journal of Interdisciplinary Studies* 9 (1997): 63-90; response by Steven Yates, pp. 91-104.

[48]Paul Davies, *The Cosmic Blueprint* (New York: Simon & Schuster, 1988), p. 203.

explorer has just stumbled into the control room for the whole universe. There he discovers an elaborate "universe creating machine," with rows and rows of dials each with many possible settings. As he investigates, he learns that each dial represents some particular parameter that has to be calibrated with a precise value in order to create a universe in which life can survive. One dial represents the possible settings for the strong nuclear force, one for the gravitational constant, one for Planck's constant, one for the ratio of the neutron mass to the proton mass, one for the strength of electromagnetic attraction and so on. As our cosmic explorer examines the dials, he finds that the dials can be easily spun to different settings—that they could have been set otherwise. Moreover, he determines by careful calculation that even slight alterations in any of the dial settings would alter the architecture of the universe such that life would cease to exist. Yet for some reason each dial sits with just the exact value necessary to keep the universe running—like a multiple-dial safe cracked open with every dial found in just the right position. What should one infer about how these dial settings came to be set?

Not surprisingly, many physicists have been asking the same question about the anthropic coincidences. As George Greenstein muses:

> The thought insistently arises that some supernatural agency, or rather Agency, must be involved. Is it possible that suddenly, without intending to, we have stumbled upon scientific proof of the existence of a Supreme Being? Was it God who stepped in and so providentially crafted the cosmos for our benefit?"[49]

For many, the design hypothesis seems the most obvious and intuitively plausible answer.[50] As Fred Hoyle commented, "A commonsense interpretation of the facts suggests that a superintellect has monkeyed with physics, as well as chemistry and biology, and that there are no blind forces worth

[49]George Greenstein, *The Symbiotic Universe: Life and Mind in the Cosmos* (New York: Morrow, 1988), p. 26-27.

[50]Greenstein himself does not favor the design hypothesis. Instead, he favors the so-called participatory universe principle or "PAP." PAP attributes the apparent design of the fine tuning of the physical constants to the universe's (alleged) need to be observed in order to exist. As he says, the universe "brought forth life in order to exist . . . that the very Cosmos does not exist unless observed" (see Greenstein, *Symbiotic Universe*, p. 223).

speaking about in nature."[51] Many physicists now concur. They would argue that—in effect—the dials in the cosmic control room appear finely tuned because someone carefully set them that way.

Yet several other types of interpretations have been proposed: (1) the so-called weak anthropic principle, which denies that the fine-tuning needs explanation; (2) explanations based upon natural law; and (3) explanations based on chance. Each of these approaches suggests that the fine-tuning of the universe represents only "apparent" design.

Of these alternate proposals perhaps the most popular approach, at least initially, was the "weak anthropic principle" (WAP). Nevertheless, the WAP has recently encountered severe criticism from philosophers of physics and cosmology. Advocates of WAP claimed that if the universe were not fine-tuned to allow for life, then humans would not be here to observe it. Thus, they claimed, the fine-tuning requires no explanation. Yet as John Leslie and William Craig argue, the origin of the fine-tuning does require explanation.[52] Though we should not be surprised to find ourselves living in a universe suited for life (by definition), we ought to be surprised to learn that the conditions necessary for life are so vastly improbable. Leslie likens our situation to that of a blindfolded man who has discovered that, against all odds, he has survived a firing squad of one hundred marksmen.[53] Though his continued existence is certainly consistent with all the marksmen having missed, it does not explain why the marksmen actually did miss. In essence, the weak anthropic principle asserts that the statement of a necessary condition of an event eliminates the need for a causal explanation of that event. Yet oxygen is a necessary condition of fire, but saying so does not provide a causal explanation of the San Francisco fire. Similarly, the fine-tuning of the physical constants is a necessary condition for the existence of life, but that does not explain or eliminate the need to explain the origin of the fine-tuning.

While some have denied the need to explain the fine-tuning coincidences, others have sought to formulate various naturalistic explanations

---

[51]Fred Hoyle, "The Universe: Past and Present Reflections," *Annual Review of Astronomy and Astrophysics* 20 (1982): 16.

[52]William Lane Craig, "Cosmos and Creator," *Origins & Design* 20, no. 2 (Spring 1996): 18-28.

[53]John Leslie, "Anthropic Principle, World Ensemble, Design," *American Philosophical Quarterly* 19, no. 2 (1982): 150.

for them. Of these, appeals to natural law have proven the least plausible for a simple reason. The precise "dial settings" of the different constants of physics represent specific features *of the laws of nature themselves*—just how strong gravitational attraction or electromagnetic attraction will be, for example. These values represent contingent features of the fundamental laws themselves. Therefore, the laws cannot explain these features; they *embody* (or possess) the features that require explanation. As Davies has observed, the laws of physics "seem themselves to be the product of exceedingly ingenious design."[54] Further, natural laws by definition describe phenomena that conform to regular or repetitive patterns. Yet the idiosyncratic values of the physical constants and initial conditions constitute a highly irregular and nonrepetitive ensemble. It seems unlikely, therefore, that any law could explain why all the fundamental constants have exactly the values they do—why, for example, the gravitational constant should have exactly the value 6.67×10^{-11} Newton-meters^2 per kilogram^2 *and* the permittivity constant in Coulomb's law the value 8.85×10^{-12} Coulombs^2 per Newton-meter^2 *and* the electron charge to mass ratio 1.76×10^{11} Coulombs per kilogram *and* Planck's constant 6.63×10^{-34} Joule-seconds and so on.[55] These values specify a highly complex array. As a group they do not seem to exhibit a regular pattern that could in principle be subsumed or explained by natural law.

The chance explanation has proven more popular but has severe liabilities as well. First, the immense improbability of the fine-tuning makes straightforward appeals to chance untenable. Physicists have discovered more than thirty separate physical or cosmological parameters that require precise calibration in order to produce a life-sustaining universe.[56] Michael Denton, in *Nature's Destiny,* has documented many other necessary condi-

---

[54]Paul Davies, *The Superforce: The Search for a Grand Unified Theory of Nature* (New York: Simon & Schuster, 1984), p. 243.

[55]David Halliday, Robert Resnick and Jearl Walker, appendix B in *Fundamentals of Physics,* 5th ed. (New York: John Wiley, 1997), p. A3.

[56]See J. Barrow and F. Tipler, *The Anthropic Cosmological Principle* (Oxford: Oxford University Press, 1986), pp. 295-356, 384-444, 510-56; John Gribbin and Martin Rees, *Cosmic Coincidences* (London: Black Swan, 1991) see especially, pp. 3-29, 241-69; Hugh Ross, "The Big Bang Model Refined by Fire," in *Mere Creation: Science, Faith & Intelligent Design,* ed. William A. Dembski (Downers Grove, Ill.: InterVarsity Press, 1998), pp. 363-84, especially pp. 372-81.

tions for specifically human life from chemistry, geology and biology.[57] Moreover, many individual parameters exhibit an extraordinarily high degree of fine-tuning. Thus our cosmic explorer not only is confronted with a large ensemble of separate dial settings but with very large dials containing a vast array of possible settings, only very few of which allow for a life-sustaining universe. In many cases the odds against finding a single correct setting by chance, let alone all the correct settings, turn out to be virtually infinitesimal. For example, the force of gravity itself requires fine-tuning to one part in 10^{40}.[58] In addition, Oxford physicist Roger Penrose has noted that a single parameter, the original "phase-space volume," required such precise fine-tuning that the "Creator's aim must have been [precise] to an accuracy of one part in $10^{10^{123}}$." Penrose goes on to remark that, "one could not possibly even write the number down in full" since "it would be '1' followed by 10^{123} successive '0's!"—more zeros than the number of elementary particles in the entire universe. Such, he concludes, is "the precision needed to set the universe on its course."[59]

To circumvent such vast improbabilities, some have postulated the existence of a quasi-infinite number of parallel universes in order to increase the probabilistic resources (roughly, the amount of time and number of trials) available to produce the fine-tuning. In these "many worlds" or "possible worlds" scenarios—which were originally developed as part of the "Everett interpretation" of quantum physics and Andrei Linde's inflationary big bang cosmology—any event that has a nonzero probability, however small, must happen somewhere in some other parallel universe.[60] So long as life has a nonzero probability of arising, it has to arise in some possible world. Therefore, sooner or later some universe had to acquire life-sustaining characteristics.

On the many worlds hypothesis our existence in the universe only appears vastly improbable, since calculations of the probability of the anthropic coincidences arising by chance only consider the "probabilistic

[57]Michael Denton, *Nature's Destiny: How the Laws of Biology Reveal Purpose in the Universe* (New York: Free Press, 1998), pp. 47-262.

[58]Paul Davies, *God and the New Physics* (New York: Simon & Schuster, 1983), p. 188.

[59]Roger Penrose, *The Emperor's New Mind* (New York: Oxford, 1989), p. 344.

[60]Andrei Linde, "The Self-Reproducing Inflationary Universe," *Scientific American* 271 (November 1994): 48-55.

resources" available within our universe and neglect the probabilistic resources available from parallel universes. Thus according to the many worlds hypothesis (MWH), chance can explain the existence of life in the universe after all.

The MWH now stands as the most popular naturalistic explanation for the anthropic fine-tuning and thus warrants detailed comment. Though ingenious, the many worlds hypothesis suffers from an overriding difficulty: we have no evidence for any universes other than our own. Moreover, since possible worlds are by definition causally inaccessible to our own world, there can be no evidence for their existence except that they allegedly render probable otherwise vastly improbable events. Of course, no one can observe God directly either, though for theists, God is not causally disconnected from our world. Even so, recent work by philosophers of science like Richard Swinburne, John Leslie, William Craig, Jay Richards and Robin Collins have established several reasons for preferring the theistic-design hypothesis over naturalistic many-worlds hypotheses.[61]

First, all current cosmological models involving multiple universes require some kind of mechanism for generating universes. Yet such a "universe generator" would itself require precisely configured physical states, thus begging the question of its initial design. As Collins describes the dilemma:

> In all currently worked out proposals for what this universe generator could be—such as the oscillating big bang and the vacuum fluctuation models . . .—the "generator" itself is governed by a complex set of laws that allow it to produce universes. It stands to reason, therefore, that if these laws were slightly different the generator probably would not be able to produce any universes that could sustain life.[62]

Indeed, from experience we know that some machines (or factories) can

---

[61]See, for example, William Lane Craig, "Barrow and Tipler on the Anthropic Principle v. Divine Design," British Journal for the Philosophy of Science, 38 (1988): 389-95; and Jay Wesley Richards, "Many Worlds Hypotheses: A Naturalistic Alternative to Design," Perspectives on Science and Christian Belief 49, no. 4 (1997): 218-27. See also Alvin Plantinga, The Nature of Necessity (Oxford: Clarendon Press, 1980).

[62]Robin Collins, "The Fine-Tuning Design Argument: A Scientific Argument for the Existence of God," in Reason for the Hope Within, ed. Michael Murray (Grand Rapids, Mich.: Eerdmans, 1999), p. 61.

produce other machines. But our experience also suggests that such machine-producing machines themselves require intelligent design.

Second, as Collins argues, all things being equal we should prefer hypotheses "that are natural extrapolations from what we already know"[63] about the causal powers of various kinds of entities. Yet when it comes to explaining the anthropic coincidences, the multiple worlds hypothesis fails this test, whereas the theistic-design hypothesis does not. To illustrate, Collins asks his reader to imagine a paleontologist who posits the existence of an electromagnetic "dinosaur-bone-producing-field," as opposed to actual dinosaurs, as the explanation for the origin of large fossilized bones. While certainly such a field qualifies as a possible explanation for the origin of the fossil bones, we have no experience of such fields, nor of their producing fossilized bones. Yet we have observed animal remains in various phases of decay and preservation in sediments and sedimentary rock. Thus most scientists rightly prefer the actual dinosaur hypothesis over the apparent dinosaur hypothesis (that is, the "dinosaur-bone-producing-field" hypothesis), as an explanation for the origin of fossils. In the same way, Collins argues, we have no experience of anything like a "universe generator" (that is not itself designed) producing either finely tuned systems or infinite and exhaustively random ensembles of possibilities. Yet we do have extensive experience of intelligent agents producing finely tuned machines such as Swiss watches. Thus Collins concludes, the postulation of "a supermind" (God) to explain the fine-tuning of the universe constitutes a natural extrapolation from our experience-based knowledge of the causal powers of intelligent agency, whereas the postulation of multiple universes lacks a similar basis.

Third, as Craig shows, for the many-worlds hypothesis to suffice as an explanation for anthropic fine-tuning, there must exist an exhaustively random distribution of physical parameters and thus an *infinite* number of parallel universes to insure that a life-producing combination of factors will eventually arise. Yet neither of the physical models that allow for a multiple-universe interpretation—Everett's quantum mechanical model or Linde's inflationary cosmology—provides a compelling justification for the existence of such an exhaustively random and infinite number of parallel

---

[63]Ibid., pp. 60-61.

universes, but instead only for a finite and nonrandom set.[64] The Everett model, for example, only generates an ensemble of material *states,* each of which exists within a parallel universe that has the same set of the physical laws and constants as our own. Since these do not vary "across universes," Everett's model, therefore, does nothing to increase the probabilistic resources available to explain the improbably fine-tuning of laws and constants within our own universe. Though Linde's model does envision a variable ensemble of physical constants in each of his individual "bubble universes," his model fails to generate either an exhaustively random set of such conditions or the infinite number of universes required to render probable the fine-tuning of our universe.

Fourth, Richard Swinburne argues that the theistic-design hypothesis constitutes a simpler and less ad hoc hypothesis than the MWH.[65] He notes that virtually the only evidence for many worlds is the very anthropic fine-tuning the hypothesis was formulated to explain. On the other hand, the theistic-design hypothesis, though also supported by indirect evidences, can explain many separate and independent features of the universe that a many-worlds scenario cannot, including the origin of the universe itself, the mathematical beauty and elegance of physical laws, and personal religious experience. Swinburne argues that the God hypothesis constitutes a simpler as well as a more comprehensive explanation in that it requires the postulation of only one explanatory entity rather than the multiple entities, including a finely tuned universe generator and an infinite number of causally separate universes, required by the MWH.

Clifford Longley of the *London Times* wrote in 1989 that the use of such an unparsimonious explanation to avoid the theistic-design argument seems to betray a kind of metaphysical special pleading and desperation.[66] Few people would accept such a far-fetched explanation in any other domain of life. That some scientists dignify MWH with serious discussion may speak more to an unimpeachable commitment to naturalistic philosophy than to any compelling merit for the idea itself.

As the twentieth century comes to a close, the design argument has

[64]Craig, "Cosmos and Creator," p. 24.
[65]Richard Swinburne, "Argument from the Fine Tuning of Universe," in *Physical Cosmology and Philosophy,* ed. John Leslie (New York: Macmillan, 1990), pp. 154-73.
[66]Clifford Longley, "Focusing on Theism," *London Times,* January 21, 1989, p. A10.

reemerged from its premature retirement at the hands of biologists in the nineteenth century. Physics, astronomy, cosmology and chemistry have each revealed that life depends on a very precise set of design parameters, which, as it happens, have been built into our universe. The fine-tuning evidence has led to a persuasive reformulation of the design argument, though not a formal deductive proof of God's existence. As a result, physicist John Polkinghorne notes that

> we are living in an age where there is a great revival of natural theology taking place. That revival of natural theology is taking place not on the whole among theologians, who have lost their nerve in that area, but among the scientists.[67]

Polkinghorne also notes that this revived natural theology generally has more modest ambitions than the natural theology of the Middle Ages. Nevertheless, his statement suggests that a profound intellectual shift has begun taking place as physics and related disciplines reveal new evidence that appears to support theistic belief.

3.3. Evidence of Intelligent Design in Biology
Despite renewed interest in the design hypothesis among physicists and cosmologists, many biologists have long-remained reluctant to consider such notions. Indeed, since the late-nineteenth century, biologists have mostly rejected the idea that biological organisms manifest evidence of intelligent design. While many acknowledge the *appearance* of design in biological systems, they insist that purely naturalistic mechanisms such as natural selection acting on random variations can give a full account of how this appearance arose.

3.3.1. Molecular Machines
In spite of the misgivings of many, the rumblings about design have begun to spread to biology. In 1998 for example, the leading journal *Cell* featured a special issue on macromolecular machines. Molecular machines are incredibly complex devices that all cells use to process information, build

---

[67]John Polkinghorne, "So Finely Tuned a Universe of Atoms, Stars, Quanta & God," *Commonweal,* August 16, 1996, p. 16.

proteins and move materials back and forth across their membranes. Bruce Alberts, president of the National Academy of Sciences, notes that molecular machines strongly resemble machines designed by human engineers, although as an orthodox neo-Darwinian he denies any role for actual, as opposed to apparent, design in the origin of these systems.

In recent years, however, a formidable challenge to this view has arisen within biology. In *Darwin's Black Box*, Lehigh University biochemist Michael Behe shows that neo-Darwinists have failed to explain the origin of complex molecular machines in living systems. For example, Behe looks at the ion-powered rotary engines that turn the whiplike flagella of certain bacteria.[68] He shows that the intricate machinery in this molecular motor—including a rotor, a stator, O-rings, bushings and a drive shaft—requires the coordinated interaction of some forty complex protein parts. Yet the absence of any one of these proteins result in the complete loss of motor function. To assert that such an "irreducibly complex" engine emerged gradually in a Darwinian fashion strains credulity. Natural selection selects functionally advantageous systems. Yet motor function only ensues *after* all necessary parts have independently self-assembled—an astronomically improbable event. Thus Behe insists that Darwinian mechanisms cannot account for the origin of molecular motors and other "irreducibly complex systems" that require the coordinated interaction of multiple, independent protein parts.

To emphasize his point Behe conducted a literature search of relevant technical journals.[69] He found a pervasive absence of gradualistic Darwinian explanations for the origin of the systems and motors that he discusses. Behe concludes that neo-Darwinists have neither explained nor, in most cases, even attempted to explain how the appearance of design in "irreducibly complex" systems arose naturalistically. Instead, he notes that we know of only one cause sufficient to produce functionally integrated, irreducibly complex systems—intelligent design. Whenever we encounter irreducibly complex systems and we know how they arose, invariably a designer played a causal role. Thus Behe concludes on strong uniformitarian grounds that the molecular machines and complex systems we observe in cells must

---

[68]Michael J. Behe, *Darwin's Black Box* (New York: Free Press, 1996), pp. 51-73.
[69]Ibid., pp. 165-86.

have also had an intelligent source. In brief, molecular motors appear designed because they were designed.

3.3.2. The Complex Specificity of Cellular Components

Other developments in biology reinforce Behe's argument. The molecular machines that Behe examines inside the cell are built from smaller components known as proteins. In addition to building motors and other biological structures, proteins perform vital biochemical functions—information processing, metabolic regulation, signal transduction—necessary to maintain cellular life. Biologists, from Darwin's time to the late 1930s, assumed that proteins had simple, regular structures explicable by reference to mathematical laws.

Beginning in the 1950s, however, biologists made a series of discoveries that caused this simplistic view of proteins to change. Molecular biologist Fred Sanger determined the sequence of constituents in the protein molecule insulin. Sanger's work showed that proteins are made of long nonrepetitive sequences of amino acids, rather like an irregular arrangement of colored beads on a string.[70] Later in the 1950s, work by John Kendrew on the structure of the protein myoglobin showed that proteins also exhibit a surprising three-dimensional complexity. Far from the simple structures that biologists had imagined, Kendrew's work revealed an extraordinarily complex and irregular three-dimensional shape—a twisting, turning, tangled chain of amino acids.

During the 1950s scientists quickly realized that proteins possess another remarkable property. In addition to their complexity, proteins also exhibit specificity, both as one-dimensional arrays and as three-dimensional structures. Whereas proteins are built from rather simple chemical building blocks known as amino acids, their function—whether as enzymes, signal transducers or structural components in the cell—depends crucially on the complex but specific sequencing of these building blocks.[71]

---

[70]Horace Judson, *Eighth Day of Creation* (New York: Simon & Schuster, 1979), pp. 213, 229-35, 255-61, 304, 334-35; Fred Sanger and Hans Tuppy, "The Amino Acid Sequence in the Phenylalanyl Chain of Insulin, 1 and 2," *Biochemical Journal* 49, no. 4 (1951): 463-80; Fred Sanger and E. O. P. Thompson, "The Amino Acid Sequence in the Glycyl Chain of Insulin, 1 and 2," *Biochemical Journal* 53, no. 3 (1953): 353-66, 366-74.

[71]Bruce Alberts et al., *Molecular Biology of the Cell* (New York: Garland, 1983), pp. 91-141.

Molecular biologists like Francis Crick quickly likened this feature of proteins to a linguistic text. Just as the meaning (or function) of an English text depends on the sequential arrangement of letters in a text, so too does the function of a polypeptide (a sequence of amino acids) depend on its specific sequencing. Moreover, in both cases slight alterations in sequencing can quickly result in loss of function.

In the biological case the specific sequencing of amino acids gives rise to specific three-dimensional structures. This structure or shape in turn determines what function, if any, the amino acid chain can perform within the cell. For a functioning protein its three-dimensional shape gives it a hand-in-glove fit with other molecules in the cell, enabling it to catalyze specific chemical reactions or to build specific structures within the cell. Due to this specificity one protein can usually no more substitute for another than one type of tool can substitute for another type. Proteins can perform functions only by virtue of their three-dimensional specificity of fit with other equally specified and complex molecules within the cell. This three-dimensional specificity derives in turn from a one-dimensional specificity of sequencing in the arrangement of the amino acids that form proteins.

3.3.3. The Sequence Specificity of DNA

The complexity and specificity of proteins both as one-dimensional arrays and three-dimensional structures raised an important question. How did such complex but specific structures arise in the cell? This question recurred with particular urgency after Sanger revealed his results in the early 1950s. Clearly, proteins were too complex and functionally specific to arise "by chance." Moreover, given their irregularity it seemed unlikely that a general chemical law or regularity governed their assembly. Instead, as Jacques Monod recalled, molecular biologists began to look for some source of information within the cell that could direct the construction of these highly specific structures. To explain the presence of all that information in the protein "you absolutely needed a code," as Monod would later explain.[72]

In 1953 James Watson and Francis Crick elucidated the structure of the

---

[72]Jacques Monod, cited in Judson, *Eighth Day*, p. 611.

DNA molecule.[73] Soon thereafter molecular biologists discovered how DNA stores the information necessary to direct protein synthesis. In 1955 Crick first proposed the "sequence hypothesis," suggesting that the specificity of amino acids in proteins derives from the specific arrangement of chemical constituents in the DNA molecule.[74] According to the sequence hypothesis, information on the DNA molecule is stored in the form of specifically arranged chemicals called nucleotide bases along the spine of DNA's helical strands. Chemists represent these four nucleotides with the letters A, T, G and C (for adenine, thymine, guanine and cytosine). By 1961 the sequence hypothesis became part of the so-called central dogma of molecular biology after a series of brilliant experiments confirmed DNA's information-bearing properties.

As it turns out, specific regions of the DNA molecule called *coding regions* have the same property of "sequence specificity" or "specified complexity" that characterizes written codes, linguistic texts and protein molecules. Just as the letters in the alphabet of a written language may perform a communication function depending on their sequencing, so too may the nucleotide bases in DNA produce a functional protein depending on their precise sequential arrangement. The nucleotide bases in DNA function in precisely the same way as symbols in a computer code or alphabetic characters in a book. In each case the arrangement of the characters determines the function of the sequence as a whole. As Dawkins notes, "The machine code of the genes is uncannily computer-like."[75] Or as Bill Gates avers, "DNA is like a computer program, but far, far more advanced than any software we've ever created."[76] In the case of a computer code the specific arrangement of just two symbols (0 and 1) suffices to carry information. In the case of an English text the twenty-six letters of the alphabet do the job. In the case of DNA, the complex but precise sequencing of the four nucleotide bases (A, T, G and C) stores and transmits genetic information—information that finds expression in the construction of specific proteins.

---

[73]James Watson and Francis Crick, "A Structure for Deoxyribose Nucleic Acid," *Nature* 171 (1953): 737-38.

[74]Judson, *Eighth Day*, pp. 335-36; Alberts et al., *Molecular Biology*, pp. 106-10.

[75]Richard Dawkins, *River Out of Eden* (New York: BasicBooks, 1995), p. 10.

[76]Bill Gates, *The Road Ahead* (Boulder, Colo.: Blue Penguin, 1996), p. 228.

Developments in molecular biology have raised the question of the ultimate origin of the specific sequencing—the information content—in both DNA and proteins. These developments have also created severe difficulties for all strictly naturalistic theories of the origin of the first cellular life. Since the late 1920s naturalistically minded scientists have sought to explain the origin of the very first life as the result of a completely undirected process of "chemical evolution." Chemical evolutionary theorists such as Alexander I. Oparin envisioned life arising by a slow process of transformation starting from simple chemicals on the early earth.[77] Unlike Darwinism, which sought to explain the origin and diversification of new and more complex living forms from simpler preexisting forms, chemical evolutionary theory seeks to explain the origin of the very first cellular life. Yet since the late 1950s naturalistic chemical evolutionary theories have been unable to account for the origin of the specified complexity or information content necessary to build a living cell.[78]

Chance-based models of chemical evolution have failed since the amount of specified information present in even a single protein or gene—a section of DNA for building a single protein—typically exceeds the probabilistic resources of the entire universe.[79] Models based on "pre-biotic natural selection" have failed since they presuppose the existence of a self-

---

[77]Alexander I. Oparin, *The Origin of Life,* trans. S. Morgulis (New York: Macmillan, 1938), see esp. pp. 64-103, 98-108, 133-35, 148-59, 195-96.

[78]For a good summary and critique of different naturalistic models see especially K. Dose, "The Origin of Life: More Questions Than Answers," *Interdisciplinary Science Review* 13, no. 4 (1988): 348-56; H. P. Yockey, *Information Theory and Molecular Biology* (Cambridge: Cambridge University Press, 1992), pp. 259-93; C. Thaxton, W. Bradley and R. Olsen, *The Mystery of Life's Origin* (Dallas: Lewis & Stanley, 1992); R. Shapiro, *Origins* (London: Heinemann, 1986); Stephen C. Meyer, "The Explanatory Power of Design: DNA and the Origin of Information," in *Mere Creation: Science, Faith & Intelligent Design,* ed. William A. Dembski (Downers Grove, Ill.: InterVarsity Press, 1998), pp. 203-17.

[79]William A. Dembski, *The Design Inference* (Cambridge University Press, 1998), pp. 203-17; Meyer, "Explanatory Power," pp. 124-26; Yockey, *Information Theory and Molecular Biology,* pp. 246-58; H. J. Morowitz, *Energy Flow in Biology* (New York: Academic Press, 1968), pp. 5-12; A. G. Cairns-Smith, *The Life Puzzle* (Edinburgh: Oliver & Boyd, 1971), pp. 92-96; Shapiro, *Origins,* pp. 117-31; J. Bowie and R. Sauer, "Identifying Determinants of Folding and Activity for a Protein of Unknown Structure," *Proceedings of the National Academy of Sciences USA* 86 (1989): 2152-56.

replicating system.[80] Yet this in turn presupposes the presence of information-rich DNA and protein molecules—the very entities that require explanation in the first place. Finally, self-organizational models have failed since the information content of DNA defies explanation by reference to the physical and chemical properties of its constituent parts.[81] Just as the chemistry of ink does not explain the origin of the specific sequencing of letters in a newspaper headline, so too the properties of the chemical constituents of DNA text—the four nucleotide bases—do not explain the specific sequencing of the genetic text. As Michael Polanyi put it, "As the arrangement of a printed page is extraneous to the chemistry of the printed page, so is the base sequence in a DNA molecule extraneous to the chemical forces at work in the DNA molecule."[82]

3.4. DNA by Design

The presence of specified information in DNA suggests a source extrinsic to physics and chemistry. When one seeks the source of the information in this morning's newspaper or in an ancient inscription, one comes ultimately to a writer or scribe. When a computer user traces the information on a screen back to its source, a writer, software engineer or programmer invariably comes to mind. If, as Gates states, DNA is similar to but more complex than a software program (in its information content), it makes sense to infer that it too had an intelligent source.

Though DNA is similar to a computer program, the case for its design does not depend on mere resemblance. Classical design arguments in biol-

---

[80]Meyer, "Explanatory Power," pp. 126-28; Mora, "The Folly of Probability," pp. 311-12; L. V. Bertalanffy, *Robots, Men and Minds* (New York: George Braziller, 1967), p. 82; T. Dobzhansky, "Discussion of G. Schramm's Paper," in *The Origins of Prebiological Systems and of Their Molecular Matrices,* ed. S. W. Fox (New York: Academic Press, 1965), p. 310; H. H. Pattee, "The Problem of Biological Hierarchy," in *Towards a Theoretical Biology,* ed. C. H. Waddington (Edinburgh: Edinburgh University Press, 1970), 3:123.

[81]Meyer, "Explanatory Power," pp. 128-34; Thaxton, Bradley and Olson, *The Mystery of Life's Origin,* pp. 113-66; H. P. Yockey, "Self-Organization Origin of Life Scenarios and Information Theory," *Journal of Theoretical Biology* 91 (1981): 13-31; Michael Polanyi, "Life's Irreducible Structure," *Science* 160 (1968): 1309; B. Kuppers, "On the Prior Probability of the Existence of Life," in *The Probabilistic Revolution,* ed. Kruger et al. (Cambridge, Mass.: MIT Press, 1987), p. 364; R. A. Kok, J. A. Taylor and Walter L. Bradley, "A Statistical Examination of Self-Ordering of Amino Acids in Proteins," *Origins of Life and Evolution of the Biosphere* 18 (1988): 135-42.

[82]Polanyi, "Life's Irreducible Structure," p. 1309.

ogy typically sought to draw *analogies* between whole organisms and machines based on certain similar features that each held in common. These arguments sought to reason from similar effects back to similar causes. The status of such design arguments thus turned on the degree of similarity that actually obtained between the effects in question. Yet since even advocates of these classical arguments admitted dissimilarities as well as similarities, the status of these arguments always appeared uncertain. Advocates would argue that the similarities between organisms and machines outweighed dissimilarities; critics would claim the opposite.

The design argument from the information in DNA does not depend on such analogical reasoning since it does not depend on claims of similarity.[83] The coding regions of DNA have the very same property of "sequence specificity" or "information content" that computer codes and linguistic texts have. Though DNA does not possess all the properties of natural language or "semantic information"—that is, information that is subjectively meaningful to human agents—it does have precisely those properties that jointly imply a prior intelligence.

William Dembski has shown in his recent book *The Design Inference* that systems or sequences that have the joint properties of "high complexity and specification" invariably result from intelligent causes, not chance or physical-chemical necessity. Complex sequences are those that exhibit an irregular and improbable arrangement that defies expression by a simple rule or algorithm. A specification, on the other hand, is a match or correspondence between a physical system or sequence and a set of independent functional requirements or constraints. As it turns out, the base sequences in the coding regions of DNA are both highly complex and specified. The sequences of bases in DNA are highly irregular, nonrepetitive and improbable—and, therefore, also complex. Moreover, the coding regions of DNA exhibit sequential arrangements of bases that are necessary (within certain tolerances) to produce functional proteins—that is, they are highly specified with respect to the independent requirements of protein function and protein synthesis.[84] Thus, as nearly all molecular biologists now recognize, the coding regions of DNA possess a

[83]Elliot Sober, *Philosophy of Biology* (San Francisco: Westview, 1993), pp. 26-47.
[83]Thaxton and Bradley, "Information," pp. 173-210; Thaxton, *Mystery*, pp. 127-66.
[84]Yockey, *Information Theory*, pp. 242-93.

high information content—where "information content" in a biological context means precisely "complexity and specificity."[85]

Thus the design argument from information content in DNA does not depend on analogical reasoning, since it does not depend on assessments of degree of similarity. The argument does not depend on the *similarity* of DNA to a computer program or human language but on the presence of an identical feature ("information content" defined as "complexity and specification") in both DNA and all other designed systems, languages or artifacts. While a computer program may be similar to DNA in many respects and dissimilar in others, it exhibits a precise identity to DNA in its ability to store information content.

As such, this argument does not represent an argument from analogy, of the sort that Hume criticized, but an "inference to the best explanation." Such arguments turn not on assessments of the degree of similarity between effects but instead on an assessment of the adequacy of competing possible causes for the same effect. Since we know intelligent agents can (and do) produce functionally specified sequences of symbols or arrangements of matter (information content), intelligent agency qualifies as a sufficient causal explanation for the origin of this effect. In addition, since naturalistic scenarios have proven universally inadequate for explaining the origin of information content, mind or creative intelligence now stands as the best and only entity with the causal power to produce this feature of living systems.

---

[85]The term *information content* is used variously to denote both specified complexity and unspecified complexity. Yet a sequence of symbols that is merely complex but not specified (such as "wnsgdtej38ejdfmfcksdncnmd") would not necessarily indicate the activity of a designing intelligence. Thus it may be argued that design arguments based on the presence of information commit a fallacy of equivocation by inferring design from a type of "information" (i.e., unspecified information) that could result from random natural processes. Ambiguities in the definition of information and information content do leave open this possibility. One can foreclose this possibility, however, by defining information content as equivalent to the joint properties of complexity and specification. Though the term is not used this way universally in information theory, it has been used this way by biologists from the beginning of the molecular biological revolution. As Sarkar points out, since the mid-1950s Francis Crick and others have equated "information" not only with complexity but also with what they called "specificity"—where they understood specificity to mean "necessary to function." See Sahotra Sarkar, ed., "Biological Information: A Skeptical Look at Some Central Dogmas of Molecular Biology," in *The Philosophy and History of Molecular Biology: New Perspectives* (Dordrecht: Kluwer, 1996), p. 191.

Indeed, experience teaches that whenever we encounter specified complexity or high information content in an artifact or entity whose causal story is known, invariably creative intelligence has played a causal role in the origin of that entity. In other words, since experience suggests that intelligent design is an empirically *necessary* cause of an information-rich system (the only cause known to be capable of producing the effect), one can detect (or, logically, retrodict) the past action of an intelligent cause from the presence of such an effect, even if the cause itself cannot be directly observed.[86] The specified pattern of red and yellow flowers spelling "Welcome to Victoria" in the gardens of Victoria harbor in Canada lead visitors to infer the activity of intelligent agents (gardeners), even if they did not see the flowers planted and arranged. The arrangement of symbols on the Rosetta Stone led archaeologists to infer the work of scribes, though archaeologists could make no direct observations of them working. Similarly, the specifically arranged nucleotide sequences—the information content—in DNA suggests the past action of an intelligent mind, even though such mental agency cannot be directly observed. Intelligent agents have unique causal powers that nature does not. Since DNA displays precisely an effect—information content—that in our experience only intelligent agents can produce, intelligent design—not apparent design—stands as the best explanation for the information content (or specified complexity) in DNA.

Part 4: Reconceptualizing Epistemic Support

Despite the rather dramatic developments in cosmology and biology during the twentieth century, many scientists and theologians remain reluctant to revise their understanding of the relationship between science and theistic belief. True, there are perhaps fewer scientists today than in the late nineteenth century who would assert that science and religion stand in overt conflict. Yet many scientists and theologians still deny that science can provide evidential or epistemic support for Judeo-Christian or theistic belief. Instead, they express skepticism about what they see as a return to the failed "natural theology" of the nineteenth century or to rationalistic attempts to prove the existence of God. They point out, perhaps rightly, that

---

[86]Stephen C. Meyer, "Of Clues and Causes: A Methodological Interpretation of Origin of Life Studies," (Ph.D. dissertation, University of Cambridge, 1990), pp. 77-140; Meyer, "Explanatory Power," pp. 82-97.

neither the evidence for a cosmological singularity nor the evidence of design in physics and biology can prove God's existence. Thus many theologians and scientists continue to affirm the strict neutrality of science and deny that science does (or can) support theistic belief.

Consider the view of Ernan McMullin, a prominent philosopher of science and a theologian at the University of Notre Dame. McMullin explicitly denies that the big bang theory provides any evidential support for Christian theism, though he admits that if one assumed the Christian doctrine of creation, one might expect to find evidence for a beginning to time. As he explains:

> What one could say . . . is that if the universe began in time through the act of a Creator, from our vantage point it would look something like the Big Bang that cosmologists are talking about. What one cannot say is . . . that the Big Bang model "supports" the Christian doctrine of Creation.[87]

4.1. Deduction and The Logic of Entailment

Many philosophers, scientists and theologians assume that scientific evidence (represented here as A) can provide epistemological support for, or grounds for, believing a theological proposition B only if the theological proposition B follows from evidence A with deductive certainty. They assume that to succeed in providing epistemic support for God's existence or other propositional commitments of theism, arguments must necessarily take a deductive logical form such as:

If A, then B

A

Therefore B

Of course, many arguments for God's existence have been framed in precisely such a deductive manner. Recall, for example, the classic statement of the *kalam* cosmological argument for God's existence.[88]

---

[87]Ernan McMullin, "How Should Cosmology Relate to Theology?" in *The Sciences and Theology in the Twentieth Century*, ed. Arthur R. Peacocke (Notre Dame, Ind.: University of Notre Dame Press, 1981), p. 39.

[88]Craig, *Reasonable Faith*, p. 92.

> Whatever begins to exist has a cause.
> *The universe began to exist.*
> ───────────────────────────────
> Therefore, the universe has a cause.

Such deductive arguments utilize the standard *modus ponens* logical form. Thus they are logically valid. If the premises of such arguments are true and can be known to be true with certainty, then the conclusion follows with certainty as well. In such arguments, logicians say the premises "entail" the conclusions. Of course, finding premises that can be known to be true with certainty can be very difficult, especially in an empirically based inquiry such as natural science. Many deductive arguments for God's existence failed for exactly this reason. Nevertheless, deductive entailment from true premises does constitute a perfectly legitimate, if infrequently attained, form of epistemic support. If *A* logically compels *B*, then it is irrational to deny *B* if one affirms *A*. In such cases *A* clearly provides support for *B*.[89] Even so, deductive entailment involves a far stronger notion of support than empirical science requires. Scientists rarely prove their theories deductively from empirical evidence. Indeed, no field of inquiry short of mathematics could progress if it limited itself to the logic of entailment. Rather, most fields of inquiry employ alternate forms of inference known variously as the method of hypothesis, abduction, hypothetico-deductive method or inference to the best explanation.

4.2. Abduction and the Logic of Confirmation of Hypothesis

During the nineteenth century a logician named C. S. Peirce described the modes of inference that we use to derive conclusions from data.[90] Peirce noted that in addition to deductive arguments, we often employ a mode of logic he called "abduction" or "the method of hypothesis." To see the difference between these two types of inference, consider the following argument schemata.[91]

───────────────────────────────

[89]Dembski and Meyer, "Fruitful Interchange or Polite Chitchat?" 418-22.

[90]C. S. Peirce, *Collected Papers,* ed. Charles Hartshorne and Paul Weiss (Cambridge: Harvard University Press, 1931), 2:375.

[91]Meyer, "Of Clues and Causes," p. 25.

Deductive schema
> Data: A is given and plainly true.
> Logic: *But if A is true, then B is a matter of course.*
> Conclusion: Hence, B must be true as well.

Abductive schema
> Data: The surprising fact B is observed.
> Logic: *But if A were true, then B would be a matter of course.*
> Conclusion: Hence, there is reason to suspect that A is true.

In the logic of the deductive schema, if the premises are true, the conclusion follows with certainty. The logic of the abductive schema, however, does not produce certainty but instead plausibility or possibility. Unlike deduction, in which the minor premise affirms the antecedent variable A, abductive logic affirms the consequent variable B. In deductive logic, affirming the consequent variable (with certainty) constitutes a fallacy—a fallacy that derives from the failure to acknowledge that more than one antecedent might explain or produce the same consequent. To see why, consider the following argument:

> If it rains the streets will get wet.
> *The streets are wet.*
> _____
> Therefore, it rained.

Or symbolically:

> If R, then W
> W
> _____
> Therefore R

Obviously this argument has a problem as it stands. It does not follow that because the streets are wet, it necessarily rained. The streets may have gotten wet in some other way. A fire hydrant may have burst, a snow bank may have melted or a street sweeper may have doused the street before beginning a cleaning operation. Nevertheless, that the streets are wet *might* indicate that it has rained. Thus amending the argument as follows does not commit the fallacy:

If it rains, then we would expect the streets to get wet.
The streets are wet.
_____

Therefore *perhaps* it rained.

Or symbolically:

If R, then W
W
_____

Perhaps R

Even if one may not affirm the consequent with certainty, one may affirm it as a possibility. And this is precisely what abductive logic does. It provides a reason for considering that a hypothesis may be true. Indeed, it gives a reason for believing a hypothesis, even if one cannot affirm the hypothesis (or conclusion) with certainty.

The natural and historical sciences employ such logic routinely. In the natural sciences, if we have reason to expect that some state of affairs will ensue given some hypothesis, and we find that such a state of affairs has ensued, then we say that our hypothesis has been confirmed. This method of "confirmation of hypothesis" functions to provide evidential support for many scientific hypotheses. Given Copernicus' heliocentric theory of the solar system, astronomers in the seventeenth century had reason to expect that the planet Venus should exhibit phases. Galileo's discovery that Venus does exhibit phases, therefore, supported (though it did not prove) the heliocentric view. The discovery did not prove the heliocentric theory since other theories might—and in fact could—explain the same fact.[92]

Peirce acknowledged that abductive inferences on their own may constitute a rather weak form of epistemic support. Yet as a practical matter Peirce acknowledged that abduction often yields conclusions that are difficult to doubt even if they lack the airtight certainty that accompanies the logic of deduction. For instance, Peirce argued that skepticism about the existence of Napoleon Bonaparte was unjustified even though Napoleon's existence could

_____

[92]Owen Gingerich, "The Galileo Affair," *Scientific American* 247, no. 2 (1982): 133-43.

be known only by abduction. As Peirce put it, "Numberless documents refer to a conqueror called Napoleon Bonaparte. Though we have not seen the man, yet we cannot explain what we have seen, namely, all these documents and monuments, without supposing that he really existed."[93] Thus Peirce suggested that by considering the explanatory power of a hypothesis, the logic of abduction might underwrite more robust relations of epistemic support.

4.3. The Logic of Comparative Explanatory Power: Inference to the Best Explanation

Since Peirce's time, philosophers of science have refined his abductive logic to show how abductive inferences (or confirmation of hypothesis) can provide a stronger form of epistemic support. The abductive framework of logic employed by natural scientists and others often provides a weak form of epistemic support, since it leaves open many possible explanations for the same evidence. Philosophers of science have recognized that scientists often have to evaluate the explanatory power of competing possible hypotheses. This method, alternatively called "the method of multiple competing hypotheses"[94] or "inference to the best explanation,"[95] often reduces, at least for practical purposes, the uncertainty or "underdetermination" associated with abductive inference. In this method of reasoning the explanatory or predictive virtues of a potential hypothesis determine which among a competing set of possible explanations constitutes the best.[96] Scientists infer that hypothesis among a competing group of hypotheses that would, if true, provide the best explanation of some set of relevant data. True, both an earthquake and a bomb could explain the destruction of the building, but only the bomb can explain the presence of charring and

---

[93]Peirce, *Collected Papers*, p. 375.

[94]T. C. Chamberlin, "The Method of Multiple Working Hypotheses," *Science* 148 (1890; reprint, 1965): 754-59.

[95]Meyer, "Of Clues and Causes," pp. 90-97; Peter Lipton, *Inference to the Best Explanation* (London: Routledge, 1991), pp. 1-5, 6-8, 56-74; Sober, *Philosophy of Biology*, pp. 1-8, 27-46, 56-74, 92-96.

[96]Recent work in the philosophy of science suggests that predictive success constitutes a special case of explanatory power in which a theory's ability to predict an event stands as evidence of its ability to explain it. See Lipton, *Inference*; Michael Scriven, "Explanation and Prediction in Evolutionary Theory," *Science* 130 (1959): 477-82; and Stephen Brush, "Prediction and Theory Evaluation: the Case of Light Bending," *Science* 246 (December 1989): 1124-27.

shrapnel at the scene of the rubble.

This example suggests that considerations of causal adequacy often determine which among a set of possible explanations will constitute the best. Indeed, recent work on the method of "inference to the best explanation" suggests that determining which among a set of competing possible explanations constitutes the best depends on assessments of the causal powers of competing explanatory entities.[97] Entities or events that have the capability to produce the evidence in question constitute better explanations of that evidence than those that do not. It follows that the process of determining the best explanation often involves generating a list of possible hypotheses, comparison of their known (or theoretically plausible) causal powers with respect to the relevant data, and the progressive elimination of potential but inadequate explanations. Of course, in some situations more than one hypothesis may serve as an adequate explanation for a given fact. Typically in such situations scientists expand their evaluation to include an ensemble of relevant data to discriminate between the explanatory power of various abductive hypotheses.[98]

Inference to the best explanation (IBE) as a method of reasoning has a number of advantages over either deduction or simple abduction. First, IBE can provide a strong form of epistemic support without having to achieve the often unrealistic standard of deductive certainty. If the logic of confirmation provides a weak form of epistemic support by suggesting a reason for believing that a hypothesis might be true, then the logic of comparative explanatory power—the method of IBE—can provide a stronger form of support by giving a reason for preferring a possibly true hypothesis over all competitors. As Peirce noted in his discussion of the evidence for Napoleon, considerations of explanatory power may establish an inference beyond reasonable doubt, even if the abductive form of argument cannot categorically exclude other logical possibilities.

Second, in discussions of reason (or science) and faith, IBE provides a way of avoiding fideism—belief without justification, or faith in faith

---

[97]Lipton, *Inference,* pp. 72-88; Stephen Meyer, "The Methodological Equivalence of Design & Descent: Can There be a Scientific Theory of Creation?" in *The Creation Hypothesis,* ed. J. P. Moreland (Downers Grove, Ill.: InterVarsity Press, 1994), pp. 67-112, 300-312, especially pp. 88-94.

[98]Meyer, "Of Clues and Causes," pp. 99-108, esp. p. 102.

alone—on the one hand or a return to strict rationalism on the other. If as both rationalists and fideists assume, deductive proofs provide the only way to support a Christian worldview, then if such proofs fail, fideism or skepticism stand as the only alternatives. If, however, scientific or other evidences suggest theism as a better explanation than competing metaphysical systems or worldviews, then one can affirm an evidential basis for theistic belief without embracing the failed rationalism of the past.

Part 5: Theism as an Inference to the Best Explanation

With confirmation of hypothesis and explanatory power rather than deductive entailment constituting epistemic support, we can now see how recent developments in modern science provide support for theism. Curiously, in the very passage in which he denies that the big bang model supports the Christian doctrine of creation, McMullin suggests this very possibility: "If the universe began in time through the act of a Creator ... it would look something like the Big Bang that cosmologists are talking about."[99] But does this not simply mean that if we assume the Christian doctrine of creation (or theism) as a kind of metaphysical hypothesis, then the big bang is the kind of cosmological theory we have reason to expect? As Arno Penzias has said, "the best data we have (concerning the big bang) are exactly what I would have predicted had I nothing to go on but the first five books of Moses, the Psalms and the Bible as a whole."[100] But again, doesn't this statement and McMullin's imply that the big bang theory provides a kind of confirmation of the Judeo-Christian understanding of creation and with it a theistic worldview? The previous discussion of confirmation would certainly seem to suggest as much. Explicating the above statements as an abductive syllogism helps to explain why.

> If theism and the Judeo-Christian view of creation are true, then we have reason to expect evidence of a finite universe.
> *We have evidence of a finite universe.*
> Therefore, theism and the Judeo-Christian view of creation may be true.

---

[99]McMullin, "Cosmology," p. 39.
[100]Arno Penzias, quoted in Malcolm W. Browne, "Clues to Universe Origin Expected," *New York Times,* March 12, 1978, p. 54.

This syllogism suggests that the big bang theory functions to confirm the metaphysical hypothesis of theism in much the same way that empirical observations confirm scientific theories. It follows that the big bang does provide epistemic support for theism, at least in this limited way.

Yet the big bang theory may provide an even stronger form of epistemic support. Metaphysics offers a multitude of competing explanations for the nature and origin of the material universe, everything from naturalism to pantheism, deism to theism. Let us initially compare the explanatory power of theism and naturalism, perhaps the two most influential worldviews in the West.

First theism, with its notion of a transcendent Creator, provides a more causally adequate explanation of the big bang singularity than a fully naturalistic explanation can offer. Since naturalism assumes that, in Sagan's formulation, "the Cosmos is all that is, or ever was or ever will be," naturalism denies the existence of any entity with the causal powers capable of explaining the origin of the universe as a whole.[101] Since the big bang in conjunction with general relativity implies a singular beginning for matter, space, time and energy, it follows that any entity capable of explaining this singularity must transcend these four dimensions or domains.[102] Insofar as God as conceived by Judeo-Christian theists possesses precisely such transcendent causal powers, theism provides a better explanation than naturalism for the singularity affirmed by the big bang cosmology. Theism also provides a better explanation for the origin of the universe than does pantheism, for much the same reason. Though a pantheistic worldview affirms the existence of an impersonal god, the god of pantheistic religions and philosophies exists within and is coextensive with the physical universe. God as conceived by pantheists cannot act to bring the physical universe into being from nothing (physical) since such a god does not exist independently of the physical universe. If initially the physical universe did not exist, the pantheistic god would not have existed either. If it did not exist, it could not cause the universe to exist.

Many scientists have acknowledged the challenge that the big bang theory poses for a naturalistic worldview. Thus many naturalistically minded

[101]Carl Sagan, *Cosmos* (New York: Random House, 1980), p. 4.
[102]Hawking and Penrose, "Singularities," pp. 529-48.

scientists—Einstein, Hoyle and Eddington, for example—either formulated alternative cosmological models to preserve an infinite universe or simply repudiated the big bang model on philosophical grounds. Most contemporary naturalists have adopted a slightly different approach. Many claim to have resolved the dissonance between the big bang theory and a naturalistic worldview by coupling the big bang theory to speculative quantum cosmologies or to many-worlds hypotheses. Yet ironically, to the extent that even these cosmological ideas may have validity, they themselves may also have latent theistic implications.[103] In any case, if the universe is finite, as the big bang and general relativity affirm, at least on the most straightforward rendering of each, then these theories provide confirmation of and epistemic support for the metaphysical hypothesis of theism. Further, theism provides a better, more causally adequate explanation for the evidence of a finite universe than its main metaphysical competitors. Hence, if we explicate epistemic support in terms of confirmation of hypothesis or explanatory power rather than deductive entailment, then the big bang theory provides support for theism and indeed for a Judeo-Christian understanding of creation.

While the big bang seems best explained by a transcendent cause, it may not by itself imply an intelligent or rational cause. Nevertheless, other types of scientific evidence may provide support for other attributes of a theistic God or a theistic worldview. Physics and cosmology suggest intelligent design as a highly plausible and arguably best explanation for the exquisite fine-tuning of the physical laws and constants of the universe and for the precise configuration of its initial conditions. Since the fine-tuning and initial conditions date from the very origin of the universe itself, this evidence suggests the need for an intelligent as well as a transcendent cause for the origin of the universe. Since God as conceived by Judeo-Christian (and other) theists possesses

---

[103]For example, on the standard Copenhagen interpretation of the so-called collapse of the wave packet, a wave function only acquires discrete values on observation. Thus, if the whole universe existed prior to Planck time as an (eternally existing) wave function as some quantum cosmologies suggest, the universe could not have acquired discrete characteristics until some "cosmic observer" had actualized one of its potential combination of states by observing it. See Richards, "Many Worlds," pp. 224-26; Plantinga, *Nature of Necessity*, pp. 213-17; Craig, "Barrow and Tipler," pp. 389-95; Craig, "Cosmos," pp. 26-27.

precisely these attributes, his creative action can adequately explain the origin of the cosmological singularity and the anthropic fine-tuning. Since naturalism denies a transcendent and preexistent intelligent cause, it follows that theism provides a better explanation than naturalism for these two evidences taken jointly. Since pantheism, with its belief in an immanent and impersonal god, also denies the existence of a transcendent and preexistent intelligence, it too lacks causal adequacy as an explanation for these evidences. Thus theism stands as the best explanation of the three major worldviews—theism, pantheism and naturalism—for the origin of the big bang singularity and anthropic fine-tuning taken jointly.

Admittedly theism, naturalism and pantheism are not the only worldviews that can be offered as metaphysical explanations for the classes of evidences discussed above. Deism, like theism, for example, can explain the cosmological singularity and the anthropic fine-tuning. Like theism, deism conceives of God as both a transcendent and intelligent Creator. Nevertheless, deism denies that God has continued to participate in his creation either as a sustaining presence or as an actor within creation after the origin of the universe. Thus deism would have difficulty accounting for any evidence of discrete acts of design or creation during the history of the cosmos (that is, after the big bang). Yet, precisely such evidence now exists in the biological realm.

Current fossil evidence puts the origin of life on earth at 3.5-3.8 billion years ago, clearly well after the origin of the universe. If the presence of a high information content in the cell provides compelling evidence for the intelligent design of the first life, then that suggests the need for an act of creative intelligence or a period of creative activity well after the big bang. One could argue against this by asserting that the information necessary to build life was present in the initial configuration of matter at the big bang. Yet the implausibility of such a view can be clearly demonstrated empirically.[104] On the other hand, theism can explain the origin of biological information as the result of God's creative activity, within a natural order

---

[104]Meyer, "Explanatory Power," pp. 113-47; Stephen C. Meyer, "Teleological Evolution: The Difference It Doesn't Make," in *Darwinism Defeated? The Johnson-Lamoureaux Debate on Biological Origins,* ed. Robert Clements (Vancouver, B.C.: Regent Publishing, n.d.), pp. 89-100.

that he otherwise sustains, at some point after his initial creation. Deism, on the other hand, cannot account for evidence of creation or design after the big bang since deism stipulates that God (the "absentee landlord") chose not to involve himself in the events or workings of the universe he created.

Interestingly, some philosophical naturalists have postulated an immanent intelligence as an explanation for the origin of the first life on earth. Francis Crick and Fred Hoyle, for example, have both proposed so-called directed panspermia models.[105] These suggest that life was intelligently designed (or seeded) by an intelligence within the cosmos—a space alien or extra-terrestrial agent—rather than by a transcendent, intelligent God. Thus their proposal suggests that even if the origin of life cannot be accounted for by a naturalistic process of chemical evolution, it can be explained by reference to a purely natural intelligence within the cosmos.

This explanation does not revive naturalism as an adequate metaphysical explanation for biological design, however, since no naturalistic explanations can account for the ultimate origin of specified biological information from simpler chemical constituents. Instead, it suggests that *if* naturalism could give an account of the origin of the specified complexity or information content required to make life somewhere, it might also be able to explain the origin of life at a specific time on earth. Yet naturalistic theories have failed precisely to explain the origin of the information necessary for life's origin. Thus, explaining the origin of life by reference to other life, albeit intelligent and extraterrestrial, only begs the question of the ultimate origin of life somewhere within the cosmos. In any case, naturalism has difficulty explaining other relevant evidences such as the cosmological singularity and anthropic fine-tuning as adequately or coherently as theism.

In 1992 the historian of science Frederic Burnham stated that the God hypothesis "is now a more respectable hypothesis than at any time in the last one hundred years."[106] Burnham's comment came in response to the discovery of the so-called COBE background radiation, which provided yet another dramatic confirmation of the big bang cosmology. Yet it is not only

---

[105]Francis Crick, *Life Itself* (New York: Simon & Schuster, 1981), pp. 95-166; Hoyle, *Evolution from Space*, pp. 24-51, 96-150.

[106]Frederic Burnham, quoted in David Briggs, "Science, Religion, Are Discovering Commonality in Big Bang Theory," *Los Angeles Times*, May 2, 1992, pp. B6-B7.

cosmology that has rendered the "God hypothesis" again respectable. A survey of several classes of evidence from the natural sciences—from cosmology, physics, biochemistry and molecular biology—finds theism emerging as a worldview with extraordinary explanatory scope and power. Theism explains a wide ensemble of metaphysically significant scientific evidences and theoretical results more simply, adequately and comprehensively than other major competing worldviews or metaphysical systems. This does not, of course, *prove* God's existence, since superior explanatory power does not constitute deductive certainty. It does suggest, however, that the natural sciences now provide strong *epistemological support* for the existence of God as affirmed by both a theistic and Christian worldview.

A Creationist Response

Gary D. Patterson and Wayne Frair

We join Stephen Meyer in affirming that God's revelations to humankind are consistent. It is our shared hope that progress in the understanding of the physical universe and the interpretation of the Bible will eliminate areas of apparent conflict.

An important distinction should be addressed immediately when considering the design argument for God's existence. Although there was a time when natural philosophy and science were considered to be the same activity, modern practice has tended to restrict the domain of science to a discussion of observable phenomena in terms of other observables. This limitation on the practice of science does not inhibit philosophers from using any reasonably well-established premise in the construction of an argument. The game of science is not the only game in town. The inherent problem in using scientific premises in the construction of an argument for the existence of God is that the deduction of an absolute conclusion from contingent premises is logically absurd. The results of science are far too weak to be used as the basis for the existence of the omnipotent God. As Christians we proclaim the good news that God exists and that he cares about humankind rather than depending on the latest round in a never-ending argument.

Many scientists believe that God is the Creator and are not surprised to observe a world that appears designed. But the existence of God does not depend on the existence of scientists. We believe that design is a coherent explanation for the observations of the physical world, but the presupposition of design is a metaphysical issue rather than a scientific one. Many of the classic design arguments are appeals to ignorance. Any material artifact in biology could be constructed one atom at a time, at least in a thought experiment. To assert that because we do not know how it actually arose, there must be a God, links a majestic conclusion to a meagerly premise. The Bible reveals that God is the creator of life, but it does not give the material details. A parallel fallacy is to assert that just because one highly unlikely mechanism for the appearance of biological life can be proposed, there can be no God. One bad philosophical argument often provokes another!

We join Meyer in stressing the importance of both synoptic design, which refers to the basic structure and properties of matter, and specific design, which discusses the creation of complex structures out of the raw materials of the universe. Both kinds of design are discussed in the Bible. The methods of science can discover and quantify the measurable properties of matter, and such efforts have produced a profound wonder in those who have investigated the fundamental structure of our world. But the fact that God is the source of the remarkable regularities of nature is revealed in the Bible and is not a scientific conclusion. God did not leave such an important conclusion to be discovered by human methods. The general properties of matter allow an enormous number of specific structures and dynamic systems to be formed. It is an empirical fact that many of these organized forms of matter are so complex that they appear designed. The Bible reveals some examples where God is said to be directly involved in the creation of specific artifacts such as stars or mountains (Ps 19:1). The methods of science cannot tell us whether God was involved. Nor does the discovery of specific mechanisms that could lead to the formation of mountains on the surface of the earth rule out participation by the designer of the earth in the realization of his plans. The methods of science are extremely useful in the discovery and systematization of the regularities of nature, but actual history revealed in the Bible should not be dismissed merely because other theoretical possibilities can be envisioned by scientists. It is the pleasure of scientists to consider all the possibilities, but the Bible deals with fundamental realities.

We commend Meyer's careful analysis of the philosophical presuppositions inherent in the arguments of many historical thinkers. While empirical evidence currently favors a universe of finite geometrical measure and limited historical duration, there is a strong philosophical driving force to elucidate new mechanisms that obscure the uniqueness of our world by proposing the existence of many worlds and the cyclic character of each of them. While speculative theory is an important part of the practice of science, it is well known that a clever theorist can explain false data as easily as reliable measurements. Wishful thinking has motivated many premises that were used to establish or refute favorite conclusions. Since the methods of philosophy, like the methods of thermodynamics, depend on the quality of the input data, philosophers must constantly reassess the validity of the premises used in their arguments.

Much of the conflict in the public discussion of Darwinism comes from a failure to distinguish the scientific observations of past and present organisms from the materialist philosophical presuppositions advocated by some atheists in the name of science. The methods of science can tell us what exists physically and perhaps what could exist in material form, but we cannot know why anything exists without historical input. A thorough scientific analysis of a hammer still does not entail the existence of nails. The results of scientific activity, while valuable in themselves, are not sufficient to construct a coherent framework for all that is known by humankind. The science of nuclear physics does not entail the construction and detonation of a nuclear bomb. When we observe the effects of a thermonuclear blast on earth, we infer that humans have been at work in the design and construction of a bomb. While a God who is so removed from us that no observable interaction is possible is philosophically more appealing to some people, the Bible constantly presents observable evidences for the activity of God. When Jesus was asked what evidence he could cite in support of his claims, he pointed to specific historical activities such as his miracles. We join Meyer in encouraging Christians to look for evidence of God's activity when the Bible reveals a good reason to believe that it will be found.

The basic program in natural theology is to observe the natural world and to construct conclusions that transcend the observations. But what constraints are there on this process? The methods of science itself restrict the conclusions to those that comprehend the observations or extend slightly the range that should be searched. When an atheist studies the stars, two possible responses are to worship the universe as the Cosmos (all that is, or was, or ever shall be) or to be frightened by the insignificance of humankind in the face of the awesome power and extent of space. Study of the stars does not compel belief in the God of the Bible, nor does it prevent it. In the light of the Bible the existence of stars is interpreted as evidence of God's creative activity. In the darkness of atheism, stars are proposed to be just another fluctuation in the succession of fluctuations that characterize the meaningless history of the universe. The methods of science do not help us make the choice between a purposeful set of fluctuations in the mass density of space that preserves the balance needed for the observed universe, and a remarkably uniform set of random fluctuations that just happened to wait long enough to avoid the growth of catastrophically large fluctuations but not so long that the fluctuations just dissipated. The fact that the known universe is characterized by a long list of fortuitous circumstances is very suggestive to us as Christians, and we agree with Meyer that it was by design. But it is not the methods of science that compel this conclusion. We must still live by faith. However, the external evidence is indeed fully consistent with our faith.

The greatest challenge to the "intelligent design" community in biology is not to continue presenting new scenarios that evidence irreducible complexity but to address the full range of biological observations. Most biological artifacts evidence both design and imperfection. Standard evolutionary arguments appeal to ignorance. If the function of some structure is not understood, then it is described as a vestigial remnant of the evolutionary process. Rather than chronicle past efforts to deal with apparent imperfection in biology, we present here a few concepts that may be useful in the future consideration of this issue.

Biological systems are sufficiently complex that they operate under multiple constraints. Optimization of one parameter by itself often degrades overall system performance. The assessment of biological systems will require many tools derived from multiple sources. The use of a multidisciplinary approach in the study of biological structure and function seems appropriate to us.

The current state of a biological organism is a function of the full history of itself and of previous generations. The history of the external environment is often reflected in the current internal state, but observations made in the present are not sufficient to fully reconstruct the history. Even with identical DNA the current state of any particular organism can vary over wide ranges, depending on the response of the organism to its environment. Internal conditions developed in response to a particular external stimulus can persist long after the outside influence has changed. Some changes are reversible and some are irreversible, which means that there is no simple pathway that returns the organism to the previous state. While popular views of biology envision history as a series of beneficial irreversible processes, actual observations of biological populations are much more complicated. The normal course of any species includes extinction when the population can no longer effectively adapt to its environment. One part of an intelligent design is a mechanism for adaptation to change that allows for improvements or which minimizes the damage caused by deleterious events. While much effort has focused on the steady state behavior of biological systems, the future may yield remarkable progress in understanding the actual mechanisms for biological change.

One of the most profound problems for the "intelligent design" community is the existence of not just biological imperfection but moral evil. Even materialist philosophers, who deny the fundamental meaning of any act, rant about attempts to introduce standards of morality. Will observations of the biological world lead to ethical standards? Is the second law of thermodynamics a moral imperative? Where will we look for explanations of acts that are not in the interest of anyone, including the actor? The Bible provides the clear light to understand that sin has deleterious consequences in the history of humankind and in the lives of individual people. We do not know exactly why God created a world where sin is a possibility, even as we do not know why God created a world where biological imperfection is the norm. But we do know that God is God, and we are not. Atheists often point to the existence of moral evil as a sign that there can be no God, but in a godless world there would be no goodness. Atheists often point to the existence of biological imperfection as a sign that there can be no God, but in a godless world we believe there would be no biology.

The theologically certain conclusion that God is the Creator still leaves unanswered the question of how God carried out his plans. The methods of science yield a set of possible processes for the behavior of material systems. This information could enable humans to carry out their plans, but it does not restrict God. As Christians we are truly thankful that God has enabled humankind to gain a measure of understanding of the material world that he created. The efforts of some atheists to denigrate the character of this world in an effort to dismiss the existence of God does not flow from the methods of science. The certainty of God's existence frees us as scientists to properly assess our observations without the distortions introduced by an atheistic worldview.

An Independence Response

Jean Pond

Stephen Meyer presents a well-articulated narrative of Western science in which we move from the early modern scientists, who approached their disciplines from a theistic perspective (good), to a post-Darwinian science, in which God becomes passé (bad), to a bold new contemporary science, which features "the return of the God hypothesis" (good). There is a sweep and symmetry to this story in which we can combine our love of the good old (pre-Darwin) days with the excitement of young crusaders (see especially Phillip Johnson's comments on "the Wedge")[1] fighting against the old fogeydom of entrenched atheistic science.

But the devil, as they say, is in the details.

Before moving on to more substantive criticism, let me start with one of those bothersome particulars. In a discussion of the "many-worlds hypothesis" (MWH) in cosmology, Meyer writes: "That some scientists dignify MWH with serious discussion may speak more to an unimpeachable commitment to naturalistic philosophy than to any compelling merit for the idea itself" (pp. 152).

---

[1]Phillip Johnson's remarks on "the Wedge" can be found in "Keeping the Darwinists Honest," *Citizen*, April 1999 <www.arn.org/docs/johnson/citmag99.html>.

How dare we scientists *discuss a hypothesis?*

Meyer has complained so often about the unwillingness of scientists to dignify the intelligent design hypothesis with serious discussion that I was amazed to read this declaration, which I suggest is not helpful to the debate at hand.

The remainder of this critique will focus on two issues raised by Meyer's chapter: (1) Finite versus infinite universes—is one more Christian than the other? and (2) What is "intelligent design," and do we really need it to explain the complex structures of life?

Finite and Infinite

Meyer states that "theism provides a better explanation than naturalism for the singularity affirmed by the big bang cosmology" (p. 170). It is true that some scientists and philosophers have regarded a finite universe—for example, one that began with a big bang—as more in need of a transcendent creator than an infinite universe (although see Quentin Smith, who argues that big bang cosmology proves God *doesn't* exist).[2]

But why? Let me pose a question. Assume that current cosmology suggested (in error, if you will) that the universe was infinite in space and time. Would theism also provide a better explanation than naturalism for an *infinite* universe? If the answer is no, we have put limits on the creative activity of God by claiming that a transcendent creator is incapable—or somehow less capable—of creating a particular kind of universe. If the answer is yes, then we are saying that theism is the better explanation for a universe whether it is finite or infinite in character, so what's the point? "Why is there anything instead of nothing?" is a question that applies equally well to any version of reality, and I see no reason that an infinite universe is ultimately any less mysterious than a finite one.

Meyer is also assuming that in one sense we have reached the end of cosmology; that is, it is impossible that future data or theories may point us back in the direction of an infinite universe. I am much more wary of calling any science finished and assuming that the universe ran out of major surprises during my lifetime.

---

[2]William Lane Craig and Quentin Smith, *Theism, Atheism and Big Bang Cosmology* (New York: Oxford University Press, 1993).

Intelligent Design: God or a Really Smart Guy?

When I was an undergraduate, I had a friend who had been reared in a very conservative evangelical church in rural Minnesota. This particular church had emphasized the influence of the devil in every mistake he made growing up, and possibly as a result, he had developed a bitter hatred of Christianity. He majored in mathematics at the university and was, when I knew him, almost a poster boy for scientific materialism.

Although he had little use for Christian beliefs in general, my friend had an interesting take on miracles. The parting of the Red Sea, manna from heaven, the blind restored to sight, Lazarus raised from the dead—he was quite willing to believe that any or all of them really occurred as described in the Bible.

How? He felt that (in theory anyway) an extremely powerful being could have performed these miracles, using highly advanced technologies of some sort. These powers or technologies—although far beyond current human understanding—were *natural* powers or technologies. That is, once our own science became advanced enough, we could explain each "miracle" in terms of natural law.

In other words, the Bible does not speak of God, just some really smart guy.[3]

I am reminded of my friend every time I read the arguments for "intelligent design." Because as I see the problem, the only designers we *really* know and understand are people. So the only design we can really contemplate is human design. Each time we talk about design in biological systems, we inevitably consider it in terms of human capabilities, not divine ones. And God becomes just a really smart guy. Robert Pennock calls this the "naturalizing" of God:

> The intelligent-design theorists have given us a scientifically gussied-up version of Paley's venerable argument: God becomes a big watchmaker in the sky, a divine genetic engineer, or a souped-up "intelligence." . . . When they try to infer God's "intelligent design" by naturalizing God, IDCs [intelligent-design creationists] are making God a part of the machine.[4]

---

[3]My friend didn't believe that "the really smart guy" actually existed, by the way, only that this was one hypothesis to explain the miracles described in Scripture.

[4]Robert T. Pennock, *Tower of Babel: The Evidence Against the New Creationism* (Cambridge, Mass.: MIT Press, 1999), pp. 303-4, 308.

The "really smart guy" issue is the underlying and critical source of my opposition to intelligent design theory, but I have other problems with Meyer's presentation as well, both major and minor.

Meyer identifies current evolution theory in biology with classical Darwinism or neo-Darwinism. As a result readers may get the impression that only gradualistic mechanisms (e.g., natural selection working on point mutations) are available for evolutionary change. He does not mention endosymbiosis, for example, even though some researchers (I don't claim all) consider this to be "the most important and powerful force in evolution."[5] This is not to say that neo-Darwinian explanations for evolution have been abandoned, of course, rather that current evolutionary theory is much richer and deeper than Meyer seems willing to acknowledge.

Meyer makes reference to Michael Behe's declaration that "there has never been a meeting, or a book, or a paper on details of the evolution of complex biochemical systems." This allegation, together with Behe's statement that "the theory of Darwinian molecular evolution has not published, and so it should perish"[6] has mystified workers in these fields, and John Catalano has developed a website that, by referencing the supposedly nonexistent research, refutes Behe's claim.[7]

I have a larger quarrel with his treatment of the origins of biological complexity. Meyer seems to be saying that the intelligent design hypothesis wins not just because it's a possible hypothesis (for a Christian, "God did it" is generally a *possible* hypothesis) but because all naturalistic explanations are so poor. In other words, we are talking about inference to the *best* explanation, not the only one. But it then follows that if naturalistic explanations improve, God may no longer be the best hypothesis.

Meyer does not worry about this because he feels he has proof that there can be no naturalistic explanation of, for example, the emergence of first life on earth. Consider his statement about the origin of macromolecules: "Chance-based models of chemical evolution have failed since the amount of specified information present in even a single protein or gene

[5]Jan Sapp, *Evolution by Association: A History of Symbiosis* (New York: Oxford University Press, 1994), p. 204.

[6]Michael J. Behe, *Darwin's Black Box* (New York: Free Press, 1996), pp. 179, 186.

[7]John Catalano, "Publish or Perish: Some Published Works on Biochemical Evolution" <www.talkorigins.org/faqs/behe/publish.html>.

. . . typically exceeds the probabilistic resources of the entire universe" (p. 158). But is Meyer correct? Are naturalistic explanations for biological systems really as weak as he makes them out to be? The idea that chance-based models have failed to account for the origin of life is based in part on probability calculations that are hopelessly flawed. For example, as Ian Musgrave[8] has pointed out:

1. Probability calculations concerning the production of some macromolecule by "chance" typically assume sequential trials when it is clearly more reasonable to use simultaneous trials.

2. These probability calculations typically overstate the specificity in amino acid sequencing needed to make a functioning protein. It is true that the tertiary (three-dimensional) structure of a protein is largely determined by its primary (linear) sequence of amino acids. In some cases (as in sickle-cell anemia) a single amino acid substitution has a profound effect on function, but it does not follow that this is always true. A given protein isn't necessarily unique in the sense that there are only one or two ways to make a string of amino acids function in a particular way. There might be thousands of ways, or even more, to make a similar molecule with that function.

Take an example from RNA. Eckland and others have looked for actively catalytic RNAs (ribozymes) in randomly generated sequences of ribonucleotides. Their results indicate that out of all possible sequences of 220 nucleotides (approximately 10^{132} sequences), at least 1 out of every 10^{12} can carry out a particular RNA self-ligation reaction. They conclude that "even the most complex natural ribozymes . . . could have arisen in one step from long random sequences."[9]

In more familiar terms, it is not necessarily the case of finding a single needle in the haystack but of finding any one of a very large number of needles in a haystack. This point is related to what is perhaps the most significant error in these calculations of probability: the specification of a fixed end point in advance of the chance-based operation in question.

---

[8]Ian Musgrave, "Lies, Damned Lies, Statistics, and Probability of Abiogenesis Calculations" <www.talkorigins.org/faqs/abioprob.html>.

[9]Eric H. Ekland, Jack W. Szostak and David P. Bartel, "Structurally Complex and Highly Active RNA Ligases Derived from Random RNA Sequences," *Science* 269 (1995): 364-70.

Consider a typical lotto game. What is it, exactly, that is so improbable about the winning sequence of numbers? Is its very existence improbable? Well, no—the lotto machine comes up with these sequences every week. The improbability of the whole thing lies in the sequence *matching another sequence* which you, the hapless player, have selected in advance.

But no hypothesis of chemical evolution says: start from a prebiotic "soup" and construct a protein *to match* a predesignated protein of x number of amino acids. All any theory of chemical evolution needs to say is this: we will start from the prebiotic soup and construct something—anything—that *works*. Works in what way? *Any* way—any way that advances us closer to the first cell. How many such "anythings" are there? How many "any ways"? We don't know, do we? And without knowing how many needles there are in that haystack, any calculation about the probability of finding one is meaningless.

In conclusion, let me say that I agree with Meyer about one thing: the systems of life are stupefyingly, mind-bogglingly complex. Here's the irony: no one knows this better than biologists. And yet we remain—the great majority of us, Christian or non-Christian—evolutionists, committed to the elucidation of these systems without recourse to the supernatural. Why? Part of the answer lies in the reason we went into science in the first place: the personal satisfaction involved in *figuring things out*. As I pointed out in my own chapter, it is no more satisfying for most scientists to say "God did it" in answer to a tough scientific problem than it is for a detective to say "God did it" in solving a murder mystery.

Another part of the answer probably relates to a disinclination by most scientists to use what P. S. Churchland calls the "I-cannot-imagine" gambit. The fact that a given person cannot imagine how the bacterial flagellum evolved says more about that person than it does about the question at hand. Churchland gives good advice here: "Learn the science, do the science, and see what happens."[10]

For me as a Christian, there is also a very important third part to this

---

[10]P. S. Churchland, "The Hornswoggle Problem," in *Explaining Consciousness: The "Hard Problem,"* ed. Jonathan Shear (Cambridge, Mass.: MIT Press, 1997), pp. 42-43. Richard Dawkins has another name for the "I-cannot-imagine" gambit: he calls it the "argument from personal incredulity" (Dawkins, *The Blind Watchmaker* [New York: W. W. Norton, 1996], p. 38).

answer. Some creationists claim that the supporters of evolution have been brainwashed by a creed of scientific materialism, but this is a judgment on their part and an offensive, unsupported one at that. *How many times do we have to say this?* Believing that evolution has occurred—that humans and all other living things are related as part of creation's giant family tree, that it is possible that the first cell arose by the natural processes of chemical evolution—neither requires nor even promotes an atheistic worldview.

I reject the hypothesis of intelligent design both on the basis of what I know as a scientist *and on the basis of what I believe as a Christian.* I find myself unwilling to reduce God to a really smart guy. I refuse to try to fit God into a scientific box.

A Partnership Response

Howard J. Van Till

On the Broad Strategy

Not surprisingly the term "intelligent design" (ID) appears already in the first paragraph of Stephen Meyer's chapter. Additional references to "design," "intelligent design" and "the design argument" permeate the remainder of his contribution to this discussion. This is precisely as it should be. Meyer is one the members of a group of scholars who call themselves "Intelligent Design Theorists," and he has done much to shape the philosophical strategies of the ID movement.

Meyer's zeal for his preferred approach to questions about the formational history of the universe is clearly evident. But that is true of each of our contributions to this volume. It is obvious that anxiety over these questions has come to dominate most discussions regarding the relationship of Christian belief and the natural sciences in North America.

The central theme of Meyer's essay is that the relationship of natural science and Christian theology is one of "qualified agreement." He refers to this as the "classical" way of envisioning the science and religion relationship and states his intention to stand in that tradition and to "reformulate this view by showing that contemporary scientific evidence from cosmology, physics and biology now supports a theistic worldview" (p. 131).

I suppose that if I were given opportunity to define the meanings of the key terms in this statement of Meyer's thesis, I could easily assent to it. In fact, I find Meyer's application of this approach to the phenomenon of "anthropic fine-tuning" to be a well-crafted argument of the general sort that I would be inclined to use myself in the "partners in theorizing" strategy that I propose in my own chapter.

On the Need for Better Definitions

In discussions regarding the sensitive issue of the science and theology relationship, I have long found it essential to establish clear operative definitions of certain key words. Without explicit clarification, differing meanings soon become confused, and emotion-charged shouting matches take the place of fruitful intellectual discourse. Consider, for example, words like *origin, naturalistic* and *design.*

On numerous occasions Meyer uses the term *origin* where I find the word *formation* to be far more fitting. Given the sense of ultimacy suggested by "origin," I ordinarily choose to reserve this important term for the meaning "ultimate source of being." Thus I would say, for instance, that questions regarding the "origin" of the universe are beyond the competence of the natural sciences and demand that we employ the resources of theology and metaphysics in our search for an answer. I think Meyer would agree.

But note what happens when our attention is shifted from the universe as a whole to particular structures within it. Meyer speaks, for instance, of Laplace's "ingenious theory known as the nebular hypothesis to account for the origin of the solar system as the outcome of purely natural gravitational forces" and of Lyell's efforts to explain "the origin of the earth's most dramatic topographical features—mountain ranges and canyons—as the result of slow, gradual and completely naturalistic processes of change" (p. 128). Here "origin" means no more than "formation" and represents a topic that has been fruitfully investigated by the natural sciences.

What does Meyer here (and elsewhere) mean by his reference to "completely naturalistic processes"? For instance, does *naturalistic* mean "without need for divine action of any sort"? If so, then it would entail the rejection of theism and its belief that without God's action of giving and sustaining the being of something, it could neither exist nor participate in any creaturely process whatsoever. On the other hand, if *naturalistic* is taken to have the more limited meaning of "creaturely" or "without need for irruptive divine intervention," then no denial of theism is entailed by its use. Given the importance of knowing whether or not the denial of theism is entailed in the definition of a word like *naturalistic,* I would think that its operative meaning must be clarified far more carefully than I find in Meyer's chapter.

What Does It Mean to Be (or Have Been) *Intelligently Designed?*

In this essay Meyer offers several arguments leading to the conclusion that an appeal to specific empirical evidence could lead a person to affirm the idea that the universe, or some particular physical or biotic system within it, is or has been "intelligently designed." The question is, What particular sort of action does "intelligent design" entail? At least the following two possibilities must here be considered.

1. To be intelligently designed is to be, or have been, thoughtfully conceptualized for the accomplishment of a purpose. This would be the intentional action of a mind or of a Mind.

2. To be intelligently designed is to be, or have been, *both* purposefully conceptualized, as in (1) above, *and* assembled, shaped or constructed in conformity with that conceptualization. This would be an action of both mind and something like "hands."

This second concept of intelligent design is based on the artisan metaphor, in which one agent, the artisan, does *both* the conceptualization *and* the construction of some artifact. One of my chief complaints about the current ID movement is its persistent choice to downplay the distinction between these two very different meanings or to ignore the difference altogether and to move silently from one concept to the other without even acknowledging the move.

Meyer begins his development of the idea of design by appeal to history. "The classical design argument begins by noting certain highly ordered or complex features within nature, such as the configuration of planets or the architecture of the vertebrate eye. It then proceeds to argue that such features could not have arisen without the activity of a preexistent intelligence (which has typically been equated with God)" (p. 131). My question is, What type of activity—the action of mind or hands or both?

Continuing his reference to the classical notion of design, Meyer notes that "Paley's work catalogued a host of biological systems that suggested the work of a superintending intelligence. He argued that the astonishing complexity and superb adaptation of means to ends in such systems could not originate strictly through the blind forces of nature" (p. 135). I presume that Meyer here intends the term "superintending intelligence" to convey the idea that Paley's classical concept of design included "hand" action along with the action of mind.

Meyer is correct to place Paley in the camp that employed "design" in a manner consistent with the artisan metaphor and the second definition above. The classical Paleyan concept of design included the action of both mind (in conceptualization) and hands (in the construction of what was conceptualized). Meyer is also correct to note that there have been other proponents of natural theology who chose to locate design entirely in the fruitful functioning of creaturely systems operating in accord with "the workings of natural law"—an approach consistent with the first definition above.

Speaking of this development in the nineteenth century, Meyer says, "By locating design more in natural law and less in complex contrivances that could be understood by direct analogy to human creativity, later British natural theologians ultimately made their research program indistinguishable from the positivistic and fully naturalistic science of the Darwinians. . . . Thus by the end of the nineteenth century, natural theologians could no longer point to any specific artifact of nature that required intelligence as a necessary explanation. Intelligent design became undetectable except 'through the eyes of faith' " (p. 136).

Notice what has happened. The meaning of "intelligent design," as this term is most commonly employed in the modern ID movement, has been effectively identified with the Paleyan picture based on the artisan metaphor. Mind action is not enough. It must be supplemented with hand action. On this view, the giving of being to a creation gifted with all of the requisite formational capabilities to make possible its evolutionary development fails to provide sufficiently convincing evidence of "design." The only form of design that would be apologetically convincing to most proponents of ID would be the Paleyan version, which includes episodes of form-imposing divine intervention.

Heads I Win, Tails You Lose

But there is a mystifying ambivalence on the matter of what counts as evidence for Meyer's claims of scientific support for ID. Suppose we take two of Meyer's arguments in favor of his thesis that "contemporary scientific evidence from cosmology, physics and biology now supports a theistic worldview" (p. 131).

In section 3.2 Meyer calls our attention to the familiar list of "anthropic cosmological coincidences" that characterize this universe. The values of numerous fundamental physical parameters appear to be "just right" for the development of life and of the materials of which living organisms are composed. If the values of any of these parameters had been different, even by relatively small amounts, processes essential to the formation of living systems could not have taken place. The actual values appear, we say, to have been "fine-tuned" for the historical development of life.

As remarkable as this fine-tuning feature is, I think Meyer has overlooked something even more remarkable. It is not simply the *numerical values of certain parameters* that must be "just right" in order for life to develop. No, it's the entire *formational economy* of the universe that must be "just right." The full menu of the universe's formational capabilities must be sufficiently robust to make possible the actualization of carbon-based life in the continuous manner now envisioned by the natural sciences. In fact, I would argue that the *formational capabilities* of the universe are more fundamental than are the *numerical values* of certain physical parameters that apply to the details of their efficacy.

It is important to note that the fine-tuning of the universe to which Meyer calls attention is necessary only in the context of the robust formational economy (RFE) principle being applicable to the universe's formational history (see my chapter in this book for the definition of this term). If, on the other hand, life and the materials of which living organisms are made could have been introduced instead by occasional irruptive divine acts, then the fine-tuning of the properties of the universe would be unnecessary. Any failure of fine-tuning could simply have been compensated for by another episode of divine intervention.

However, given the occurrence of fine-tuning, Meyer does ask the correct question: How did this fine-tuning come about? He considers a number of hypotheses and argues that the best one available is the one that proceeds from theism: the universe has the remarkable character that it has, including the fine-tuning feature, as the outcome of its having been thoughtfully conceptualized by an intelligent Creator. To put Meyer's thesis in my preferred vocabulary, if the universe has sufficient formational capabilities to satisfy the RFE principle (which includes the fine-tuning of all relevant physical parameters), then theism is affirmed. The truth of the RFE principle serves as an affirmation that this universe is the outcome of purposeful conceptualization by an intelligent Creator. I wholeheartedly agree with the spirit of this affirmation.

Suppose, however, we were to move from cosmological matters, like anthropic cosmological coincidences and fine-tuning, to biological concerns. What sort of *biological* evidence does Meyer select as offering support for the thesis that the system of terrestrial life bears the marks of having been intelligently designed? Noteworthy features of several types of systems are considered by Meyer—"the origin ['formation'] of complex molecular machines," the achievement of the "complex specificity of cellular components" and the configuring of "the sequence specificity of DNA" (pp. 154, 155, 156).

In each case Meyer's line of argumentation is essentially the same. Here is a sample: "Developments in molecular biology have raised the question of the ultimate origin of the specific sequencing—the information content—in both DNA and proteins. These developments have also created severe difficulties for strictly naturalistic theories of the origin of the first cellular life. Since the late 1920s naturalistically minded scientists have sought to explain the origin of the very first life as the result of a completely undirected process of 'chemical evolution.' " The result? All such "naturalistic chemical evolutionary theories have been unable to account for the origin of" these structures (p. 158).[1]

What's the point that Meyer wishes to make? That the particular structures of certain component parts of living systems could not have come to be assembled by the use of their own formational capabilities alone. Therefore they must have been formed by discrete acts of "intelligent design," which is here used as a synonym for "assembly by some extranatural

---

[1] Note that here, as elsewhere, Meyer consistently uses *origin* where *formation* is meant, and the ambiguity in the meaning of *naturalistic* is left unresolved.

agent." Meyer speaks only of mental action, but the "hand" action of assembly is essential to his case. "The specifically arranged nucleotide sequences—the information content—in DNA suggests the past action of an intelligent mind, even though such mental agency cannot be directly observed" (p. 162). Since Meyer considers physical, chemical and biological processes to be unable to accomplish the desired arrangement, it must be accomplished by the "hands" of an intelligent agent having "unique causal powers that nature does not" (p. 162).

The idea of self-organizational processes is wrapped by Meyer in the derogatory vocabulary of "naturalistic evolution" instead of the language of "God-given capabilities." In essence, it appears to me that Meyer has granted the preachers of naturalism exactly what they wish—acceptance of the assertion that if atoms and molecules are equipped to accomplish the assembly of life forms, then a Creator God is unnecessary. Or, as I have stated, the common *naturalistic challenge:* If there are no gaps in the formational economy of the universe, then what need is there for a Creator?

Hence, in his employment of biological examples in arguments favoring the need for intelligent design, Meyer's strategy is to deny the possibility that atoms and molecules have been equipped (by their Creator) to do the work of actualizing life on earth. Or, to put Meyer's thesis in my language, if the robust formational economy principle is false, then naturalism is unable to account for the formation and evolution of life on earth and the assembling action of an "intelligent agent" is essential. The need for an intelligent designer is evident in what formational capabilities are missing in the universe's formational economy.

Here then is the puzzling ambivalence. In his reflections on the cosmological fine-tuning of the universe, Meyer's conclusion of the need for ID is based on an appeal to the remarkable features (special values of cosmological parameters) that the universe *does* exhibit. As I noted above, Meyer argues, in essence, that if the RFE principle is *true*, then ID is also true. But in his reflection on the character of *biological* structures, the argument seems based on an appeal to certain features (specific formational capabilities) that the universe *does not* exhibit. In essence Meyer appeals to biological examples to argue that if the RFE principle is *false*, then ID must be true. Putting these two arguments side by side, it looks like the old trick line "heads I win, tails you lose."

4 Partnership
Science & Christian Theology as Partners in Theorizing

Howard J. Van Till

First a Christian, then a scientist. Born into a Christian family, educated in Christian schools from day one, I was a full member of the Christian community long before I became a professional scientist. My inclination, therefore, is to approach questions regarding the relationship between theology and science from the starting point of my commitment to the Christian faith and my respect for historic Christian theology, particularly its doctrine of creation.

To a person who is not committed to Christianity, this may sound as though I were effectively disqualifying myself from the arena of critical thinking. Especially to a member of the secular academy, my admission of commitment to a religious belief system might be taken as a confession of being infected with an intellectually disabling bias. How could one who holds to the historic Christian faith actually be open to honest scientific inquiry? Is it not the case, for instance, that a faith commitment of this sort precludes any critical examination of certain beliefs about the universe, especially regarding its being a creation? Is that not why there is so much sentiment against the scientific theory of evolution in North America today? How could intellectual integrity possibly survive in the environment of a religious belief system?

That question about intellectual integrity is fair. Persons outside of the

Christian faith have a right to ask it because in all likelihood they have seen numerous examples of transparently shoddy scholarship presented in the name of Christianity. They have seen striking examples of tortuously twisted data presented in the guise of "scientific evidence," gross misrepresentations of professional scientific judgment, outrageously contrived conclusions and utterly silly theories presented in the name of Christian scholarship. Especially in the arena of what has become popularly known as "the creation-evolution debate," the Christian community has cause for deep embarrassment.

But there is also some good news. Substantial portions of the Christian community have long been committed to sound thinking and to intellectual integrity, not in defiance of the Christian faith but as the natural expression of a proper Christian confidence that authentic knowledge is not a competitor to faith but a valuable partner in the quest for a well-informed understanding of what is true and real. As it was modeled to me by numerous mentors—parents, teachers, pastors and colleagues—the characteristic activity of this kind of faith is not the blind acceptance or strident proclamation of some unexamined dogma but the eager and open-minded development of a well-informed and carefully articulated body of beliefs. My intention is to make a constructive contribution to that enterprise.

The Cosmos: Nature or Creation?

The questions put to me by the editor of this volume focus on the relationship of Christian theology and the natural sciences. The question of the faith-science relationship and the fact that there are many differing viewpoints regarding it is not new. Many of us have been talking and writing about these matters for some time. However, I submit that it is not the most important or fundamental question that is at issue in the various versions of the science-faith dialogue or the more narrowly conceived creation-evolution debate that seems never to end (nor even to make progress).

As I see it, the more fundamental question at issue is one that has been around as long as reflective human beings have been around: Who are we, and what is the identity and character of the universe in which we find ourselves? About fifteen years ago I spent an entire month speaking to audiences consisting mostly of Calvin College supporters and members of my denomination, the Christian Reformed Church in North America. Because Carl Sagan's television series *Cosmos* was still fresh in our collective memories, I entitled my lecture "The Cosmos: Nature or Creation?"

That choice—nature or creation?—is still with us. What is the proper identity-specifying name for the cosmos (that is, the universe considered as a magnificently structured and harmoniously integrated whole)? Is it *nature*, a name that would imply its status as being that of the ultimate and self-existent reality envisioned by Sagan and other popular proponents of naturalism? Or is it *creation*, a name that would signify its having the status not of something that is self-existent but rather of something that has being only because it has been given being by a transcendent Creator? These two names represent, I believe, the two principal options presented to our culture. One is theistic—God is the Creator; all else has the status of creature. The other is naturalistic—nature is all there is; the universe is self-existent and has no need for a Creator.

Putting the Question of Relationship in Its Place

Having recognized that the question regarding the identity and character of the universe is the primary one, we can proceed to a number of secondary questions that relate closely to our present concerns: What is the relevance and probative force of biblically informed Christian theology, and what does it contribute toward an answer to our primary question? What is the relevance and probative force of the empirically informed natural sciences, and what do they contribute toward an answer to our primary question?

The focus of these two broad categories of secondary questions provides the occasion for asking questions at yet a third level: What is the nature of the scientific enterprise, and what is the epistemological status of scientific theorizing? What is the nature of the theological enterprise, and what is the epistemological status of theological theorizing? Finally, given that science and theology are intellectual endeavors carried out by communities of scholars, what is the relationship of these two scholarly enterprises?

How are the disciplined activities of Christian theology and the natural sciences related? Numerous possibilities regarding their relationship and consequent style of engagement could be considered. Do these two enterprises address a common set of questions? If so, how are their answers related? Are they in agreement so that a concord between scientifically and theologically derived perspectives could be displayed? Or are the answers provided by science and theology so different from one another as to place them in competition over the same piece of intellectual turf?

Some persons see Christian theology and the natural sciences as enterprises that address two differing sets of questions. If that is so, is there any basis left for substantive interaction, or are the scientific and theological enterprises best advised to ignore one other as scholarly endeavors that are mutually irrelevant—each concerned with matters having no relevance to the other?

My own place in this spectrum of possible relationships follows from a number of judgments made concerning the character and competence of these two enterprises, each of which is to be seen as an attempt by a community of persons engaged in applying the tools of their trade to the task of making progress in developing a better answer to our original questions: Who are we, and what is the identity and character of the universe in which we find ourselves?

To the best of my knowledge, both science and theology are honestly seeking growth in authentic human knowledge about ourselves and about the universe in which we reside. Furthermore, I shall presume that each of these two enterprises is committed to maintaining high standards of both professional competence and intellectual integrity. To do otherwise would be a waste of one's effort. How are these two professional enterprises related? My approach will be based on the premise that they are neither enemies engaged in a competitive battle nor independent endeavors that should function in isolation from one another, but *partners in theorizing*— each engaged in a constructive effort to make its own unique contribution toward a better understanding of the nature of humanity and of the universe that we inhabit.

First Things First

I was tempted at this point to continue this chapter with formal reflections regarding the nature of science and the nature of theology, in each case making some comments on the presuppositions that are commonly made, the sources of information ordinarily consulted, the methodologies usually employed by the professional communities and the outcomes of these professional activities. That formal approach could be fruitfully taken, but the point of my remarks so far is that these are matters of secondary or tertiary importance. So let us return to the questions that I consider more fundamental, the questions that are unsettling to the Christian community, the questions that get many people agitated and drive the more inquisitive among them to explore the subtleties of the science-faith dialogue in the first place. An appeal to the sciences or to theology can then be made in the context of our struggle to grow in the understanding of issues far more fundamental than the relationship of two professional, scholarly enterprises.

What are these questions that lead the broad community of Christians to be concerned about the faith-science relationship? Are they primarily philosophical questions about the presuppositions or the methodology of science? No! Are they theological questions regarding the temporality or atemporality of divine action? Not a chance! Cosmological questions regarding the formation of the elements? I doubt it. Geological questions about continental drift? Not very likely. Biological questions regarding genetic variability or natural selection or common ancestry? Now we are getting a bit closer, aren't we?

We all know that the most problematic issue is the *creation-evolution* question. I see no need whatsoever to hide it from direct view or to sneak up on it via some obscure intellectualized pathway. Let us get the real issue out into the open where it can be examined for what it actually is—a complex set of difficult questions that few persons in the pew are prepared scientifically, philosophically or theologically to examine with professional competence, but nonetheless questions that most people feel strongly inclined to answer. Furthermore, there is a great deal of pressure placed on Christians to answer in a way that takes a judgmental poke at "those evolutionists," or "those Darwinists," or "those 'theistic naturalists' who teach in Christian colleges but refuse to badmouth the scientific concept of evolution."

The source of this prevalent anti-evolution sentiment varies from person to person. For some it may be the result of reading the science-faith literature commonly found in Christian bookstores or in popular Christian magazines. Since the writers of these books and articles are Christians, perhaps even with impressive-looking affiliations with big-name universities, it would be easy to presume that their anti-evolution stance represents Christian orthodoxy. For others the negative attitude toward evolution may proceed from peer pressure or from impressions made on them during childhood. For some persons the anti-evolution sentiment may be the outcome of thoughtful and knowledgeable judgment based on a critical examination of the relevant data, but that appears to be rare. (Pardon my candor here; I have been at this discussion for a long time and find the general quality of popular argumentation extremely discouraging.)

My strategy for this chapter, therefore, is to use the creation-evolution debate as a type of case study and as the prime example of a cultural phenomenon that demonstrates the urgent need for more careful reflection about the ways in which Christian theology and the natural sciences contribute to our self-understanding. Having long been frustrated by the structure and the conventional rhetoric of the debate, I will do my best to offer an alternative approach to the fundamental concerns beneath the surface of the familiar but fruitless shouting match between "creationists" and "evolutionists."

Is the Cosmos All There Is?

Some readers may remember the opening line of the *Cosmos* series on public television nearly two decades ago. In his characteristically confident and captivating tone of voice Carl Sagan declared, "The cosmos is all that is or ever was or ever will be."[1] In the context of the full thirteen-hour presentation the term *cosmos* was employed as a synonym for what we who are less inclined toward dramatic amplification would simply call the "universe"—the physical/material world of spiral-structured galaxies and uniformly expanding space, of luminous fusion-powered stars and glowing interstellar nebulae, of orbiting planets and the astoundingly rich array of living organisms that inhabit at least one of them.

One could rightly, I believe, take this dramatic line of script as an indicator of the program's "worldview"—that is, its comprehensive concept regarding the character of reality, of our identity and status within

---

[1]Carl Sagan, *Cosmos* (New York: Random House, 1980), p. 4. Although Sagan is ordinarily credited with (or blamed for) this line, it was apparently a sentence supplied by the scriptwriters, who wanted an especially dramatic opening line.

it, and the significance of it all. The label ordinarily employed to identify the type of worldview presented by Sagan is "naturalism."[2] Its foundational tenet of faith is that nature is all there is. The physical/material universe is itself the ultimate reality. The universe is self-existent and needs no transcendent Creator to give it being or to sustain it in being. There is no Creator of whom creatures could be aware and hence no possibility of a Creator-creature relationship that could serve as the source of meaning or purpose. Significance or value, if they are to be found at all, must be found within the bounds of the universe's own physical/material nature.

Other spokespersons for naturalism are not difficult to find. Zoologist Richard Dawkins, chemist P. W. Atkins, biochemist Jacques Monod, molecular biologist Francis Crick, philosopher Daniel Dennett and numerous other writers could be cited as proponents of this particular religious (although not theistic) perspective. What often confuses the issue, however, is the fact that this particular "religion" of naturalism is so commonly embedded in works that are presented to readers as being no more than popularizations of modern science. Answers to ultimate questions regarding purpose, meaning, value, significance or source of being are, when offered in this context, treated as if they were either self-evident or easily derivable from simple and logically unassailable extensions of scientific reasoning alone.[3]

What do its proponents offer as the basis for a naturalistic worldview? Why would a person come to believe the fundamental tenets of this religious perspective? I must confess that I have great difficulty in coming to a clear answer to this question, and I make no claim to deal thoroughly with it here. I will, however, make a suggestion regarding one possibly significant factor—that in reaction to the shallow rhetoric offered by some Christian writers the preachers of naturalism have mistakenly concluded

---

[2]Other possibilities include "materialism" and "atheism."

[3]For my own critique of writings of Atkins and Sagan see chaps. 8 and 9 in Howard J. Van Till, *Science Held Hostage: What's Wrong with Creation Science and Evolutionism* (Downers Grove, Ill.: InterVarsity Press, 1988). For my critique of philosopher Daniel Dennett's book *Darwin's Dangerous Idea,* see Howard J. Van Till, "No Place for a Small God," chap. 8 in *How Large Is God?* ed. John Marks Templeton (Radnor, Penn.: Templeton Foundation Press, 1997).

that if the failure of episodic (special) creationism can be demonstrated, then naturalism has been proved.[4] More on this later.

Is the cosmos all there is? Is nature the ultimate reality? Is the existence of the universe self-caused, as numerous proponents of naturalism have argued?[5] British chemist P. W. Atkins seems to think that a yes answer makes perfectly good sense and that the idea of an "absolute nothing" transforming its nothingness into something as marvelous as this universe is a perfectly reasonable and defensible proposition.

> In the beginning there was nothing. Absolute void, not merely empty space. There was no space; nor was there time, for this was before time. The universe was without form and void.
>
> By chance there was a fluctuation, and a set of points, emerging from nothing and taking their existence from the pattern they formed, defined a time. The chance formation of a pattern resulted in the emergence of time from coalesced opposites, its emergence from nothing. From absolute nothing, absolutely without intervention, there came into being rudimentary existence. The emergence of the dust of points and their chance organization into time was the haphazard, unmotivated action that brought them into being.[6]

Is the cosmos all there is? Was there only "nothing" in the beginning? Yes, says Atkins. In the beginning was an "absolute nothing" that had the remarkable capacity to transform its nothingness into the universe of which we are amusing artifacts but no more. Looking for a second opinion? The apostle John has something considerably more substantive to offer:

> In the beginning was the Word, and the Word was with God, and the Word was God. He was in the beginning with God. All things came into being through him, and without him not one thing came into being. (John 1:1-3)

In these words from the Gospel of John we have the essence of the his-

---

[4]For an example of the reasoning by which I have reached this conclusion, see Van Till, "No Place for a Small God."

[5]For an especially strident articulation of this assertion see P. W. Atkins, *The Creation* (San Francisco: W. H. Freeman, 1981).

[6]P. W. Atkins, *Creation Revisited* (New York: W. H. Freeman, 1992), p. 149.

toric Christian doctrine of creation: there are only two kinds of being—
God, who through his Word (Christ) is the Creator; and *everything else*—all
of which has the identity and status of "creature." God is the ultimate and
only self-existent reality. The universe—all that is not God—has being only
because God has given it being and continues to sustain it in being from
moment to moment. To be a creation is to have been given being by a transcendent Creator. To say, as we find in Genesis 1:1, "In the beginning God
created the heavens and the earth" (NIV) is to say that all that is not God
has been given its being by the uniquely divine creative act of the God of
whom the Scriptures speak. For Christians the truth of that declaration is
affirmed not only by the text but by the totality of life's experiences, which
include experiences of God's presence. The universe is not self-explanatory and its existence is not self-caused. The universe is not the ultimate
reality but the creation of a Creator who is. We are not merely amusing artifacts of the workings of an impersonal physical/material universe that just
happens to exist, but we are the outcome of divine intention. The universe
is the actualization of God's thoughtful conceptualization for the accomplishment of his gracious and comprehensive purpose. In other words, we
and the entire universe, of which we are a part, are here both by God's
design (intention) and by his act of creation (the giving of being). This is
what I understand to be the essential core of the doctrine of creation. It is
distinctly theological in focus and constitutes one of the "fundamentals of
the faith," and it would be difficult for me to imagine any Christian dis-
agreeing with any portion of it.

One Doctrine but Many Portraits

Although there is but one historic Christian *doctrine* of creation, there are
numerous and remarkably varied *portraits* of the creation—narratives that
either depict in an artistic and figurative style what the Creator has accomplished, or attempt to chronicle in a documentary style the formational history of the creation. The elements of artistic portraits might emphasize the
essential role and transcendent status of the Creator, while the elements of
a chronicle might focus attention on the historical manifestation of the
Creator's work. Artistic portraits would be read primarily as a call to stand
in awe before the Creator and to take comfort in the knowledge of being a
member of his good creation. Chronicle-style portraits would be read as a

listing of the particulars (the specific events and processes that took place, along with a timetable) of how the multifarious physical structures (from subatomic particles to gigantic galaxies) and the diversity of life forms came to be actualized in the course of time from a temporal beginning.

Several and varied portraits, highly artistic in character, could be drawn from the biblical text. The book of Isaiah, for instance, employs the imagery of tentmaker, artisan and military commander as it speaks about God as the Creator who "stretches out the heavens like a curtain, and spreads them like a tent to live in" (40:22), and as the One who "created the heavens and stretched them out, who spread out the earth and what comes from it" (42:5), and as the One who could say, "I made the earth, and created humankind upon it; it was my hands that stretched out the heavens, and I commanded all their host" (45:12).

A similarly artistic employment of the artisan, craftsman and builder metaphors can be found in some of the psalms. Recall such familiar words as "When I look at your heavens, the work of your fingers, the moon and the stars that you have established" (8:3), and "Long ago you laid the foundation of the earth, and the heavens are the work of your hands" (102:25).

In other instances the Bible artfully portrays the Creator's action in the conceptual vocabulary of reference to the effective power of wisdom, discernment and knowledge—qualities often personified in other ancient Near Eastern religious literature. "The LORD by wisdom founded the earth; by understanding he established the heavens; by his knowledge the deeps broke open, and the clouds drop down the dew" (Prov 3:19-20). "It is he who made the earth by his power, who established the world by his wisdom, and by his understanding stretched out the heavens" (Jer 51:15).

Perhaps the most familiar and frequently employed form of literary artistry to be found among the Scripture's portrayals of God's creative work is the *royal* metaphor, in which God's creative actions and his relationship to all creatures are portrayed in the conceptual vocabulary of the king, who has the authority to give commands to his subjects. The king speaks, and all who fear him—that is, all subjects who revere him and over whom he has unquestionable authority—must carry out his orders.

By the word of the LORD the heavens were made,
and all their host by the breath of his mouth.

He gathered the waters of the sea as in a bottle;
he put the deeps in storehouses.

Let all the earth fear the LORD;
let all the inhabitants of the world stand in awe of him.
For he spoke, and it came to be;
he commanded, and it stood firm. (Ps 33:6-9)

Essentially the same royal metaphor is found in the language of Genesis 1, "Let there be light" (1:3), and "Let there be an expanse between the waters to separate water from water" (1:6 NIV), and "Let the earth put forth vegetation" (1:11), and "Let there be lights in the expanse of the sky" (1:14 NIV), and "Let the waters bring forth swarms of living creatures" (1:20), and "Let the earth bring forth living creatures" (1:24).[7]

From these and other scriptural references, as they have been read through the spectacles of differing interpretive programs, whether consciously examined or not, Christian communities have often drawn conclusions regarding the particular manner in which the creation came to be actualized in the course of time. Without here claiming to be exhaustive, the following two basic families of portraits of creation's formational history can be found well-represented in communities of faith today.

Episodic (Special) Creationism

The portraits of creation's formational history that seem to be held by the vast majority of persons in the conservative evangelical Christian community fall into the general category of *episodic creationism,* perhaps more commonly referred to as *special* creationism. In its formulation of a narrative intended to chronicle the particulars of the creation's formational history, the episodic creationist portrait focuses attention on a succession of instances (distributed over time) in which an extraordinary creative act of God (that is, an act of "special creation" or a creative "intervention") is believed to have brought about the actualization of some distinctively new

---

[7]For an extensive commentary on Scriptural references to God's creative activity and to the character of the creation, see John H. Stek, "What Says the Scripture?" chap. 8 of Howard J. Van Till, Robert E. Snow, John H. Stek and Davis A. Young, *Portraits of Creation: Biblical and Scientific Perspectives on the World's Formation* (Grand Rapids, Mich.: Eerdmans, 1990).

type of creature, whether that creature be a fundamental category of being (like light or space), or a physical/material structure (like sun, moon and stars), or a form of life (like fish, birds and land animals). Each of these episodes of special creation (or of creative intervention) is ordinarily presumed to correspond to one of the "days" in the creation narrative of Genesis 1.

There is, however, a strong division of the episodic creationist community that proceeds from differing judgments regarding both the flexibility of biblical interpretation and the probative force of modern natural science. On the one hand, *recent episodic creationism* (or young-earth special creationism) places high priority on the presumption that Genesis 1 is not to be read as an *artistic portrait* crafted for the primary purpose of introducing humanity to the one and only God who is Creator of all else (a portrait that stands in remarkably bold contrast to the ancient Near Eastern polytheism of Israel's neighbors) but rather as a concise *chronicle*—more like a documentary photograph than an artistic portrait—listing a succession of special creation episodes. Furthermore, it is also held that the temporal structuring of the Genesis 1 narrative into a series of six ordinary calendar days constitutes a normative revelation regarding the actual timetable of God's creative acts and of the creation's formational history. The creation of the universe and its subsequent formation into galaxies, stars, planets, plants, animals and humans is believed to be bound to the framework of a standard week of six twenty-four-hour days that took place about six thousand to ten thousand years ago.

The other family of episodic creationist portraits could be given the generic label *old-earth episodic creationism.* They belong in the category "episodic creationist" because of their holding to the belief that the actualization of some creaturely forms—the basic "kinds" of living creatures are most commonly listed—required episodes of extraordinary action on the part of the Creator in the course of time. However, although they share with young-earth episodic creationists their commitment to the necessity of occasional creative interventions by God, they reject their recent creation timetable. In place of the six-thousand-year timetable derived by the application of literalistic presuppositions regarding the character of biblical genealogies and of the creation narratives, old-earth episodic creationism is willing to adopt the fifteen-billion-year chronology derived by the natural sciences, using its standard approach for the interpretation of empirical data.

In these two versions of episodic creationism we have both significant similarities and interesting differences in judgment regarding the answers to some of the "secondary questions" that we identified early in this chapter, questions having to do with the relevance and probative force of (a) biblically informed Christian theology and (b) the empirically informed natural sciences, especially in regard to questions about the character of the created universe and about the particulars of the creation's formational history. Proponents of all forms of episodic creationism agree that biblically informed Christian theology, most notably the historic Christian doctrine of creation, is essential for coming to know the true identity of the universe as the creation—that which has being only as a gift from the Creator (a perspective shared, of course, by all Christians).

Furthermore, recent episodic creationism and old-earth episodic creationism agree that although there may be a diversity of biblical portraits of God's creative action, the Genesis narratives take precedence over all others and must be read as a succinct chronicle in which faithful readers of the Bible are presented with a revelation regarding occasional episodes of creative intervention by God in the course of time. But then, however, there comes a major fork in the episodic creationist road. For the recent creationists, both the *creative-intervention* picture and the *six-ordinary-day* chronology are taken to be normative. For the old-earth episodic creationists, however, only the creative intervention portion of the Genesis narratives is normative. The six-day chronology, on the other hand, is considered by the old-earth creationists to be figurative, referring perhaps to six extended periods of time. Much has been written by the proponents of each chronology to argue the correctness of one and the folly of the other.

What about the relevance and probative force of the empirically informed natural sciences? Both forms of episodic creationism reject such scientific concepts as biotic evolution and the common ancestry of all extant life forms. This major scientific paradigm, the broad outline of which is accepted by the vast majority of natural scientists working in relevant fields of investigation, is judged by episodic creationists to be explicitly ruled out by biblical requirements, and that being the case, it is presumed also to be demonstrably deficient on scientific grounds as well. Consequently, much episodic-creationist literature, whether of the young- or old-earth version, is dedicated to the goal of demonstrating that an unbiased reexamination of the empirical evidence would actually discredit the concept of biotic evolution.

At this point, however, episodic creationists come once again to a major fork in the road. For old-earth special creationists, the judgment of the scientific community regarding the *timetable* of the universe's formational history is considered to be so highly credible that it must be allowed to inform the interpretation of what many consider to be a pivotal portion of biblical text. To recent episodic creationists, however, such a hermeneutical move is judged to be a disastrous capitulation to an essentially secular (or naturalistic) scientific enterprise. The epithets, "accommodation," "compromise" and "sell-out" are likely to surface in exchanges between the two camps.

My own stance on the question of biblical relevance can be stated rather succinctly in the context of this discussion.[8] I begin with the recognition that the Scriptures, especially the Hebrew Scriptures, were written in a cultural and historical context radically different from the modern Western culture in which we are now immersed. *It is unavoidable, therefore, that the Scriptures were written in a* conceptual vocabulary *substantially different from the one we now employ in daily discourse.* I say "conceptual vocabulary" because not only do the words of the original biblical text differ from the words employed in modern English, but the concepts that the Hebrew words represented differ substantially from the concepts now signified by our own vocabulary.

Because of this intimate and unavoidable relationship between one's conceptual vocabulary and the historical-cultural context in which one lives, it is necessary for us to exercise extreme caution in reading modern translations of an ancient text. At the very least we must be on guard against imposing our modern Western conceptual vocabulary on ancient Near Eastern textual material. We must be equally on guard against imposing our modern Western, scientifically influenced agenda of inquiry on any biblical text that was written in the context of questions and concerns most immediately relevant to the ancient Near Eastern world. That was a

---

[8]For a more extensive presentation of this (as articulated more than a decade ago), see the first five chapters of Howard J. Van Till, *The Fourth Day: What the Bible and the Heavens Are Telling Us About the Creation* (Grand Rapids, Mich.: Eerdmans, 1986).

world concerned with intense, religion-amplified rivalries—rivalries experienced not merely as power struggles between competing national or religious groups but as power struggles between the very deities (whether real or imagined) on whom the groups depended for their respective identities.

Given the substantive differences between the modern Western world and the ancient Near Eastern world, I would judge it extraordinarily improbable that answers to modern scientific questions regarding the particulars of the creation's formational history—*questions totally foreign to the conceptual vocabularies of the very people to whom the original text was directed*—were somehow cleverly hidden in the ancient text, only to be discovered in the twentieth century. Yes, I have seen numerous and piously presented claims to the contrary. I have seen claims, offered in support of the idea that the Bible is scientifically inerrant, that Moses (in Gen 1) taught that the universe was expanding and that Job's reference (in Job 38:7) to an occasion on which "the morning stars sang together" has recently been confirmed by radio astronomers.[9] In all honesty, I count claims of this sort to be utterly without merit. Ironically, I suspect that people outside of the Christian community see the meritless nature of these claims even more quickly than many Christians do. It is sobering to think about the effect this may have on the concept of Scripture that is being conveyed to the scientifically informed culture to which we wish to present the good news.

From these and other considerations, it is my deeply held conviction that questions regarding the particulars of the creation's formational history should not be directed to the Scriptures. For instance, questions regarding the timetable of cosmic history, drawn from modern arguments about the age of the creation (is it six thousand years old or fifteen billion years old?), are questions that I count as utterly foreign to the agenda of the biblical text. In my judgment, therefore, all arguments about the specific age of the creation based on differing interpretations of early Genesis constitute a trivialization of an important portion of biblical text. Likewise, I find numerous other questions that are prominent in the creation-evolution debate to be questions that should never be addressed to the biblical

---

[9]These and similar claims can be found in the sixth-grade textbook *Observing God's World* (Pensacola, Fla.: A Beka, 1978).

text with the expectation of being provided with normative answers. Is the theory of common ancestry valid? Did stars suddenly appear by divine fiat (cf. Ps 33:6)? Is natural selection in combination with other extant biotic phenomena capable of accounting for macroevolution as now envisioned by biological theorists? Was the earth originally endowed with the capability to organize into all of the different "kinds" of creatures side by side as Augustine envisioned? Interesting questions all, but not, I believe, questions that a Christian would have any right whatsoever to expect to be normatively answered by the biblical text.

Nonepisodic Creationism

The second major family of portraits of creation's formational history is based on the expectation that this history was not punctuated by occasional episodes of divine intervention but was instead *continuously and at all times expressive of the Creator's effective will for the actualization of forms and structures.* As in the case of episodic creationism the historic Christian doctrine of creation is the starting point for these portraits. The universe, complete with its formational capabilities, has being only because God has given it being. However, in contrast to special creationism, nonepisodic creationist portraits of the creation's formational history do not focus attention on the formation of any particular creaturely structures or forms as being any more or less expressive of God's creativity than any others. The formation of all creatures at all times—even to this day—is, from the nonepisodic creationist perspective, equally to be perceived as the manifestation of God's will for the formational history of the creation.

Within the scope of these broad and defining features of nonepisodic portraits, let me here propose two more specific versions of continuous formational histories that would fall into this general category.

Contemporary (or independent) actualization. The elements of the first portrait can be found in the writings of Augustine, especially in *De Genesi ad Litteram (The Literal Meaning of Genesis),* which is his commentary on the first three chapters of Genesis.[10] In this commentary written late in Augustine's career, the goal was to demonstrate a one-to-one correspondence

---

[10]Augustine, *The Literal Meaning of Genesis,* trans. John Hammond Taylor, Ancient Christian Writers 41 and 42 (New York: Newman Press, 1982).

between the text of these chapters and what actually took place in the creative work of God; in fact, this is precisely how he defined the term *literal* in this endeavor.[11] Following his principles for this literal reading, Augustine concluded that the six-day form of Genesis 1 was neither to be taken as a specification of the chronology of God's creative work nor that this work was episodic in nature. Instead, and in marked contrast to modern episodic creationist interpretations, he concluded that God created "all things together" in one initial, all-inclusive and instantaneous creative act. But this conclusion did not lead Augustine to a picture in which all created things suddenly materialized in mature form at the beginning.

In order to understand how Augustine could envision all things to have been created at the beginning but yet not have all things appear in mature material form at that beginning, we must come to understand Augustine's use of the distinction between *potential* form and *actual* form. In the beginning, according to Augustine, all created forms existed both in the mind of God and in the formable substances of the created world. But in the formable substances the creaturely forms existed not actually but only potentially. Although the creaturely forms were not initially expressed in visible material beings, these forms were present *potentially* in the capabilities for actualization, called by Augustine "causal reasons" or "seed principles," with which the Creator had originally endowed the created substances.

In the course of time these capabilities for actualization functioned as God intended, and the full array of potential structures and forms became actualized into material structures and life forms. As envisioned by Augustine, who lived at a time when spontaneous generation was considered to be an acceptable notion, the full array of life forms could be actualized cotemporally, side by side, as the earth's "seed principles" functioned to transform ordinary earthly substances into living creatures. No episodes of divine intervention were necessary; no acts of special creation needed to be performed. Augustine made it abundantly clear that his portrait of creation's formational history was not of the episodic creationist type.

---

[11]Although I find many of Augustine's theological perspectives fruitful, I would be so bold as to suggest that given the nature of the text, this particular goal may be unattainable. For more extensive comments on this work of Augustine, along with comments on St. Basil's *Hexaemeron*, see Howard J. Van Till, "Basil, Augustine and the Doctrine of Creation's Functional Integrity," *Science and Christian Belief* 8, no. 1 (1996): 21-38.

Sequential actualization. But neither was it of the modern evolutionary type, which constitutes our second example of a nonepisodic creationist portrait of creation's formational history. The evolutionary creation picture is one in which the diversity of physical/material structures and life forms become actualized in time as the outcome of a rich array of creaturely processes for the effective accomplishment of self-organization and self-transformation. However, in contrast to Augustine's side-by-side actualization picture, the evolutionary creation picture envisions the actualization of new forms in the creation, especially of life forms, as occurring sequentially over time.

Clearly this evolutionary (sequential) creation portrait can be recognized as one that proceeds from the judgment that modern scientific concepts such as cosmic evolution, elemental evolution, galactic evolution, stellar evolution, planetary evolution, chemical evolution and biotic evolution have substantial merit as theories in which considerable confidence is warranted by the empirical evidence *as interpreted by those persons most competent to do so.* In the arena of biotic evolution this portrait incorporates the concepts of the genealogical continuity of life and the common ancestry of all extant life forms, which, of course, entails the idea that we humans are in some meaningful way related to all the rest of God's living creatures.

So Where's the Beef?
There is raging within the Christian community today an intense argument regarding the relative merits of episodic creationist and evolutionary creationist portraits of the creation's formational history. Having been engaged in portions of this disagreement for many years, I have reached the judgment that this argument, commonly called the "creation-evolution controversy," is currently structured in a way that makes progress unlikely. Dissipative confusion has arisen, I believe, because the Christian community, especially the conservative evangelical portion of it, has not been educated on how to distinguish this argument between episodic and evolutionary creationism (differing portraits favored by persons who are equally committed to the historic Christian doctrine of creation) from the authentic battle between the worldviews of naturalism and theism. Literature that exemplifies this failure to distinguish the two can often be recognized by its presumption that Christians, in order to be faithful, must reject

the scientific concept of evolution. Hence the common misperception that the "creation-evolution debate" correctly pits all faithful Christians against those diabolical "evolutionists" and those profoundly misguided "theistic naturalists" who fail to recognize the evils of "scientific naturalism."

It is my deep conviction that since the current format of discussion is not likely to be fruitful for Christianity in the long run, we must do the difficult work of restructuring it. In order to attempt that, I first propose a few modifications in the conceptual vocabulary to be employed in future discussions. The old and familiar vocabulary, centered on the "creation versus evolution" theme, has failed. Therefore, a new set of concepts must be tried.

I have argued in this chapter that the most fundamental questions at issue are neither questions about the relationship of the scientific and theological enterprises nor questions about the nature of either one of these professionalized disciplines, but rather questions about the character of the universe about which both, to one degree or another, theorize. Suppose then we ask ourselves, What is the most fundamental difference that distinguishes the episodic creationist from the evolutionary creationist visions of the character of the universe? Or to employ a question that was made momentarily famous some years ago in a television commercial, "Where's the beef?" Why the intense argumentation between the proponents of the two major schools of portraiture regarding the creation's formational history?

In the context of noting the presence of two "forks in the episodic creationist road," we earlier made brief reference to differing judgments regarding the relevance and probative force of both the biblical text and the empirical data. Quite obviously, differences of a similar sort play substantial roles in the argumentation between episodic creationists and evolutionary creationists. But those differences are familiar by now and have been discussed at length elsewhere. Consequently, what I choose to do here is to dig beneath the surface of these epistemological arguments (whether biblical data or empirical data is relevant; what can be inferred from either data set; whether biblically informed theology or empirically informed science has priority) to see what fundamental differences there might be on questions regarding the very character of the creation. My expectation is that differences between the two principal categories of portraits of the creation's formational history (episodic versus nonepisodic) proceed from a more fundamental difference regarding the nature of the universe to which God gave being in the beginning.

What more basic difference? My thesis is that *the argument between defenders of episodic and evolutionary portraits of creation's formational history proceeds from differing concepts of creation's formational economy.* In the statement of this thesis there appears the term "formational economy," which is the first example of a new conceptual vocabulary element that I judge to be essential if the continuing discussion is to be fruitful.

To develop this concept, begin by thinking of all of the creaturely capabilities for action that contribute to the being that God has given to the various elemental units and structures of the creation. Then focus attention especially on all of those capabilities that might in some way contribute to the formational history of the creation, especially capabilities for self-organization or transformation. Examples of such creaturely capabilities would include the following:

☐ Protons and neutrons have the capabilities to interact and combine in such a way as to form atomic nuclei—from the simple hydrogen nucleus, with only one proton, to more massive nuclei like that of uranium, with its ninety-two protons and an even larger number of neutrons.

☐ Atomic nuclei, in turn, have the capabilities to act and interact in ways that lead to the formation of other nuclei, including larger and more complex nuclei.

☐ Atoms, active structures formed by the combination of electrons with nuclei, have the capabilities to interact and to organize themselves into a vast spectrum of molecules, which have the capabilities to interact in ways that lead to the formation of an even more vast array of other molecules, including those required for the functioning of living organisms.

☐ Molecules possess the capabilities to interact in ways that lead to their organizing themselves into molecular ensembles having still more remarkable capabilities, perhaps even the capabilities that constitute life, as exhibited by a unicellular organism. (At the present time there is no scientific consensus on how the first living molecular ensemble came to be actualized, but the expectation is that one or more candidates will some day be judged highly credible.)

☐ Living cells exhibit an astounding menu of capabilities for metabolism, reproduction, differentiation, variation, adaptation and the like. Far more capabilities are likely to be found in the future.

☐ Multicellular organisms exhibit a mind-boggling array of capabilities, most of which far exceed the capabilities of individual cells and most of which far exceed those that the human mind could have imagined from a knowledge of single cell behavior alone. The "possibility space" of potential life forms and the dynamic pathways that make possible their actualization is a truly awesome feature of the creation.

Now imagine that it were possible to construct an exhaustive list of all such creaturely capabilities for self-organization and transformation that could conceivably contribute to the formational history of the creation. Call that immense encyclopedia of capabilities the *creation's formational economy*—the set of all of the resources and capabilities that characterize the creation's abilities for actualizing new structures and forms in the course of time. Although we may at this time have knowledge of only a small portion of that dynamic economy, we can nonetheless form the concept of it for the sake of reflecting on the character of the being that God has given to the creation.

Given the addition of this new term to our conceptual vocabulary, I believe that we are now in a position to ask an especially important question about the character of the creation: *Is the formational economy of the creation sufficiently robust (that is, gifted with all of the requisite capabilities) to make possible the actualization of all of the different physical/material structures and all forms of life that have ever existed since the beginning of time?* It is on the answer to this question that episodic creationists and evolutionary creationists experience one of their most intense disagreements. In effect, episodic (special) creationists are saying no, the creation does *not* have the requisite capabilities; that is why uninterrupted evolutionary development is impossible. Nonepisodic creationists (whether of the Augustinian, independent actualization variety or the sequential, evolutionary actualization variety) are saying yes, we believe that the formational economy of the creation *is* sufficiently robust, and that is why irruptive acts of creative intervention are unnecessary.

Another way to speak of the different concepts of the creation is to ask, Are there any "ontological gaps" (formed by the absence of key capabilities) in the creation's formational economy that would prevent the creation from actualizing the full array of physical/material structures or life forms that have existed since the beginning? If the answer is yes, as the episodic creationist position would entail, then occasional episodes of creative intervention are absolutely necessary for the bridging of those gaps. If on the other hand there are no such gaps to be bridged, then there is also no need for episodes of special creation in the course of time.

Suppose we were to take our question to the professional scientific community. The first thing we would have to do is to rephrase the question. In place of the word *creation*, a term that has meaning only in the context of a theistic worldview, we would have to use the religiously noncommittal term *universe*. So what do scientists ordinarily presume about the universe's formational economy? Is it sufficiently robust to make possible the actualization of all structures and forms in time? If so, would that actualization in time be like Augustine's independent, contemporary scenario, or of the evolutionary, sequential type, or some other scenario?

I think we all know how nearly all professional natural scientists, including the vast majority of those who are Christians, would answer this question. Scientific theorizing regarding the formational history of the universe, whether attention is focused on the formation of the chemical elements or of galaxies or of stars or of planets or of the forms of life that we find on our own planet, proceeds on the presumed applicability of what I have come to call the *robust formational economy principle*. For the sake of scientific theorizing *we assume that the formational economy of the universe is sufficiently robust to account for the actualization in time of all of the types of physical/material structures and all of the forms of life that have ever existed.* That presupposed principle, in spite of its extremely important and fundamental nature, is almost never stated as explicitly as we have stated it here. Why not? I do not think that the usual silence stems from any devious intent to hide it from plain view. I think it is more a matter of oversight. When something is taken to be universally accepted within a community, its employment is likely to be taken for granted rather than explicitly stated.

Why is it taken for granted and not repeatedly held up for reexamination? For essentially the same reason, I believe, that the heliocentric structure of the solar system is no longer brought up for public scrutiny in the way that it was in the time of Galileo. Scientific theorizing based on the robust formational economy (RFE) principle has been extraordinarily fruitful at a variety of levels, from the formation of the elements to the formational history of primates. In scientific theorizing, fruitfulness of such overwhelming proportions breeds confidence. That does not, of course, have the logical status of unassailable proof as is commonly sought in a court of law, but it is the best line of judgment that will ever be available to the natural sciences. It is also the way in which we all proceed in our daily living. There is nothing esoteric or unusual or mischievous in this state of affairs.

Ironically, the RFE principle that has come, by its fruitfulness and its success in numerous applications, to be highly appreciated within the professional scientific community is at the same time an especially problematic aspect of modern natural science for the conservative evangelical Christian community. As I have reflected on the strongly negative attitude that a large segment of the Christian community holds for scientific theorizing about the formational history of the universe (although apparently not for the scientific theorizing that provides the basis for advances in medical science or electronic gadgetry or other contributors to our health, wealth, convenience or creature comforts), I have often asked myself what feature of contemporary scientific theorizing these Christians find especially distasteful or threatening. I think a strong case could be made that it is the robust formational economy principle.

Why? That is not a simple question to answer, but I think one very significant factor is that, for a complex of reasons, the RFE principle is treated, both within and outside of Christian community, as if it were a principle owned not by the Christian theological heritage but by today's strident preachers of naturalism.

Who Owns the Robust Formational Economy Principle?

If a person were required to answer this question on the basis of popular rhetoric alone, whether of the pro-evolution or anti-evolution variety, the rhetorical consensus would likely favor the answer that the RFE principle belongs exclusively to the worldview of naturalism. Furthermore, vocal Christian critics of evolution would likely add that the "scientific establishment" (whatever that term is intended to represent), since it appears to accept robust formational economy as a valid working principle, has sold out to this antitheistic worldview. Christian anti-evolution literature is frequently punctuated with accusations that contemporary science is thoroughly committed to naturalism. The preachers of naturalism would, of course, like very much for that to be true, but simply desiring something to be true does not make it so. Neither does gaining the endorsement of popular distributors of misinformation make it so.

I think that the popular rhetoric on this question is profoundly wrong and that Christians and non-Christians alike are being led down the road of misunderstanding by rhetoric that, no matter how pious or attractive it may appear, proceeds from fundamentally flawed concepts regarding (1) what Christians have a right to presuppose about the character of the creation that the sciences investigate, and (2) what constitutes, for the Christian, an appropriate scientific methodology.

To gain a sense of the reasoning that provides the warrant for these candidly expressed conclusions, suppose that we were to begin with a commitment to the historic Christian doctrine of creation—the starting point that I recommended already in the first paragraph of this chapter—and to proceed from that commitment to the evaluation of the RFE principle and its implications for scientific methodology. As I stated earlier, all Christians agree that the entire universe, every aspect of it, has being only because God, its Creator, has given it being. That means, of course, that *every creaturely capability that the creation possesses must be seen as a gift from the Creator.* Therefore, from the standpoint of a commitment to the historic Christian doctrine of creation, the formational economy of the universe is not something that has any independent existence, nor does it contain any creaturely capabilities that God did not choose to give it. Furthermore, if it is as remarkably complete as the RFE principle describes it, that would be recognized by a Christian as none other than *affirmative evidence for the unfathomable creativity and unlimited generosity of the Creator.* For a Christian to discover that the RFE principle is highly encouraged by the empirical evidence would, it seems to me, provide the occasion for the conclusion not that naturalism is therefore warranted but rather that God is to be praised for God's creativity and generosity. Scientific theorizing about the creation's formational history would therefore proceed on the assumption that the RFE principle is true.

Suppose, on the other hand, that a person were to begin with a commitment to the worldview of naturalism—nature is all there is. There is no Creator; nature is its own source of being. How does something—a universe, say—come to exist in place of "absolute nothing"? If Atkins's rhetoric is taken to be representative, then naturalism's answer is simply "chance," or to repeat his more colorful prose, "the haphazard, unmotivated action" of nothingness. (Other spokespersons might have the courage to say, We don't know.) These are not very satisfying or convincing answers from Mr. Atkins. But there is far more that naturalism must yet explain. Naturalism must account for the existence not merely of a nondescript something in place of nothing but rather of a _something_ as remarkable as a universe that contains us. In other words, naturalism must accept the challenge of explaining the existence of a universe that is equipped with a formational economy sufficiently robust to account for the formation of the elements, of space, of galaxies, of stars, of planets, of plants, of animals and of human beings. How does the "haphazard, unmotivated action" of nothingness do _that?_

Some proponents of naturalism have tried to take comfort in the "anthropic principle," one form of which says that there is no mystery that the universe is as it is (and thus no cause to marvel at its robust formational economy) because if it were not precisely as robust as it appears to be, we would not even be here to ask the question. But of course this is no answer to the original question. The anthropic principle may well give an answer to the question, Given that we do exist, what must be the character of the universe of which we are a part? But the anthropic principle is utterly unable to tell us how we, and this universe of which we are a part, come to have existence in place of nonexistence. The bottom line is that naturalism can point to no source whatsoever for the existence of any universe, certainly not one to which the RFE principle applies.

So who owns the robust formational economy principle? The preachers of naturalism? No. And the last thing a Christian ought to do is to give in to their claims that they do. The historic Christian doctrine of creation provides a far more substantial basis for this principle than naturalism could ever hope to provide. _If the RFE principle correctly describes the way the universe is, how could anything less than the Creator's unfathomable creativity and unlimited generosity account for it?_ All of the familiar rhetoric of the creation-evolution debate that suggests that naturalism owns this principle is, I believe, as far off the mark of truth as it could possibly be. I can easily see why the preachers of naturalism would love to have ownership of the RFE principle conceded to them and why they try their best to promote the claim that they actually deserve it, but why do so many Christians let them get by with such a transparent inversion of sound reasoning? Why allow anyone to get by with the claim that the *more* robust the formational economy of the universe is, the *less* it needs a Creator to give it being?[12] How did we come to accept such a sorry state of argumentation as this?

Destined for Failure: The Creation-Evolution Debate

Perhaps a large part of the answer to that last question can be found in the twisted and tangled structure of the creation-evolution debate. By "creation-evolution *debate*" I am referring not to the controversy within the Christian community between episodic and evolutionary creationists but rather to the popular debate in which the words *creation* and *evolution* are employed as if they were labels for two opposing and irreconcilable perspectives, one Christian, the other naturalistic.

The most common format for this largely North American cultural phenomenon pits episodic creationist theism against evolutionary naturalism. It is a format I find to be egregiously misleading for participants and observers alike. It is not simply a debate concerning whether or not the *scientific* concept of evolution is warranted by the empirical evidence. Neither is it simply a debate concerning whether or not the formational history of the universe was punctuated by occasional episodes of divine creative intervention. Neither is it limited to a debate between proponents of the historic Christian *doctrine* of creation and proponents of the "no Creator thesis" of naturalism.

---

[12]Some critics have interpreted the robust formational economy principle as equivalent to a prohibition of all divine action in the creation—as one would expect to find in strong forms of deism. But that is not the case at all. The question at issue here is not, Does God act in or interact with the creation? With the vast majority of Christians, I presume that God does act in and interact with the creation. The actual question here is, What is the character of the creation in which God acts and with which God interacts? Now, since the possibility of divine action is in no way dependent on the existence of gaps in either the formational or operational economies of the creation, the absence of gaps in no way precludes divine action. While the absence of gaps makes certain types of divine action unnecessary, God is no less free to act as God chooses, provided only that such action is consistent with God's own being. To the best of my knowledge, historic Christian theology has never restricted the locus of divine action to gaps in the creation's formational or operational economies. Neither should we do so now.

As it is most commonly structured and as it is most commonly reported by journalists in the popular media, this debate is a public contest in which the worldview of Christianity is represented by proponents of episodic creationism (very often of the young-earth variety) and the scientific concept of evolution (which presumes that the RFE principle is warranted) is represented by proponents of a naturalistic worldview. There are other versions of the debate, but this is, I believe, the most common and the most flagrantly misguided version. Note that each of these two positions is constituted by the conflation of a worldview *and* a specific portrait of the universe's formational history. Christianity is fused to an episodic creationist portrait of God's creative action (only one portrait among many permitted by the doctrine of creation), and the evolutionary portrait of the formational history of the universe is coupled with naturalism (which, tragically, has been allowed to usurp ownership of the robust formational economy principle).

This debate, presented in a way that demands an either-or choice between only two alternative positions, is doomed to failure for many reasons. On a technical level this either-or format suffers from the deadly disease of "the fallacy of many questions." Relevant to each of the two comprehensive positions offered are questions on a diversity of topics. Some of these are authentic scientific questions (for example, on chronology, on speciation, on the fossil record, etc.) while others are authentic theological questions (regarding the source of the universe's being, regarding the character of divine creative action, regarding divine purposes, etc.). In the standard debate format, however, observers are presented with only two packages of answers to a lengthy list of categorically diverse questions, and they must choose either one package or the other. This places perceptive people in a serious dilemma. If a person feels religiously obligated to side with Christian theism, then the episodic creationist portrait must be accepted as part of the package. On the other hand, if a person feels bound by intellectual integrity to side with the scientific concept of evolution, the worldview of naturalism must be accepted as part of the package. An either-or choice of this sort makes no sense, of course, and no observer should ever accept the demand to make that choice. Answers to each of the diverse questions at issue, whether scientific or religious, must be evaluated on their own terms and not simply packaged with a set of answers to other questions belonging to very different categories.

Why does the debate continue to be conducted in this fallacious either-or format? No single factor would exhaustively explain so complex a cultural phenomenon as the creation-evolution debate, and it would take a team of well-informed intellectual and social historians to untangle the web of relevant factors. For the moment, however, let me call attention to one strand of the web that is related to our present concerns—the strand of rhetorical action and reaction in which both sides of the debate have become entangled.

For a substantial portion of the Christian community (for lack of a better label, let us call this the "conservative evangelical" branch) the historic Christian doctrine of creation has come, for a number of reasons, to be closely associated with one particular portrait of the creation's formational history—the young-earth episodic creationist portrait. For many Christians this particular picture is experienced as being one of the fundamentals of the faith revealed by an inerrant biblical text.

Meanwhile, the professional scientific community has come to be highly respected for the probative force of its methodology of rigorously disciplined theorizing that is informed and tested by empirical research. Over an extended period of time the judgment of this professional enterprise regarding cosmic chronology has become increasingly firm: the duration of cosmic history is neither infinite nor limited to the brief span of thousands of years but is extended over billions of years from a singular beginning. This conclusion regarding chronology is disturbing enough to the young-earth episodic creationists. Even more disturbing, I suspect, is the fact that the same scientific methodology (which includes the working assumption that the RFE principle is warranted) has led the scientific community to the conviction that not only have life forms appeared sequentially in time, but they are related to one another in a genealogically continuous manner. Theories regarding the various creaturely capabilities that make this remarkable evolutionary phenomenon possible are still under development, but with each discovery of the capabilities of atoms, molecules, cells and organisms, the prospect for success seems brighter. Gaps in our knowledge of these capabilities remain, but the probability that there are corresponding gaps in the formational economy of life itself appears to diminish as such sciences as genetics and developmental biology continue their programs of research.

To the preachers of naturalism this state of affairs makes it look as if their apologetic victory over Christian theism has been handed to them on a silver platter. The Christian doctrine of creation, one of the fundamentals of the faith on which all Christians agree, has come to be packaged with young-earth episodic creationism. So if the growing prestige of the natural sciences can be exploited to discredit the recent episodic creationist portrait, then it can be made to appear as if the whole of Christian theism has been defeated.

Given the state of scientific judgment regarding cosmic chronology and given the growing scientific confidence regarding the warrant for the RFE principle, young-earth creationism with its anti-evolution stance is in deep trouble on two counts: (1) its chronology is off by a factor of more than a million, and (2) its postulation of gaps in the formational economy of the creation becomes weakened with each discovery of another remarkable capability for self-organization or transformation exhibited by atoms, molecules, cells or organisms. So the reasoning of naturalism's preachers might be that their best strategy is to challenge the Christian community with this taunt: _If there are no gaps in the formational economy of the universe, then what need is there for a Creator?_[13]

Now what? How should the Christian community respond to this naturalistic taunt? Many differing responses have been documented by historians. But the one that seems to have fanned the flames of the creation-evolution debate to its greatest heat output (far more heat than light, I would say) is this one, offered primarily by episodic creationism: let naturalism have evolution if it wants it. (After all, who really wants to be related to chimpanzees?) Let naturalism also have the RFE principle and encourage Christians to hold to the expectation of gaps in the creation's formational economy. Defeat evolutionary naturalism not by attacking the faulty rhetoric that attempts to link naturalism with the possibility of a gapless for-

---

[13]Although this is not a direct quotation (after all, the term "formational economy" is not yet a household term), it does, I believe, capture the thrust of some of the most strident rhetoric of the preachers of naturalism. Falsely thinking that defeating episodic creationism is equivalent to defeating the historic Christian doctrine of creation, they exploit scientific judgment favoring the evolutionary scenario for the universe's formational history as if it bolstered the credibility of naturalism.

mational economy, but by launching a campaign to discredit the scientific concept of evolution itself.

What should be done about the advantage that the natural sciences appear to give to naturalism? The popular answer seems to be to see what Christianity might do to weaken that advantage. Among Christians, try to discredit scientific methodology by asserting that it is rigged to favor naturalism. Apply the labels "methodological naturalism" and "provisional atheism" to its methodology so that its claim to probative force can be called into question within the Christian community. Apply the oxymoronic label "theistic naturalism" to those Christian scientists who find no fundamental fault with scientific methodology. If necessary, invent a "creation-science" or a "theistic science" to replace conventional science. Promote a variant of science that welcomes the postulating of occasional divine interventions to account for things that "secular science" cannot (yet) explain—perhaps the formation of the first living creature, or perhaps the "Cambrian explosion" of new life forms and certainly the formation of the human species.

There is no need to extend this recitation any further. I presume that the readers of this volume are abundantly familiar with this line of thought. It is selling well in the Christian marketplace. My hope is, however, that readers will soon recognize this anti-evolution strategy as a sincere but profoundly misguided response to the naturalistic taunt. A response is certainly called for, and I commend those writers who are encouraging the Christian community to become more bold in articulating that response. But the Christian response to this offensive taunt must be something far more substantive and well-informed than a knee-jerk reaction, and it certainly should not be shaped by ground rules chosen by the adversary. It should not, for instance, allow naturalism to steal ownership of the RFE principle or the scientific concept of genealogical continuity among the living creatures of God's creation. In other words, the Christian response should be shaped not by the faulty presumptions or strong-arm tactics that characterize the naturalistic taunt but by the fundamental tenets of the historic Christian doctrine of creation. The heart of the Christian response to the naturalistic taunt should not be a negative attack on the scientific theorizing that naturalism seeks to exploit but an affirming demonstration of the continuing relevance of historic Christian doctrine.

There is no substantial reason for continuing to hold to a portrait of the creation's formational history that is in serious trouble, and rightly so, on purely scientific grounds. The energy of the Christian community should be spent not on attempting to defeat the scientific concept of biotic evolution but on exposing the transparently hollow claims commonly made by the preachers of naturalism. The robust formational economy principle is *not* the property of naturalism, and the scientific concept of biotic evolution does *not* in any way make a Creator unnecessary. Quite the contrary on both counts. Who but a Creator having unfathomable creativity and unlimited generosity could both thoughtfully conceptualize and give being to a universe having so robust a formational economy that its astounding diversity of structures and life forms could be actualized in time by the employment of those capabilities? Is a fully gifted universe less in need of a Creator than a universe with gaps in its formational economy? If one's response to the naturalistic taunt is founded not on the presumptions of naturalism but on the historic Christian doctrine of creation, then the clear answer is, surely not; in fact, it is even more in need of a Creator's thoughtful conceptualization and generous gifting.

The scoring system of the contemporary creation-evolution debate is as upside down as one could imagine. As it now stands, each scientific discovery of a creaturely capability that makes the formational economy of the universe look more robust is credited to the account of evolutionary naturalism. Meanwhile, the truth of the Christian doctrine of creation, by its having been coupled with the episodic creationist picture, is made to appear as if it were dependent on the presence of gaps in that formational economy, gaps formed by the absence of selected creaturely capabilities. Some Christians even encourage the development of a science-like enterprise that searches for empirical evidence for the presence of such gaps. Instead of joy at the discovery of creaturely gifts given by the Creator to the creation, will there be joy over evidence of gifts withheld? What an irony it would be if the preachers of naturalism had a higher view of the creation's giftedness than did the preachers of Christ.

Intelligent Design to the Rescue? Not Likely

During the past few years there have appeared a number of books and articles promoting the thesis that there is empirical evidence favoring the conclusion that the universe has been "intelligently designed."

I have often been cited as a critic of the intelligent design (ID) movement now under way. Why would I be critical of such a movement? Have I not already made it abundantly clear that as one who holds to the historic Christian doctrine of creation, I do heartily believe that the universe was designed by an intelligent Creator? I certainly hope that I have. Then, to use a line employed earlier, "Where's the beef?" Would not a creation gifted with a robust formational economy exhibit, in a manner accessible to the empirical natural sciences, the marks of having been "intelligently designed"? Evidently not, according to the literature of the intelligent design movement.

The relationship of "robust formational economy" and the concept of "intelligent design" depends, of course, on the current working definition of ID, which may differ considerably from one's first impression of the term's meaning. Given my involvement in the evaluation of the ID movement, I recently conducted an experiment on the students enrolled in my physical science course, a course designed for students not majoring in any of the natural sciences. About a month or two into the course and without having yet made any reference to the term "intelligent design," I placed the following question on the blackboard at the beginning of class: "Do you think there is any empirical evidence that would support the conclusion that the universe was intelligently designed?"

The students, all Christians to the best of my knowledge, began to respond very positively to this question, citing as evidence such features of the universe as its orderliness, its beauty, the intricately patterned character of its behavior as described by the laws of physics, its coherence—all taken to be evidence that the Designer of the universe was not *stupid* but rather *intelligent*. After allowing this listing of evidences to go on for a while, I interrupted the process and asked, "Before listing evidence that the universe possesses character trait X, shouldn't we make certain that we know exactly what trait X is?"

The students had little choice but to agree, so I wrote a second question on the board: "What does it mean to be 'intelligently designed'?" I also explained to them that this term "intelligent design" was being used as a label for the defining concept of a movement in the arena of Christian thought regarding the relevance of natural science to matters of religious significance and that I was curious to know what this term would convey to them if its specific meaning in this context were not spelled out ahead of time. We spent a good share of the remaining class time collecting answers to my second question. Certain themes began to characterize their unprompted responses. (I did my best not to steer them in any particular direction.) To be intelligently designed, they offered, was to have been "carefully planned," to have been "thoroughly thought out," to have been "intended" and so on. Furthermore, the intelligent designing of something would require having some specific "purposes or goals" in mind.

Looking at the full list of their contributions and finding them clustered around a limited number of themes, I proposed the following as a statement that incorporated all of them: "To be 'intelligently designed' is to be thoughtfully conceptualized for the accomplishment of some comprehensive purpose." They agreed that this brief statement captured well the essence of what they perceived to be what it meant to be "intelligently designed."

I found this response of my students very informative and fascinating, especially so because it affirmed something that I had earlier concluded. To a person in the late twentieth century, saying that something has been "intelligently designed" would ordinarily be taken to mean that something has been purposefully intended and thoughtfully conceptualized. In other words, "intelligent design" is presumed to be the action of *mind*.

The designing action of the *mind* is to be distinguished from the various actions performed by *hands*. An artisan or a skilled craftsman works with his or her hands to assemble some structure from its component parts or to mold materials into some new form, shape or configuration. It is an action in which form is imposed on raw materials or one in which parts are assembled by an agent into some new structure. This forming or structuring action of the artisan's hands is necessary because neither the raw materials nor the component parts have been equipped with the capabilities to actualize that form or structure.

As I expected, my students took the meaning of "intelligent design" from the current usage of the word *design*. But this meaning is different from earlier meanings of the term. In traditional natural theology the action of "design" was generally thought to require both mind and hands. The traditional "design argument," perhaps most often associated with the name of eighteenth-century clergyman William Paley, is based on the artisan metaphor. One person, the artisan, did both the designing (planning, or thoughtful conceptualization for the accomplishment of some chosen purpose) and the assembling of what had first been conceptualized. The mind of Paley's watchmaker did the conceptualization of the watch's mechanism, and his hands did the forming of the parts and the assembling of them into a complete and functioning timepiece. When Paley and others who advocated a form of natural theology argue from the recognition of "design" in the natural world to the existence of a Designer, the work of the Designer required the action of both Mind and the divine equivalent of "hands."

As I understand their literature, today's proponents of intelligent design argue that there is empirical evidence that clearly indicates that certain specific organisms or biotic subsystems possess the property of "irreducible complexity."[14] An "irreducibly complex" system is made up of several interacting parts, all of which must be present for the system to function in its characteristic manner. The standard mousetrap is taken as the exemplar of irreducible complexity; take away any one of its functioning parts and it ceases to be a mousetrap. It is further argued that there is no conceivable way in which the several parts of the organisms or biotic subsystems cited *could have been assembled by known natural processes* (with special emphasis on biochemical processes), especially if natural processes are restricted to gradual or small stepwise modification. Presuming that case to have been made, it is concluded that systems displaying irreducible complexity must therefore be the product of intelligent design. That is to say, these systems could have been actualized for the first time *only as the outcome of an act of extra-natural assembly.* By "extra-natural assembly" I here mean the action of some unidentified agent that manipulates or coerces certain extant substructures into a new configuration—specifically a new configuration that would not have been actualized by the use of the inadequate capabilities of its component parts or materials.

The bottom line is that what is being called a theory of intelligent design is in actuality a theory claiming to have demonstrated the necessity of "extra-natural assembly." Why would extra-natural assembly be required? Because the formational economy of the universe is missing the particular

<hr>

[14]See Michael J. Behe, *Darwin's Black Box* (New York: Free Press, 1996).

creaturely capabilities that would be needed for self-assembly. In other words, intelligent design theory, like its cousin episodic creationism, claims to have produced empirical evidence for the presence of *gaps in the formational economy of the creation,* gaps that would require supplementary divine action in the course of time to bridge. How would the creation's formational economy come to have those gaps? By divine intention to withhold certain capabilities, I presume.

Where does ID theory take us? Some enthusiastic supporters are hailing it as a giant leap forward in the war against naturalism, a historic revolution in the making. Is that really the case? Or does ID theory take us back to the same inverted scoring system as in the creation-evolution debate and back to the search for gifts withheld from the creation? Why not instead promote the *fully gifted creation perspective* in which the search for gifts withheld is replaced with the celebration of each new creaturely capability discovered by the sciences as further evidence of God's creativity and generosity?

The Fruits of Partnership

What is this fully gifted creation perspective? Perhaps my proposing an answer to this question will serve also as a means of illustrating the concept of Christian theology and the natural sciences functioning cooperatively as "partners in theorizing."

As is the case for visual perspectives, so also for conceptual perspectives; much is determined by the initial choice of standpoint—the locus or platform of fundamental commitments, from which one views the surrounding visual or conceptual territory.

Everything that I have written here and elsewhere proceeds from my commitment to experience the universe, every element of its substance, every one of the capabilities that contribute to its formational and functional economies, as the creation that has being only as the outcome of the effective will of the Creator of whom the Judeo-Christian Scriptures speak. This commitment has an extraordinarily important implication for the scientific enterprise. In essence, though this fundamental matter seems so often overlooked, a commitment to the historic Christian doctrine of creation serves to legitimize the natural sciences as being an appropriate human endeavor. From the standpoint of ancient Near Eastern polytheism, the powers and actions of what we now conceive to be the physical/material world were not the actions of mere creatures but of numerous and often capricious deities. The actions of the storming atmosphere, of raging seas, of flooding rivers, of growing plants, of reproducing animals, of shining sun, of waxing and waning moon and of stars marching across the nighttime sky were the actions not of things having the status of creature but of deities themselves. The ancient Near Eastern polytheistic religions of Israel's neighbors had deified the powers of their environment, making fearsome gods out of those environmental powers that were often experienced as a threat to human life and well-being.

The perspective of biblically informed Christian theology stands in bold contrast to the polytheism so familiar to ancient Israel. The opening lines of the Hebrew Scriptures, in addition to their primary role of introducing the one God who comes to covenant with us as being our Creator, accomplish something else of great importance to us to this day—the "de-deification" of all environmental powers. The storms are not gods; the seas are not gods; the rivers are not gods. They are all creatures, things that have been given being and are sustained in being as members of the good creation, things whose powers and capabilities are to be experienced not as threats to human life or well-being but as gifts given by God the Creator for the accomplishment of God's good purposes and for the service of humankind. And the sun, moon and stars—the awesome lights of the daytime and nighttime skies—are not gods to be afraid of. They too are creatures having the status of servants that were gifted with the capabilities to make light, to mark seasons and to regulate the cycles of our personal, civil and ceremonial activity. No, "The sun will not harm you by day, nor the moon by night" (Ps 121:6 NIV).

In the context of perceiving the entire universe as the creation, the natural sciences need not fear that they are intruding into the realm of divine prerogative, and modern technology need not fear that it is attempting to manipulate the action of deity. Modern natural science may rest assured that the object of its investigation is none other than the creaturely world.[15] And modern technology may rest assured that the powers that it seeks to employ or regulate or manipulate are not the powers of capricious or fearsome deities but the powers, capabilities and

---

[15]One could even argue that the term "natural science" should be replaced with "creaturely science."

actions of creatures—members of the good creation.

Given this foundational and theologically grounded perspective, how might one proceed in the scientific endeavor? What more specific presuppositions might one make regarding the nature of the creaturely universe that it wishes to investigate? Focusing on a fundamental question at issue in the present context, is the creation's formational economy sufficiently robust to make possible the actualization of all of the physical/material structures and all of the life forms that have ever come to be actualized in the course of the creation's formational history? The fully gifted creation perspective is defined by a yes answer to this question—a yes that obviously must be qualified out of a concern to maintain intellectual humility.

Among the requirements that intellectual humility would impose is this one: an unqualified answer, whether yes or no, is not humanly achievable because we will never know all of the elements in the creation's formational economy. Epistemological gaps—things we do not (yet) know—may someday be filled in as the outcome of continuing scientific investigation, or they could conceivably be indicative of corresponding ontological gaps—caused by the absence of specific creaturely capabilities—that must have been bridged by divine creative interventions.

In the absence of a full knowledge of the creation's formational economy, we must make an informed judgment regarding the warrant for the RFE principle. Specifically, we must allow ourselves to be informed both by Christian theology and by the natural sciences, each of which is an enterprise that seeks to formulate and evaluate various theories and to construct a coherently integrated set of theories about the nature of reality, at least of some portion of it. Theology is the more comprehensive enterprise, and although it is concerned primarily with the natures of and interrelationships among God, humankind and the rest of the creation, it does have substantive reason to theorize concerning the character of the creation's formational history and concerning the manner in which divine creative action becomes manifest in the course of time. In the context of that concern the warrant for the robust formational economy principle should be of great interest.

Augustine evidently found ample warrant for that broad concept of the nature of the creation in his reading of Scripture. Although I find myself in hearty agreement with his general conclusion that the creation was gifted from the outset with the requisite capabilities to actualize all life forms in the course of time, I would recommend two qualifications: (1) I do not believe that the Scriptures alone give us a sufficient basis for absolute certainty, either positively or negatively, regarding the warrant for the robust formational economy principle, and (2) I believe that the natural sciences have definitively discredited Augustine's picture for the independent and contemporary actualization of each different type of creature. To this I would add, however, that if a Christian today wishes to make an informed judgment regarding the warrant for the RFE principle, I believe that the contribution of the natural sciences is essential. *Christian theology and the natural sciences must be mutually informed partners in theorizing on matters such as these.*

What does natural science have to contribute today? Considerable insight that is grounded in relevant experience, I would say. The physical sciences, for instance, have been actively engaged for nearly two centuries in theorizing about the formational history of various physical/material structures—planet earth, stars, galaxies, space, atoms, molecules. Especially in recent decades, aided by remarkably fast computational devices, the sciences of cosmology, astronomy and geology have made significant progress in coming to a more realistic portrait of the physical processes that have functioned to bring about the actualization of configurations from the minuscule structures of atomic nuclei to the vast cosmic textures formed by the spatial distribution of galaxies. Of course, many specific questions remain, but the portrait of the universe's formational history seems to be coming progressively into sharper focus. Essential to this theoretical enterprise and the key to all of the particular successes to which one might point, is the presupposition that the RFE principle is fully warranted.

I believe that this striking success in the physical sciences provides very strong encouragement for the assumption that the RFE principle would be equally warranted in theorizing about the formational history of life forms. Furthermore, it is the judgment of nearly every biologist that doing so for more than a century has been the principal reason for the progress that has been made in formulating and evaluating the several theories that constitute the evolutionary paradigm. In other words, presupposing the applicability of the RFE principle has been extraordinarily fruitful in providing reasonable accounts for why the array of extant life forms exhibits the biochemical, genetic and morphological similarities we see and how they came to be actualized in time. No one would deny the presence of significant gaps in our knowledge regarding the particulars of most evolutionary processes and lineages. But neither would anyone be warranted, I believe, in dismissing the wealth of evidence favoring the concepts of genealogical continuity throughout the history of life on earth and the common ancestry of all extant life forms. I have no hesitancy in identifying this as a human judgment that is open to critical evaluation, but it is a judgment that I have made with confidence on the basis of all of the relevant theological and scientific factors that I have been able to incorporate into the judgment-making process.

Thus I have come to believe that the creation of which we are a part was brought into being, by God's effective will, from nothing about fifteen billion years ago and that it was gifted from the outset with all of the capabilities it would need to form the full array of both physical/material structures and life forms that have ever existed. What was brought into being at the beginning, then, was not only the elemental material of which creaturely forms would be made, and not only a densely populated "potentiality space" of possible structures and forms into which these materials could be configured, but also all of the requisite dynamic creaturely pathways (processes made possible by God-given capabilities) for actualizing those forms and structures as intended by God.

I judge that the big bang scenario that has been formulated and is under continuing development by cosmologists is on the right track in its reconstruction of the formational history of space, of the elements and of galaxies. Likewise, I judge that stellar astronomy is essentially correct in its reconstruction of the formational history of stars, from gravitationally collapsing globules of interstellar gas and dust to mature stars, followed by spectacular episodes of stellar disintegration that occur at the end of their luminous lifetimes.

And if my curiosity regarding formational histories takes me beyond the arena of my professional experience in physics and astronomy, I would have no hesitancy whatsoever to ask my colleagues in biology for their best professional judgment about the formational history of terrestrial life. Furthermore, given my high expectations regarding the wealth of self-organizational and transformational gifts that the Creator has given to the creation, I am not at all surprised to hear of the confidence that biologists have come to have in the scientific concept of biotic evolution and the RFE principle that it presumes to be applicable.

It is worth noting, I believe, that the vast majority of the biologists that I know personally are Christians. Given that personal acquaintance, I have come to be fully confident that those Christian biologists have self-consciously performed their evaluation of the scientific concept of biotic evolution from the standpoint of their commitment to the historic Christian doctrine of creation. Contrary to an oft-repeated litany of reckless accusations, these are not dull-minded people who have been indoctrinated into naturalistic thought patterns by their secular university training, nor are they duplicitous persons who are willing to say anything to maintain either the respect of their non-Christian colleagues or the generosity of research funding agencies.

In summary, the fully gifted creation perspective is not the misguided outcome of "accommodation" to the forces of naturalism but the fruitful outcome of Christian theology and the natural sciences functioning as partners in theorizing. In fact, this perspective precludes any accommodation to the naturalistic worldview. Its response to the naturalistic taunt rejects the ground rules of naturalism and proceeds instead along the path of fruitful theorizing first cleared by the historic Christian doctrine of creation.

What happens when there is no partnership? What happens when each operates in isolation from the insights and contributions of the other? Perhaps some features of the present creation-evolution debate could serve as examples. Science uninformed by theology is prone to scientism, the unwarranted elevation of scientific methodology from the realistic status of being considered a fruitful means of learning about selected features of reality to the exaggerated status of being considered a superior, perhaps even the exclusive, means toward knowledge of reality. Similarly, a community in which theology is uninformed by (or misinformed about) the natural sciences is prone toward biblicism and the unwarranted elevation of one portrait of the creation's formational history from the realistic status of one artistic biblical portrait among many to the exaggerated status of being treated as a normative chronicle that rules out the concept of a fully gifted creation capable of actualizing new creaturely forms by the use of its God-given gifts. In the absence of a healthy partnership, both lose. In place of mutually informative dialogue between Christian theology and the natural sciences there are only turf wars and the fruitless shouting match known as the "creation-evolution debate."

A Creationist Response

Wayne Frair & Gary D. Patterson

We are in full agreement with Howard Van Till that an appropriate starting point for a discussion of the relationship between theology and science is a commitment to the Christian faith and its doctrine of creation. We also agree that "authentic knowledge is not a competitor to faith but a valuable partner in the quest for a well-informed understanding of what is true and real" (p. 196). We appreciate the unique contribution that both science and theology make toward a better understanding of the nature of humanity and of the universe that we inhabit.

We join in affirming the centrality of the revelation that God is the Creator and that everything else is created. We agree that the reality of divine intention must be contrasted with the naturalistic dogma of an impersonal universe. The human enterprise we call science should not be confused with the religious perspective called naturalism.

We join in celebrating the richness of the expression of God's creative activity found in the Bible. A subject as deep as this requires language that transcends our common thoughts. We applaud the emphasis on the full testimony of Scripture on the subject of creation. One common ground that unites us is a deep appreciation of the value of the Bible in the practice of Christian theology.

The Bible is a profoundly historical book. One of the most characteristic ways of describing a historical event is exemplified in Galatians 4:4-5: "But when the time had fully come, God sent his Son, born of a woman, born under law, to redeem those under law, that we might receive the full rights of sons" (NIV). The history of the heavens and the earth can be organized into actions of God with respect to his creation. The incarnation and resurrection of Jesus Christ are two central acts of God in Christian theology. The notion that God acts in history is a fundamental principle. The Bible does contain specific revelation that informs us of God's role in particular events. But proper exegesis of any text requires a partnership that we have referred to as the hermeneutical spiral. All our knowledge must be brought to bear on the interpretation of the Bible. While we may differ in detail on the interpretation of a particular passage, the principles of biblical interpretation presented in our chapter are in agreement with those presented in Van Till's chapter.

We believe that God created space-time and that he employs whatever means are needed to accomplish his plans. We also view God's activity with respect to his creation as continuous, as indicated by the specific biblical passages quoted in our chapter. But in order to describe continuous history it is common to divide time into coherent segments. While there is a history of debate that is implied by Van Till, the current discussion can be carried out without polarization into competing camps. Descriptions of God's actions using human language have inherent limitations, but since the Bible chooses to use this mode of communication, we can proceed cautiously and graciously.

Augustine is a good example of a Christian wrestling with the relationship between the Bible and physical reality. He was not necessarily correct in his assumptions or conclusions, but he was transparent and insightful. He was strongly influenced by the philosophy of Plato and sought to organize his thoughts using concepts borrowed from that source. He tried to create a unified picture that did not contradict either his interpretation of the Bible or his understanding of physical reality. In this sense, he was practicing the partnership approach. One of the strengths of this procedure is that it can continue to improve our understanding as more is known. However, progress is not always monotonic; therefore, aberrant periods in either theology or science can lead to conflict. The openness required of this approach is disquieting to many, but we join Van Till in recommending it to our Christian brethren.

We agree that the universe has a continuous history, but it is still useful to organize time into coherent parts. Before the Planck time, history is known only to God. Stephen Hawking's concept of imaginary time allows this period to be represented as continuous with the present. A plausible scenario for the first three minutes is now part of the standard lore of physics, although the details change weekly! The most important question for humankind on this subject is: Why does the universe exist? The Bible reveals that God intentionally created it. The popular view that the universe is just a big fluctuation is not consistent with actual observations of fluctuating physical systems, but is based on the philosophical notion that our history is characterized by random events with no purpose. As the number of observations that can constrain our speculations decreases, the appearance of other motivations for our positions increases. It is just as inappropriate to accept blindly all the philosophical baggage that sometimes comes with certain theories as it is to reject blindly sound experimental evidence because it appears to contradict our cherished notions. Both patience and charity are required when considering the heavens.

We stand solidly with Van Till in the desire to oppose atheism and naturalism. Rather than look back at unprofitable arguments, we desire to look together at the known history of the universe and the full text of the Bible. We believe that a partnership model, as proposed by Van Till, is also a good metaphor for describing the actions of God in history. We will try to give some examples to illustrate this principle. We join Van Till in celebrating the richness of the material world that God has given to humankind and rejoicing in every new capability discovered by science. We also choose to praise God for the specific acts revealed in the Bible. God is described in many biblical passages using an artisan metaphor. The artisan combines the material properties of his medium with intentional acts of craftsmanship. Competent artists are well aware of the possibilities inherent in their art, and they form a partnership with the materials to produce specific products. Who knows the material properties of the universe better than God? We are truly thankful that he has encouraged us to study the world around us and to apply this knowledge to accomplish our plans. God is revealed in the Bible as actively involved in his creation, actualizing his intentions when the time is full.

In order to illustrate the nature of this partnership, let us consider a common activity like baking a cake. Suppose the ingredients consist of flour, sugar, cocoa and oil. We could study the individual properties of the ingredients, but this knowledge alone would not produce a cake. We could study the properties of a series of mixtures of the ingredients, but again we would not discover a cake. A cake requires the proper ingredients, a recipe and a baker. The information contained in the recipe allows the baker to process the ingredients and produce the cake. If he chooses to ignore the time limit for exposure of the mixture to heat, nature will take its course and the cake will burn. Is it irruptive of the baker to mix the ingredients and bake the cake?

We propose that the beginning of the universe was an intentional act of God rather than an accidental fluctuation. If the standard model is followed through the first three minutes, many things happen, but there would yet be no stars. In fact, the global description of the universe employed in this approach does not lead directly to stars. The ingredients for stars could be produced, but the conditions for star formation would not yet have been realized. The Bible tells us that God deliberately made the stars to accomplish a purpose. As Christians we praise him for his gift of the stars. As scientists we look at stars to see what they are, what they were and what they shall become. These two activities are complementary and reinforce one another. The study of the stars has revealed that the universe is a very dynamic place. Mistaken notions about a static cosmology, whatever their source, have given way to a picture that more accurately reflects the temporal nature of all created things.

Our solar system is also a fascinating place. We are learning more about it every day. The Bible tells us that it had a beginning and that it will have an end, but that it is not an accident. God intentionally assembled a very diverse group of objects composed of many different substances and organized it in such a way that it possessed a high degree of stability. As Christians we praise God for his gift of a local part of the universe that was prepared for our habitation. As scientists we look at the solar system and reflect on what it was, what it is and what it will become. As Christians we acknowledge that we may not know the recipe for the production of the solar system, but we do know the artisan. As scientists we acknowledge that we may not be able to infer a plausible mechanism for the formation of the solar system because we do not know the initial conditions, nor do we have any data that was obtained directly during that time period. However, just as the observation of the microwave background radiation can be interpreted as an "echo" of the big bang, and the existence of heavy elements can be interpreted as the remnants of supernovae, there may be observations of the solar system in the present that may be interpreted in terms of a proposed history. The observation of a layer of iridium in the crust of the earth is interpreted currently as evidence of a large meteor impact at a particular point in history.

When the Bible appears to reveal a specific intentional act of God, Christians should not be afraid to look for evidence. If the evidence is consistent with the proposed interpretation of the Bible, then a measure of confidence is produced. If no evidence is found, or if contradictory evidence is found, then we must face the facts and abandon or revise our interpretation. Scientific conjectures are subject to the same protocol. Procrustean adherence to discredited speculations does not advance our understanding.

Earth is a truly remarkable place. The Bible tells us that this is not an accident. God intentionally prepared the earth as a dwelling place for humankind. Observations of the earth in the present have been interpreted in terms of a dramatic history. As Christians we admit that we may not know the recipe for the formation of a planet like ours, but we do know the artisan. As scientists we know that reconstructing a plausible history of the earth is difficult because we do not have data collected directly during that time period. However, data collected in the present have been interpreted in terms of processes observed in the present to produce a history of earth. One of the most remarkable observations of the surface of the earth is that it has changed enormously. In particular, a material called soil has been formed. It is a complex mixture of inorganic materials, organic materials and living organisms. The remarkable conditions on the earth that make life possible lead Christians to praise God for his gift of a habitation.

The Bible tells us that God created life intentionally. Atheists have been able to provide no support for the speculation that life arose as a spontaneous fluctuation. The simplest single-celled organism contains so much specific information and operates so far out of equilibrium that random fluctuations will not lead to the observed living states. As scientists we observe the cellular world and try to organize our knowledge into coherent relationships between the biological structures and functions that have been discovered. This activity is not improved by imposing the metaphysical condition that there is no God. The need for an intelligent agent to construct living cells is not due to a problem with the chemicals from which it is composed; it is a reflection of the nature of physical reality that highly nonequilibrium states require a specific recipe to produce them. Even many perceptive atheists have given up the myth that random fluctuations are enough to produce life, and they have started looking for specific pathways that could lead to self-organized structures. We believe that the robust economy is a partnership between God and his creation.

The Bible describes humankind as a partnership of flesh and spirit. The concept of a spirit that can communicate with God transcends the realm of science. The Bible asserts that God intentionally gave a spirit to us. It also addresses us as responsible agents who can choose to do good or evil. Our Christian life is described as a partnership between God and us. Without him we indeed can do nothing spiritual. Science practiced apart from God produces scientists who suffer profound alienation. One of the best gifts we can give our fellow scientists is the gospel of Jesus Christ. We share Van Till's concern that some scientists may be hindered in their path of faith by thinking that Christianity is inherently antagonistic to science. We join Van Till in affirming that we are encouraged to observe all that God has created, and we rejoice in each new discovery. We can now join in the activity of applying this knowledge as responsible agents in obedience to our God.

An Independence Response

Jean Pond

As a believer whose professional experience is in biology, let me first say how pleased and grateful I was to read Howard Van Till's spirited defense of Christian biologists against accusations that, as evolutionists, we are stupid, brainwashed by naturalism or liars (p. 234). I have elsewhere pointed out that Christian evolutionists—after years of hearing their professional competence, faith and integrity called into question—tend to get a little touchy on this subject.

I find myself in agreement with Van Till on a substantial number of other points as well. I think he makes a valuable distinction between the essential *doctrine* of creation and the various *portraits* of creation. Like Van Till I think that doctrine is a fundamental part of the Christian faith, but the portraits may vary. I am also appreciative of his forthright identification of the creation-evolution issue as a major sticking point and his willingness to step boldly into the fray. It will indeed be helpful if his attempt at a "restructuring" of the discussion is successful; I must confess, however, to some pessimism on this score.

The problem may be that the creation-evolution controversy is neither a scientific issue nor entirely a religious one. It is in part a *political* issue, and American politics (as all other politics, I suspect) remain aloof from logic. I am undoubtedly not using the term *political* in a precise way—perhaps *cultural* is a closer fit—but what I am referring to is the tendency of human beings to want to place themselves within a tribe (group, denomination, political party) where they feel accepted and where they can draw lines as to who is right and who is wrong, who is in and who is out.

In the United States the creation-evolution issue has become one of the key indicators of "in or out?" for various groups. An understanding of the science and theology involved seems to me to have become less important than the willingness to declare yourself on one side or the other. Still, hope is a virtue, so I remain hopeful that Van Till's analysis will have a beneficial effect in this debate.

Below I comment further on two topics addressed by Van Till: naturalism as a religion and the "robust formational economy" (RFE) principle. I conclude with a brief discussion of why—despite agreeing with Van Till on a variety of points—I still maintain that independence rather than partnership is the appropriate relationship between science and faith.

Are Atheists Religious?

In his discussion of Carl Sagan's *Cosmos* Van Till defines naturalism as the idea that the physical universe is all that exists, that there is no transcendent Creator and so on, and he adds that naturalism is a "religious perspective" (p. 201). I agree with his definition, but I feel we need to be careful when describing naturalism as a religion. I get the point: human beings decide whether to believe that a supernatural, transcendent God exists; to say that such an entity does *not* exist is a worldview assertion rather than a scientific one. No one is more irritated than I am to hear statements such as "science has proved God doesn't exist." Nevertheless, calling naturalism a religion always makes me uncomfortable because in the contexts where this claim tends to be used it often comes off sounding like an accusation, as if being religious was something weak or shameful. ("You're just religious too!")

In addition, Dawkins and others have clearly explained that they see no reason to believe in a supernatural deity. To believe in God requires (in my experience) faith beyond reason, and this faith is an essential element of "religion." If one must have faith to say God *does* exist, is it fair to claim that the proponents of naturalism must have "faith" to say God *doesn't* exist?

There would be no logical end to the things one might be asked to have faith in. What if a group developed a religion involving belief in leprechauns? Are we then required to describe ourselves as having a *religion* of "not believing in leprechauns"?

Now I realize that an appeal to analogy involving odd little men does not address the whole of the question. As I understand it, what Van Till is saying is this: the universe exists, but its existence is not self-explanatory. Therefore there must be an explanation for this existence outside of the universe itself, resulting in the need for a transcendent creator. I happen to agree, but I think a couple caveats are in order: (1) there is nothing in this line of argument that identifies the creator of the universe with the Christian God; (2) it is a very difficult point to *prove.*

When physicists told us that time and space themselves did not exist prior to the big bang, didn't we all try to imagine what that really *meant?* Without time and space, where . . . ? when . . . ? Hmm. Perhaps some readers have had an experience similar to mine: after a few minutes of such contemplation, metaphorical wisps of smoke begin to emerge from your ears.

The whole concept of something beyond or "outside" the universe is so mysterious and alien to our experience that we resort—quite naturally and, I think, correctly—to this answer: God did it. But what if the proponents of naturalism say they feel no such mystery? We say: The universe is not self-explanatory and requires a transcendent creator. They say: Yes, it is; and no, it doesn't. On what basis do we tell them they're wrong? Science won't work since we have just declared it unable to deal with questions at this level. Faith?—now we're back to leprechauns.

The RFE Principle

I found Van Till's presentation of the robust formational economy principle to be enlightening, although I am sorry to say that his terminology does not trip easily off the tongue! He has turned the old creation-evolution scoring system upside down, stating, as I understand it, that a universe exhibiting a robust formational economy is a universe which is that much *more* likely to require a transcendent creator.

I can agree that a God who created a universe capable, from the first nanoseconds, of coming up with human beings on its own is in some sense more powerful than a God who had to step in from time to time to jostle things on their way. Like Van Till I think the reasoning behind this argument is the same whether the jostling involved, say, the special creation of human beings five to ten thousand years ago or the "intelligent" design of sequences of DNA.

Hoimar von Ditfurth makes a similar argument. He points out that if we give the easily explicable natural phenomena to the proponents of naturalism and keep only the tough bits for God, then (science being what it is) God will be banished to the smaller and more obscure aspects of creation with every passing year.[1] Let's give this up now before it's too late.

Nevertheless I think there are problems with Christian ownership of the RFE principle. Are we saying that (1) if the RFE principle is true, theists win, and (2) if the RFE principle is not true (jostling needed), the naturalists win? The latter doesn't work, since the requirement for periodic supernatural interventions negates naturalism. So we are faced with claiming that theists win either way, which hardly seems sporting.

I can imagine a proponent of naturalism raising his or her hand and saying, "Excuse me? Are you saying that (1) if we can't explain how the vertebrate eye evolved, that is evidence for God, and (2) if we *can* explain how the vertebrate eye evolved, that is even better evidence for God? Is there *any* evidence that you would accept as arguing against the existence of God?"

Is there? I suspect not. I have often wondered, for example, what would happen if new data in physics pointed toward a return to the steady-state theory of the universe or indicated in some other way that the universe was infinite in age. (It is not necessary for my example that this new theory be *correct*, of course, only that people think it is.) Would we agree that this was evidence, now, against the existence of God? Or would we be falling all over ourselves writing articles to prove an infinite universe could only arise through the actions of a transcendent Creator?

But if there is no scientific evidence that we would accept as negating the existence of God, then we are outside of the realm of science. It is for this reason, among others, that I question whether science and Christian

[1]Hoimar von Ditfurth, *The Origins of Life: Evolution as Creation* (San Francisco: Harper & Row, 1982), pp. 105-6.

theology can be partners in theorizing.

Partnership or Independence?

I find myself much more of a mind with Van Till than creationists of either the young-earth or the old-earth variety or proponents of intelligent design. Our approach to Scripture is similar, at least in part, in that Van Till describes biblical authors speaking (on occasion) figuratively and in metaphor (pp. 204-5). We are in full agreement, I believe, on the scientific merits of the theory of biological evolution.

Van Till and I disagree to some extent, however, on the (real or potential) theological relevance of science. He suggests that what science has to tell us about the physical universe (and especially, a physical universe characterized by a robust formational economy) should be recognized as "*affirmative evidence for the unfathomable creativity and unlimited generosity of the Creator*" (p. 218).

I agree that the RFE universe is highly *compatible* with a Christian worldview, but I don't consider it actual evidence in favor of the existence of God. I tend to believe that Christians will believe in God no matter what science comes up with next, and therefore since there are no data that can disprove the existence of our Creator, so there are no data that can prove it either.

Our disagreement over the theological relevance of scientific data and theories leads to a disagreement over the appropriate relationship between science and theology in general. Van Till contends that these two human undertakings are "each engaged in a constructive effort to make its own unique contribution toward a better understanding of the nature of humanity and of the universe that we inhabit" (p. 198). This is a statement with which I agree. But he also states his premise that science and theology are not "independent endeavors that should function in isolation from one another, but *partners in theorizing*" (p. 198).

Isolation. It sounds so negative, doesn't it? Perhaps my real disagreement with Van Till is not whether science and theology should be partners in our struggle to understand human existence but only at what *level* that partnership should occur.

Van Till seems to be suggesting (and I'm willing to be corrected here) that this partnership should be developed at the scholarly/academic level.

I tend to believe that this should *not* occur: when I teach anatomy and physiology, prenursing students need to know the same things about the workings of the heart, be they Christian or non-Christian. When I walk into a molecular biology laboratory, my procedures and data must be reproducible by Christians and non-Christians alike. When I describe my physical world in scientific terms, that description must ring true for Christian and non-Christian. The universe is the way it is. It is the same universe for us all.

The integration between science and faith that occurs—as I believe it must, for Christians—should occur in the constructing of worldviews, and this happens at the level of the *individual*. Each of us makes our worldview out of all we experience and know. None of us is a bifurcated person. The human mind does its best to understand what science tells it about the nature of physical reality. The human heart has what faith it can, in the existence of a creator. We put these things together, in our individual selves, and go out to face the world.

A Qualified Agreement Response

Stephen C. Meyer

Howard Van Till begins by making a clear distinction between two world-views: naturalism and theism. He then asks whether nature is self-existent (as the naturalists claim) or dependent on a Creator for its existence (as theists claim). He asks further what the Bible and the empirical sciences have to say about these important questions. Van Till notes that the biblical writers deny the self-existence of nature and support the existence of a purposeful and transcendent Creator. Further, he makes clear that as an orthodox Christian he stands with the biblical writers in their affirmation of a theistic worldview and in their opposition to a naturalistic one. On this ultimate metaphysical question, he and I concur.

Nevertheless Van Till and I differ markedly in our epistemology, our view of science and our view of its relationship to theistic belief. Though Van Till believes that God designed the universe, he rejects specific empirically based design inferences and arguments (with one possible exception, see below). Van Till takes this view because he assumes something he calls the robust formational economy (RFE) principle. The RFE principle asserts that nature possesses "capabilities for self-organization and transformation"(p. 215). It further asserts that these capacities for self-organization are "sufficiently robust to make possible the actualization of all physical/material structures and all forms of life that have ever existed since the beginning of time" (p. 216). In brief, the RFE principle holds that God created the universe with the potential to organize itself (or to evolve) into all the complex structures and life forms that we observe today without any subsequent creative acts on God's part.

Professor Van Till does not just entertain the RFE principle as a hypothesis, instead he holds it as a regulative principle for scientific theorizing, indeed one that he claims to have derived from Christian theology.[1] For this reason he rejects (as both unscientific and theologically misguided) any hypothesis that implies the inadequacy of self-organizational laws, mechanisms or properties to produce the structures and living forms we observe in the world. Specifically, he rejects the design hypothesis as an explanation for the origin of particular biological systems on the grounds that it implies a less than fully gifted formational economy of the universe. In his view, design inferences and arguments don't celebrate the design and wisdom of the Creator, they mistakenly celebrate "gaps in the formational economy of creation" (p. 229). Thus as a result of his commitment to the RFE principle, Van Till adopts a view of science that denies the possibility of detecting divine action at any point in cosmic history after the initial creation of the universe. Accordingly, he also adopts a model for the relationship between science and Christianity that implies science provides very little (if any) evidential support for theistic belief (beyond whatever evidence it might provide for the RFE principle).[2]

---

[1]Van Till cites the theology of Basil and Augustine to justify what he elsewhere calls the doctrine of the functional integrity of the universe (roughly, the RFE principle). For a critique of his exegesis of Basil and Augustine on this point, see Jonathan Wells, "Abusing Theology: Howard Van Till's 'Forgotten Doctrine of Creation's Functional Integrity,' " *Origins & Design* 19, no. 1 (1998): 16-22.

[2]Van Till believes the RFE principle shows the design of a Creator. Thus in his view, evidence establishing the RFE principle would provide some evidence for God's existence. He says a "remarkably complete" formational economy would provide evidence against naturalism and "affirmative evidence [for] the unfathomable creativity and unlimited generosity of the Creator" (p. 218). Yet recall that by a "remarkably complete formational economy" Van Till means self-organizational laws and properties of nature that render appeals to intelligent design or divine action unnecessary. In other words, a "remarkably complete formational economy" refers to the complete sufficiency of natural processes as mechanisms for generating the "full array of both physical/material [entities] and life forms that have ever existed" (p. 215).

Van Till's view seems to contradict earlier published statements in which he insists

On the other hand, design theorists such as myself affirm what we regard as a more open philosophy of science. We think that scientists should follow the evidence wherever it leads. As a result, we think questions about whether natural self-organizational capacities or acts of intelligent design better explain particular features of the natural world ought to be decided by empirical investigation rather than by *a priori* principles (i.e., the REF principle and its secular sister, the principle of "methodological naturalism"). We accept that self-organizational laws, properties and mechanisms suffice to explain *some* features of the physical world. We are willing to consider *the possibility* that self-organizational laws, properties and mechanisms *might* explain all features of the physical and biological world. Nevertheless we do not accept that scientists must limit themselves to strictly naturalistic or self-organizational hypotheses when attempting to explain the origin of specific features of the world. We think scientists should infer the *best* explanations for the origin of a given phenomenon, not just the best self-organizational or naturalistic explanation for a phenomenon. Imagine, for example, the folly of a homicide detective deciding to con-

---

the findings of science are metaphysically neutral (see, for example, Howard Van Till, *The Fourth Day* [Grand Rapids, Mich.: Eerdmans, 1986], pp. 208-15). It also raises an obvious question. If the laws and properties of the natural world completely suffice to explain the origin of the "full array" of entities and "life forms that have ever existed," why invoke anything else? Why not assert, as philosophical naturalists do, a self-existent and self-creating natural system as the metaphysical starting point for all explanation of physical phenomena? Surely that would be a simpler and thus better explanation than invoking self-organizational properties *and* God's design. Thus many naturalists regard, with some justification, putative evidence for the sufficiency of self-organizational laws as support for their worldview.

Of course Van Till could argue that naturalists still need to explain why the universe exists at all. And indeed he could well make (though he doesn't) various cosmological arguments to show that the existence of God, as opposed to naturalism, helps explain why something exists rather than nothing. Even so, a person could still explain the existence of the universe and its putative self-organizational capacities by invoking a deistic god who designed the universe with these capacities from the beginning but who refrains from disrupting nature's "functional integrity" by any discrete acts of creation thereafter. Thus the RFE principle does not provide "affirmative evidence" of a Creator, still less a theistic one. At best, when coupled with some kind of cosmological argument, it might provide the basis for a weak deistic argument and conception of nature. Indeed, though Van Till himself repudiates deism, his view that God created the universe with a robust formational economy such that it could and did develop without subsequent creative "interruptions," strongly resembles a classical deistic view of nature.

sider only "natural causes" as a possible explanation for the deaths he investigates. Such a detective will never "get his man," even if the evidence for murder is quite compelling. Or imagine the folly of an archaeologist who upon discovering cave paintings and petroglyphs decides to reject the hypothesis of design by intelligent agents because it would imply "gaps in the formational economy of the universe" and the insufficiency of self-organizational natural processes. So it would, but wouldn't it also constitute a better explanation? Design theorists affirm the intellectual freedom of scientists to formulate design hypotheses where the evidence warrants. Van Till's "robust formational economy principle" restricts that freedom.

Do Empirical Data Support the RFE Principle? The RFE Principle and the Origin of Biological Information
Van Till not only asserts the RFE principle as a methodological principle, he also suggests that it has a strong evidential basis. Indeed he offers a partial list (pp. 214-15) of self-organization capacities that can explain the development of life on earth, starting from the elementary particles present from the first moment of creation. Van Till suggests, in accord with the RFE principle, that "atoms . . . have the capabilities to interact and to organize themselves into a vast spectrum of molecules, which have the capabilities to interact in ways that lead to the formation of an even more vast array of other molecules, *including those required for the functioning of living organisms"* (p. 214, emphasis added). Thus Van Till suggests the origin of life can be explained as the result of self-organizational properties of the chemical constituents of living cells. Yet, here Van Till's RFE principle leads him astray. Indeed, from the standpoint of contemporary molecular biology, the last part of his statement is clearly false.

Building a living cell requires information. In modern cells, information is stored in DNA and proteins. Those attempting to explain the origin of life must, therefore, explain the origin of the information in these important biomolecules. Yet contemporary molecular biology (and information theory) shows that the information in these large macromolecules cannot be explained as the result of the self-organizational properties of their constituent parts (e.g., of the smaller molecules and atoms that make up DNA).

Some try to explain the origin of the information in DNA (as expressed in the specific sequencing of its nucleotide bases) as the result of self-organizational capacities or forces of attraction between the different constituent parts of the DNA molecule. Like Van Till they assert the existence of "molecules, which have the capabilities to interact in ways that lead to the formation . . . of other molecules, including those required for the functioning of living organisms" (p. 214). Some have even stated self-organizational forces of chemical necessity or attraction between molecular constituents make the origin of life and the genetic information it requires "inevitable."[3]

Yet this assertion, like Van Till's above, contradicts well-established biological facts. The structure of DNA depends on several chemical bonds that could result from "self-organizing" forces of chemical attraction. There are chemical bonds, for example, between the sugar and the phosphate molecules that form the two twisting backbones of the DNA molecule. There are bonds fixing individual (nucleotide) bases to the sugar-phosphate backbones on each side of the molecule. There are also hydrogen bonds stretching horizontally across the molecule between nucleotide bases making so-called complementary pairs. Each of these bonds help form the structural features of the DNA molecule and *do* result (in part) from self-organizing forces of attraction between constituent molecular subunits.

Nevertheless such forces cannot explain the origin of the specific sequencing that constitutes the information in DNA. Figure 1 shows that there are *no* chemical bonds (or self-organizing forces of attraction) at work between the bases along the vertical axis in the center of the helix. Yet it is precisely along this axis of the molecule that the genetic instructions in DNA are encoded.[4] Further, just as magnetic letters can be combined and recombined in any way to form various sequences on a metal surface, so too can each of the four bases A, T, G and C attach to any site on the DNA backbone with equal facility, making all sequences equally probable (or improbable), given the laws of physics and chemistry. Indeed there are no differential forces of attraction between any of the four bases and the binding sites along the sugar-phosphate backbone.

---

[3]See, for example, Christian deDuve, "The Beginnings of Life on Earth," *American Scientist* 83 (1995): 437.

[4]Bruce Alberts and Dennis Bray et al., *Molecular Biology of the Cell* (New York: Garland, 1983), p. 105.

The same type of (so-called n-glycosidic) bond occurs between the base and the backbone regardless of which base attaches. All four bases are acceptable, none is preferred. As Bernd-Olaf Kuppers notes, "The properties of nucleic acids indicate that all the combinatorially possible nucleotide patterns of a DNA are, from a chemical point of view, equivalent."[5] Thus "self-organizing" laws or properties cannot explain the sequential ordering of the nucleotide bases in DNA because (1) there are *no* chemical bonds between bases along the message-bearing axis of the molecule, and (2) there are no *differential forces of attraction* between the backbone and the various bases that could account for variations in sequencing.

For those who want to explain the origin of the information necessary to build life as the result of self-organizing properties intrinsic to the material constituents of living systems, these rather elementary facts of molecular biology have devastating implications. Molecular biology makes clear that self-organizing forces of attraction between the constituents in DNA (as well as RNA and protein)[6] do not explain the specific sequencing of bases on these large information-bearing biomolecules. These facts also raise a very difficult question for Van Till's RFE principle. He insists that God's direct, discrete or special creative activity played no role after the initial moment of creation at the big bang. His RFE principle asserts that the laws of nature acting on elementary particles, or the self-organizational properties of those particles, were sufficient to organize matter into the complex forms we see today. Nevertheless, if the chemical subunits of DNA lack the self-organizational properties or latent self-organizing potential necessary to produce the informational sequencing of DNA, then it is difficult to see how the far less complex and biologically specific elementary particles (such as those present just after the big bang) or atoms possessed the intrinsic properties necessary to

---

[5]Bernd-Olaf Kuppers, "On the Prior Probability of the Existence of Life," in *The Probabilistic Revolution,* ed. Kruger et al. (Cambridge, Mass.: MIT Press, 1987), p. 364.

[6]See R. A. Kok, J. A. Taylor and W. L. Bradley, "A Statistical Examination of Self-Ordering of Amino Acids in Proteins," *Origins of Life and Evolution of the Biosphere* 18 (1988): 135-42; Stephen C. Meyer, "DNA by Design: An Inference to the Best Explanation for the Origin of Biological Information," *Rhetoric and Public Affairs* 1, no. 4 (1998): 519-56, esp. 535.

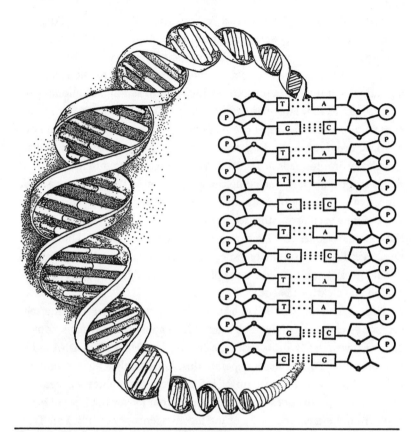

Figure 1. The bonding relationships between the chemical counstituents of the DNA molecule. Sugars (designated by the circled P's) are linked chemically. Nucleotide bases (A's, T's, G's, and C's) are bonded to the sugar-phosphate backbones. Nucleotide bases are linked by hydrogen bonds (designated by dotted double or triple lines) across the double helix. But no chemical bonds exist between the nucleotide bases along the message-bearing spine of the helix. Courtesy of Fred Hereen, Daystar Publications.

organize themselves into fully functioning organisms.

Of course, Van Till can continue to hold out hope that the necessary self-organizational properties will be found. But consider what that would mean. For such properties to be found in the constituent parts of the DNA molecule, our current understanding of the chemical structure and information-bearing properties of DNA would have to be radically altered. Based on our current understanding, however, we can say definitely that such properties simply do not exist. Perhaps scientists will find self-organizational capacities elsewhere, perhaps in some kind of external (to DNA) self-organizational process or law. Yet this possibility, as well as the one we have already considered, would require fundamental revisions in our thinking about the nature of information. Known self-organizational laws and properties inevitably describe or generate highly repetitive or redundant patterns—like the repetitive sequences of ions in crystals or the symmetrical order of a swirling vortex. They do not generate specified complexity or information. Yet the arrangements of matter in information-rich texts or molecules, including the genetic text of DNA, possess a high degree of complexity or aperiodicity—not repetitive order. (To illustrate the difference compare the sequence NaCl-NaCl-NaCl-NaCl-NaCl-NaCl-NaCl to the sequence "Time and tide wait for no man." The former sequence displays redundant order and does result from self-organizational forces of attraction, the latter displays [specified] complexity or information and clearly does not.)

Thus to assert as Van Till does that life may have arisen from the self-organizing capacities of the molecules that compose living systems, contradicts what we already know about the chemical structure of the DNA molecule on which living systems depend. Most importantly it also contradicts what we know about the origin of information. Experience teaches that specified complexity does not self-organize from matter but instead originates from the creative activity of intelligent agents—of minds. Van Till's RFE principle forbids consideration of this possibility (after the big bang) and thus blinds him to important evidence for God's creative involvement at discrete points during the history of life. It also leads him to overlook scientific evidences of design that provide epistemological support, though not proof, for a theistic worldview.

Postscript
Richard F. Carlson

What we have in the previous four chapters are four distinct views from five people—significantly different views from five different people, from people who take each other seriously and who will share eternity together in the presence of their Lord and Savior, people who value one another here on earth, and people who can disagree but who can care and respect one another. This is the way discussions should take place between Christian brothers and sisters—to the point, raising significant questions of each other and causing each other to examine his or her own positions, yet doing so in a spirit of valuing the other person and taking the other person seriously.

My conclusion is that each viewpoint represented here has important ingredients to add to the science-faith (creation-evolution) discussion within the Christian church. Even more broadly, the preceding four chapters also bring out some important principles related to how Christian believers might in general faithfully approach issues of current relevance.

As I reflect on the presentations and the responses in the previous four chapters, certain important issues have arisen. In what follows I offer some further comments.

Biblical Interpretation
All of us (contributors and me) take the Bible very seriously—it is the principal authority for our lives. However, a question arises as we do our best to take the Bible seriously and to try to derive from it teachings for our lives, including our training in righteousness and becoming equipped for "every good work" (2 Tim 3:16-17). The question is: How do we take our Book, this

ancient Book, this Book written in prescientific times, and read it with contemporary problems and issues—in particular, scientific questions—in mind so that the scriptural goals of 2 Timothy 3:16-17 are fulfilled? In my opinion we are addressing a *crucial* question here, perhaps *the* crucial question. Wayne Frair and Gary Patterson are the most explicit in calling for a careful interpretation of biblical passages. They point out that the Bible uses a variety of literary styles, and they state the importance of establishing the cultural, social and historical context of a given biblical text. They affirm the crucially important use of scholarly analyses in a proper biblical interpretation. The importance of such an approach in reading the Bible is acknowledged explicitly by Howard Van Till and Jean Pond, and implicitly by Stephen Meyer. I completely agree.

Significant progress has been made in this past century in the area of the theory of language. This has been especially helpful for biblical studies and interpretation. Earlier (in the modern period) language was seen to function in one of two ways. The first was called referential (or representative), in which groups of words were to be understood by analyzing them into their simplest parts, and the meaning of the parts was to be accounted for in terms of reference. Here language gets its meaning by describing facts or describing objects. The second theory is called the expressivist theory of language (a sort of second-class theory of language), where if language doesn't describe something in the world, then maybe it is meaningful because it expresses some inner attitude or feeling or intention of the speaker or writer. Here language has no factual meaning.[1] Theology in the modern period was forced to adopt one or the other theories of language, with the conservative church opting for the referential aspect, while the liberals adopted the expressivist version. The problem is that neither alone is adequate to describe all dimensions of how language actually works. And in particular, it left the conservative (now the evangelical) wing of the Christian church with a theory of language that left one little choice but to interpret essentially all Scripture in a literal way—all Scripture except those portions that were clearly not to be interpreted in such a way, such as the parables of Jesus. If there was any question at all, the faithful response

---

[1]Nancey Murphy, *Anglo-American Postmodernity: Philosophical Perspectives on Science, Religion, and Ethics* (Boulder, Colo.: Westview, 1997), pp. 10-11.

was to interpret a passage in a literal way.

Recent work in the theory of language[2] suggests that five aspects or dimensions of language need to be taken into account in order to understand how language works and work effectively for a given piece of writing. This is of crucial importance in doing biblical studies, for example. These dimensions are

1. *Linguistic conventions.* This involves grammatical and word studies. A person needs to know Greek and Hebrew grammar and proper word usage in order to understand the Bible. Communication between the biblical writer and the contemporary reader must be clear.

2. *Social conventions.* A person needs to know the proper forms for various types of social conventions that took place during the times in which the Bible was being formed, written and originally used. A person needs to know the social (religious) context in which biblical passages were written or used in those times. For example, recognizing that the Psalms were sung in the midst of worship is an important aspect of understanding what the Psalms are and what they are saying. A person needs to know the kinds of forms that are related to the social (religious) conventions. He or she needs to tentatively assess the *Sitz im Leben* (the setting in the life of the people). Here the form of communication (writing) should be appropriate to the social or religious context, and that form must be identified and its usage understood by the reader.

3. *Referential dimension.* In order to really understand what a biblical text is saying, a person needs to know the history going on at the time. We need to know to whom a given passage was written, when it was written, what was going on at the time it was written, what would have been the concerns of those to whom the passage was written. In other words, we need to know the historical and cultural context for a given passage—the relation between the passage and the world. The passage must bear an appropriate relation to the known state of affairs.

4. *Expressivist conditions.* Expressivist conditions include the writer's (or speaker's) intentions and even his or her attitudes and emotions. This is perhaps the main goal of biblical studies—to understand the writer's

---

[2]James Wm. McClendon Jr. and James M. Smith, *Understanding Religious Convictions* (South Bend, Ind.: University of Notre Dame Press, 1975). See also Murphy, *Anglo-American Postmodernity*, pp. 131ff.

(God's) intention in writing a particular biblical passage. For example, if a biblical writer as an editor was using a number of sources, what was the editor's intent in putting the particular chosen sources together in the way that was done—all the details of editing? In short, what was the sacred writer or editor trying to communicate as that person responded in obedience to the Holy Spirit, resulting in an inspired (God-breathed) biblical text? For example, if I read "God created the heavens and the earth," but my response is "so what?" then I really don't understand what it means to read that God created the heavens and the earth. I don't really understand what the writer of that passage was saying.

5. Up-take. The last step is the hearer or reader "getting it"—getting the point of what was being written or said. This is the equivalent of doing careful and thorough Bible study, known by some as inductive Bible study. The question is, how does the text affect you? or rather what impact does the text have on you? A more technical way of putting this is known as "reader response criticism." *Up-take* means that the reader or hearer gets it, because she or he shares the linguistic and social conventions, understands correctly the things that are being referred to and basically gets the point that the speaker or writer is trying to communicate.

In order to understand a given biblical passage, it seems to me that all five aspects of language theory must be incorporated. This forms the crux of successful and appropriate biblical hermeneutics (interpretation). In addition it appears that most if not all of these aspects have been affirmed in one way or another in the discussion of biblical interpretation by the contributors to this volume. Both the older referential aspect and expressivist aspect of language are included in this more comprehensive theory. It is clear that each has a role to play, but each in itself is wholly inadequate to give a valid biblical hermeneutic. In a nutshell, this method of Bible study is a careful, thorough (inductive) type of Bible study method, spelled out in detail.

In particular I urge all of us to apply these principles to a most crucial passage, a passage that plays a definitive role in the discussion of faith and science: Genesis 1:1—2:3. What is language doing here? How was this passage used in the life of the people of Israel? What is the historical, cultural context? When was this passage inscripturated? By whom? What situation does this passage address? What is the overall message (intent) of the passage? Why is this passage found in the first chapter of Genesis, at the beginning of the Bible? Are we to read this passage in a literal way, taking it to be a blow by blow account of creation in the contemporary scientific sense? And why is this passage followed immediately by a second creation account—one that is significantly different—in Genesis 2:4-25? For me, these are crucially important questions for a believer who wants to be a faithful and obedient servant of our Lord Jesus.

Sources of Theological Knowledge

In one way or another each of the contributors to this volume addresses this question, either directly or indirectly. Ultimately here we are addressing the question of authority: *theological authority.* Some theological traditions—for example, the Anglican (or Episcopal) and the Roman Catholic—have been explicit in affirming the threefold combination of Scripture, tradition and experience (or reason). Christians from other Protestant groups are not so quick to affirm tradition and experience, as they place what seems to be exclusive emphasis on Scripture (e.g., *sola Scriptura*). And yet in practice we all look to tradition and experience along with the Bible (as our primary source) to formulate our theological beliefs.

Tradition probably has the highest standing in the Roman Catholic Church and is spoken of as the *magisterium* and is exercised through councils, the bishops and the papacy. For Protestants the term is generalized to a body of extrabiblical material that is found to be helpful in supplementing Scripture in certain areas of absence or where Scripture needs clarification. In all cases the resulting teachings, statements, theological conclusions, theological systems, creeds and so on are subject to the test of Scripture. Examples that might fall under the category of tradition for Protestants, but perhaps not for all churches, would be the trinitarian and christological statements of Nicaea, Constantinople and Chalcedon, seen as expressions of biblical truth. In addition, the great teachers of the church such as Augustine, Aquinas, Luther, Calvin and others have produced valuable work in theological formulations, but always to be evaluated in the light of Scripture. And every sermon preached can be thought of as a possible addition to the tradition of the church.

Experience is the third component. We all integrate our individual life experiences into our theological systems, for if our Christian faith cannot account for life itself and in particular our individual lives—all our good and bad experiences—does Christian faith have any real relevance? All of the contributors to this volume affirm the importance of the scientific enterprise. We need to pay attention to the judgments of professional scientists. Science provides important data and information for both our lives and our theology, although there is not complete agreement among our contributors over the extent of the role that science plays in Christian theology. Jean Pond is the most cautious here, with the other four contributors affirming a more positive role for science in theology. I would suggest at the *very least* competent science places some helpful boundaries on theology, especially for what theology has to say in terms of scientific statements about our physical and biological universe. In at least that sense, theology should pay attention to scientific results and progress. As a result I conclude that experience in the broad sense does indeed play a role in our theological formulations and in particular in the case of science and faith.

The concept of *sola Scriptura* (Scripture alone) was the watchword of the Reformation. This concept affirms Scripture alone as the primary and absolute norm of supernatural theology. Scripture is the supreme teacher and arbiter of belief and practice. It is the norm against which all claims by any other authority are judged. However, this concept of *sola Scriptura* was never meant to deny the usefulness of Christian tradition as a subordinate norm in theology.[3] To tradition I suggest that we add experience also in a subordinate role.

My conclusion is that competent scientific knowledge ("effective" science, in the words of Wayne Frair and Gary Patterson) can and should play an important but subordinate role in our theological understanding. Of course, we must realize, as Jean Pond points out, that science progresses and that the scientific conclusions of today may be replaced by the scientific conclusions of tomorrow. We indeed need to exercise caution in our use of science in theology. However, I completely agree with the statement by Philip Clayton: "Any theological system that ignores the picture of the world pointed by scientific results is certain to be regarded with suspicion."[4]

---

[3]Richard A. Muller, "sola Scriptura," in *Dictionary of Latin and Greek Theological Terms* (Grand Rapids, Mich.: Baker, 1985), p. 284.

[4]Philip Clayton, *God and Contemporary Science* (Edinburgh: Edinburgh University Press, 1997).

Scientific Knowledge—How Far?

There seems to be a significant difference among the contributors to this volume regarding the scope of scientific knowledge. Jean Pond and Howard Van Till see natural science as a somewhat more limited enterprise than does Stephen Meyer, with the Wayne Frair-Gary Patterson team somewhere in between. Howard and Jean take a more traditional view of science.

A traditional view includes such principles as construing natural science to be an enterprise limited to the rational, empirical and objective. In particular, observational data is public, neutral and independent of the observer, and religious or metaphysical principles have no say in theory adjudication. Stephen Meyer wants to modify that view to include, as he points out, wherever the data seem to lead, including religious or metaphysical conclusions. Wayne Frair and Gary Patterson seem to be leaning in the direction of Stephen here.

A systematic presentation of developments in the philosophy of science is well beyond the scope of this volume. Let me just note that the philosophy of science has moved beyond the so-called traditional view of science, which has some connections with positivism, a philosophy that did not permit any metaphysical components within any system of knowledge. However, modern science from the time of Galileo and Newton (seventeenth century) has always had (perhaps hidden) certain metaphysical (and hence unprovable) assumptions underlying its practice—the belief that the universe is rational and that the laws of nature are the same throughout the universe and are constant in time are examples of such underlying metaphysical assumptions. But there has been a movement away from positivism on the part of the philosophers of science, although many scientists are unaware of this. For example, a number of philosophers feel that the scientific methodology of Imre Lakatos describes well the actual practice of normative science.[5] It is interesting to note that Lakatos's method explicitly points out that the core of every scientific theory is metaphysical and hence is not accessible by experiment.

It is also true that many scientists, especially theoretical physicists and cosmologists, are introducing metaphysical concepts into their theories.

---

[5]Imre Lakatos, "Falsification and the Methodology of Scientific Research Programmes," in *Criticism and the Growth of Knowledge*, ed. Imre Lakatos and Alan Musgrave (Cambridge: Cambridge University Press, 1970), pp. 91-196.

They simply cannot seem to stay away from such considerations, as the hard data seem to push them beyond purely physical (naturalistic) explanations in so many cases. Some (many) of these scientists are inexperienced or unsophisticated in terms of philosophical knowledge, yet they seem to be naturally moving beyond physics as traditionally practiced in their attempts to account for what they are learning in terms of the character and beginnings of our universe and even the direction in which our universe seems to be headed.

So it appears to me that both the actual practice of scientists (especially physicists and cosmologists) themselves and the understanding of the normative practice of science by philosophers of science seem to be indicating that science is moving beyond a strictly materialistic or empirical or naturalistic accounting, at least in certain areas of scientific interest.

Scientific Knowledge: Exclusive or Multifaceted?

Let's just suppose that metaphysical theories along with traditionally scientific theories (naturalistic, empirical, physical) are regarded as valid for trying to account for what has heretofore been regarded as strictly scientific territory. For example, let us consider the fine-tuning data that Stephen Meyer presented in his chapter. This data is recognized by physicists as valid, and most would agree that it calls for an explanation. Stephen correctly points out that there are a number of theories in physics that attempt to account for the data: many-worlds theories, quantum branching schemes, the idea of an infinite universe, various anthropic principles, the concept of mathematical necessity and even the idea of "pure chance." A number of (Christian) philosophers, including Stephen, have added another theory to the mix: the theory of God as the designer of the universe. As it stands now, none of these physics theories seem to be satisfactory under the generally accepted hypothetical-deductive scheme of evaluating scientific theories. Meyer and a number of other philosophers argue that the theistic-designer hypothesis accounts for the fine-tuning data and can account for more in terms of predictive power than any of the scientific theories. This is very good news for Christians—so far.

But what if at some point a purely physics theory is found to give an entirely satisfactory accounting of the fine-tuning data? As a physicist I see this as unlikely but definitely as a possibility. What does that do to the status of the theistic designer explanation? My suggestion is that it does nothing to destroy the designer hypothesis, that the two explanations can stand side by side. How can I make such a claim? I do so by noting some further significant work in understanding the relationship of all of the sciences, including theology.

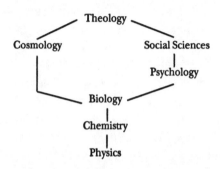

Figure 2. Nancey Murphy's classification of the sciences

It was Arthur Peacocke who, after classifying the sciences in a hierarchical order, from physics at the bottom and then chemistry, biology, psychology and the social sciences at the top, suggested that causation works in two directions—from lower to upper levels (the traditional way of understanding causation) but also from upper to lower levels (a contribution by Peacocke).[6] Bottom-up causation refers to the laws describing how the constituent parts of an entity influence the next level up, whereas top-down causation describes the influence of the higher level (a larger system) on the constituent parts of the system (at a lower level). Peacocke made an additional contribution in placing theology at the top of the hierarchy, suggesting that theology is the most encompassing science, and that the interaction between God and the universe is the most complex of all systems. Nancey Murphy, while affirming Peacocke's overall idea, has proposed a modification of the hierarchy—she divides the hierarchy into two branches and adds some components, with the resulting model as shown in figure 2.[7]

---

[6]For example, see Arthur Peacocke, *Theology for a Scientific Age: Being and Becoming— Natural, Divine, and Human,* 2nd ed. (Minneapolis: Fortress, 1993).

[7]Nancey Murphy, *Reconciling Theology and Science: A Radical Reformation Perspective* (Kitchener, Ont.: Pandora, 1997), p. 17.

Putting these ideas together, it follows that for a given set of data, for example, the cosmological fine-tuning data, a bottom-up (physics) explanation along with a top-down (theological) explanation could *both* be valid explanations; that is, the validity of one explanation would not depend on the other being shown to be invalid or less valid.

As a result, we could have, for example, mathematical necessity *and* God as explanations for our observation of the fine-tuning of the universe.

What Counts as Scientific Evidence? Gaps for God?

Here is another very important but very, very subtle topic. The actual data of science is recognized as useful by each of our contributors. This is not surprising, as the collecting and interpreting of actual data is simply the way typical science proceeds. All of the contributors recognize the crucial role data plays in formulating theories, but in addition Stephen Meyer, for example, even uses data (fine-tuning data) in formulating a metaphysical theory related to theistic design. And, of course, the more data gathered that support a given theory, the stronger the case can be made for that theory. No problem. No one will argue with that.

But what about using the *lack* of data in supporting a given theory and a metaphysical theory to boot? So-called gaps arguments have had a sad history in Christian theology, for as gaps are filled by our scientific progress, it seems (at the surface at least) that God simply gets squeezed out of our understanding of natural processes. These former gaps that become filled were clearly "epistemological" gaps, that is, gaps in our then-current knowledge, which then became former gaps when the particular question (scientific question, for example) is answered (by science being performed in the typical naturalistic way).

However, it *is indeed possible* that a gap in our knowledge could be an inherent gap in the way things actually are—an "ontological" gap, one that inherently cannot be closed because of the nature of our universe. Perhaps there simply *is* no way to account for some process or phenomenon in terms of the limitations under which science puts itself—in terms of naturalistic and empirical explanations. In this case there will never be a scientific explanation *in principle* (perhaps Jesus' incarnation and resurrection would be examples), and the only possibility is to give an explanation that goes beyond science, a metaphysical explanation (like a theistic explanation). But one must be very careful to make a compelling case that the lack of data implies an ontological rather than an epistemological gap.

A Few Final Questions and Comments

Each of the contributors had the opportunity to make comments and raise questions about each of the positions represented in this volume. It is my opinion that each position has been presented in a compelling manner and is well worth consideration as a position that a faithful Christian could hold. But having said that, I should point out that I regard each of the four positions something like a model in science. Scientific models are extremely useful in terms of developing scientific theories. A good model accounts for a certain range of data, but a model does not quite have the status of a scientific theory. Each model has a certain limited number of deficiencies, and it is the deficiencies that can motivate improvements in the model, with the hope that eventually the model will grow into an accepted theory. I regard each of the four positions presented in this volume as very good models of how science and faith are related. But I have a few questions—in fact, one question for each of the positions.

Question to Wayne Frair and Gary Patterson. Is the Bible "an essential part of the practice of science for a Christian" (p. 28)? Can that case be established? If so, what is the role of the Bible?

Question to Jean Pond. The fine-tuning data seem to require an explanation that goes beyond the limitations of naturalistic science. Is this perhaps an example in which both science and Christian theology have some mutual interests and hence might inform each other?

Question to Howard Van Till. Can the robust formational economy (RFE) principle account for God's action in the world, in particular, to answer specific prayer? In other words, does the RFE principle allow an understanding of how God can do special things (specific episodic interventions) in our world?

Question to Stephen Meyer. Most biological systems exhibit both good design and imperfection (bad design). Is it "intelligent" for a designer (such as God) to produce less than perfect products?

May God bless us and guide each of us as we press on toward our high calling, as we strive to honor him in all that we do, say and ponder as we attempt to understand the relationship between our wonderful universe— God's exceedingly excellent creation (Gen 1:31)—and God and us.

Annotated Bibliography

The contributors to this volume have recommended the following books and articles for further reading regarding the various viewpoints represented by these contributors. The comments are those of the contributors.

Recommended by Wayne Frair and Gary D. Patterson

Davis, Percival, and Dean Kenyon. *Of Pandas and People: The Central Question of Biological Origins.* 2nd ed. Dallas: Haughton, 1993. This book was written by scientists and stresses, as a scientific viewpoint, intelligent causation as contrasted with natural causation. The text covers the fields of biology, chemistry and geology, and can serve as an excellent supplement for a high school or college student taking a one-sided biology course which stresses only naturalistic evolution.

Frair, Wayne, and Percival Davis. *A Case for Creation.* 3rd ed. Lewisville, Tex.: Accelerated Christian Education, 1983. Two professional biologists have aimed this book at Christians who are biologists or have at least some background and understanding of science. A case is made for limited change and a challenge given for additional laboratory and field research.

Osborne, Grant R. *The Hermeneutical Spiral: A Comprehensive Introduction to Biblical Interpretation.* Downers Grove, Ill.: InterVarsity Press, 1991. This is the essential graduate text for modern evangelicals who wish to explore the Bible in its full context. While it may be challenging reading for many, no lesser effort will suffice to address the deeper issues involved in the interaction of Christian biblical theology with modern science.

Pearcey, Nancy, and Charles Thaxton. *The Soul of Science.* Wheaton, Ill.: Crossway, 1994. In this book Pearcy and Thaxton consider the history and development of modern science in a fully nuanced context. The value of Christian presuppositions in the practice of science is explored in detail.

Roth, Ariel A. *Origins: Linking Science and Scripture.* Hagerstown, Maryland: Review & Herald, 1998. Ariel Roth, a professional biologist and a professor, wrote this book as an attempt to harmonize the Bible and science. The author has wrestled with many crucial issues and feels that science's biggest error has been in rejecting God and accepting only mechanistic explanations. Roth prefers a recent creation.

Recommended by Jean Pond

Gould, Stephen Jay. "Nonoverlapping Magesteria." *Natural History* 106 (March 1997): 60-62; and *Rocks of Ages: Science and Religion in the Fullness of Life.* New York: Ballantine, 1999. A clear statement of the NOMA principle is given by the originator of the term in the article. In the book Gould includes and expands on his NOMA article.

Gross, Paul R., Norman Levitt and Martin W. Lewis, eds. *The Flight from Science and Reason.* Annals of the New York Academy of Sciences 775. New York: New York Academy of Sciences, 1996. This volume represents a compilation of forty-two papers from a 1995 conference of the same name. Although the papers address everything from sociology to quantum mechanics, in general they present arguments upholding traditional scientific methodologies. Particularly relevant are the articles by Eugenie C. Scott ("Creationism, Ideology, and Science") and Langdon Gilkey ("The Flight from Reason: The Religious Right"). One of the interesting things about this volume is that it demonstrates how attacks on science are currently coming from two rather different directions: the "academic left" and the "religious right." This strange bedfellowship is also the subject of an article by Matt Cartmill, "Oppressed by Evolution," *Discover,* March 1998, pp. 78-83.

Jaki, Stanley L. *Genesis 1 Through the Ages.* London: Thomas More, 1992 This book presents a survey of the various attempts—over a two-thousand year period—to conflate the teachings of the first chapter of Genesis with scientific findings. Jaki, whose style can be obscure, starts with the early Jewish sages and continues on to the present day. He calls the greatest threat to Genesis 1 "the ever-recurring temptation to make that magnificent chapter appear concordant with the science of the day in order to assure its cultural respectability" (p. 31).

Pennock, Robert T. "The Prospects for a Theistic Science." *Perspectives on Science and Christian Faith* 50 (September 1998): 205-9; and *Tower of Babel: The Evidence Against the New Creationism*. Cambridge, Mass.: MIT Press, 1999. The article, which is incorporated into one chapter of the book, originated as a paper for a conference on "Naturalism, Theism and the Scientific Enterprise" held at the University of Texas in 1997. It contains a critical appraisal of "theistic science," with a particular emphasis on the work of Phillip Johnson. Pennock argues that what Johnson—and others like him—are really doing is trying to confine God within a scientific box.

Polkinghorne, John. *Reason and Reality: The Relationship Between Science and Theology.* London: SPCK, 1991. Polkinghorne is a physicist, Anglican priest, and former president of Queens College, Cambridge University. He has written extensively on the relationship between science and faith. Although he would probably be more comfortable with the complementary (rather than the independence) view of this relationship, I would recommend any of his books for the interested reader. This volume includes a chapter ("Reason and Revelation") on the comparison between science and Christian revelation, and another chapter ("The Use of Scripture") on proper biblical interpretation.

Recommended by Stephen C. Meyer

Behe, Michael J. *Darwin's Black Box: The Biochemical Challenge to Evolution.* New York: Free Press, 1996. Behe examines the intricate "irreducibly complex" molecular machines and systems that characterize the microscopic machines of the cell. He shows why these systems cannot be explained as a result of a gradual self-assembly by the mechanism of natural selection, but instead can best be explained by intelligent design.

Dembski, William A. *The Design Inference: Eliminating Chance Through Small Probabilities.* Cambridge: Cambridge University Press, 1998. In this book mathematician and philosopher William A. Dembski articulates in rigorous mathematical fashion the criteria by which rational agents recognize the products of intelligent design. It provides a foundational theory for the detection of design, both in human history and in biological and other natural systems.

Dembski, William A., ed. *Mere Creation: Science, Faith & Intelligent Design.* Downers Grove, Ill.: InterVarsity Press, 1998. This volume is an anthology of essays by leaders in the intelligent design movement. It examines evidence for design across a range of scientific disciplines, including physics, cosmology, chemistry and biology. It also includes a chapter in which I expand my argument for intelligent design as the best explanation for the information encoded in DNA.

Heeren, Fred, and George Smoot. *Show Me God: What the Message from Space Is Telling Us About God.* Rev. ed. Wheeling, Ill.: Day Star, 2000. Heeren and Smoot investigate a number of recent discoveries in physics and cosmology that point to the reality of the Creator. The book employs an engaging conversational style—complete with sidebars, interviews with top scientists, interstellar pictures and the like—and appeals to the scientific layperson and students in particular.

Thaxton, Charles, Walter Bradley, and Roger Olsen. *The Mystery of Life's Origin.* Dallas: Lewis & Stanley, 1984. These authors scrutinize the evidence for the theory of the chemical evolution of the origin of life, and they find that it both lacks explanatory power and is inconsistent with a variety of disciplines, including chemistry, geo-chemistry, thermodynamics, molecular biology, and the information sciences. This book's provocative epilogue suggests that the design hypothesis can be profitably employed within science to explain the origin of information-rich structures.

Recommended by Howard J. Van Till

Goodwin, Brian. *How the Leopard Changed Its Spots: The Evolution of Complexity.* New York: Simon & Schuster, 1994; and Stuart Kaufmann. *At Home in the Universe: The Search for the Laws of Self-Organization and Complexity.* New York: Oxford University Press, 1996. For readers interested in being stimulated to awe and wonder at the creation's remarkable capabilities for actualizing complex structures and organisms, I heartily recommend both of these books

Miller, Kenneth R. *Finding Darwin's God: A Scientist's Search for Common Ground Between God and Evolution.* New York: HarperCollins, 1999. Is it possible that modern evolutionary biology could stimulate an enrichment of Christian theology? I believe that this is not only possible, but that the partnership of biology and theology is essential if Christianity is to regain its relevance to the modern university. Miller presents this case from his perspective as a Christian biologist.

Sarna, Nahum. *Understanding Genesis.* New York: Schocken, 1970. This book will assist readers regarding what the early chapters of Genesis can contribute to the science-faith discussion. Written by a biblical scholar from the Jewish community, Sarna assists the reader in hearing the text of Genesis as it was heard in its original ancient Near East context.

Vanstone, W. H. *The Risk of Love.* New York: Oxford University Press, 1978 (first published in Great Britain [1977] as *Love's Endeavour, Love's Expense*). I recommend this brief book as a fresh theological and pastoral approach to Christian reflection on God's creative activity. This work was especially influential in stimulating me to portray God's creative activity, not primarily in the language of form-imposing power, but rather in terms of God's infinite creativity and loving generosity in the giving of being to a creation richly gifted with dynamic capabilities.

Contributing Authors

Wayne Frair is professor (emeritus) of biology at The King's College, Tuxedo, New York. Dr. Frair graduated from Houghton College in 1950 with an A.B. in zoology and then from Wheaton College in 1951 with a B.S. also in zoology. He then completed an M.A. in embryology in 1955 at the University of Massachusetts, and a Ph.D. in biochemical taxonomy in 1962 from Rutgers, The State University. His research interests have focused on turtles, with emphasis on biochemical taxonomy. Dr. Frair is the author of more than fifty research papers, including some dealing with the topic of science and the Bible. He is a coauthor of the book *A Case for Creation*, now in its third edition. He was a witness for the defense at the 1981 creation v. evolution trial in Little Rock, Arkansas. Dr. Frair is a Fellow of the American Association for the Advancement of Science, the American Scientific Affiliation, the Society of the Sigma Xi, the Creation Research Society, the Victoria Institute (England) and a number of other scientific societies. From 1986 to 1993 he was the president of the Creation Research Society and is a current member of its board.

Stephen C. Meyer received his Ph.D. in history and the philosophy of science from Cambridge University in 1990. He is currently associate professor of philosophy at Whitworth College, Spokane, Washington; a Senior Research Fellow at the Discovery Institute (Seattle); and director of the Discovery Institute's Center for the Renewal of Science and Culture. Formerly a geo-physicist with the Atlantic Richfield Company, Dr. Meyer completed a Ph.D. dissertation on origin-of-life biology and the methodology of the historical sciences. He has contributed to several scholarly books and anthologies, including *The History of Science and Religion in the Western Tradition: An Encyclopedia; Darwinism: Science or Philosophy; Of Pandas and People: The Central Question in Biological Origins; The Creation Hypothesis: Scientific Evidence* _for an Intelligent Designer; Mere Creation: Science, Faith & Intelligent Design; Facets of Faith and Science: Interpreting God's Action in the World._ In addition to his technical articles on design Dr. Meyer has written many editorial features in newspapers and magazines, including _The Wall Street Journal, Los Angeles Times_ and _Chicago Tribune._ He has appeared on national TV and radio programs such as _Technopolitics,_ PBS's _Freedom Speaks,_ CNBC's _Hardball with Chris Matthews_ and National Public Radio's _Talk of the Nation._

Gary D. Patterson is professor of chemical physics and polymer science at Carnegie Mellon University, Pittsburgh, Pennsylvania. He received his B.S. in chemistry from Harvey Mudd College in 1968 and his Ph.D. in physical chemistry from Stanford University in 1972. He was a member of the technical staff in the chemical physics department at AT&T Bell Laboratories from 1972 until 1984. Dr. Patterson is a fellow of the American Physical Society and the Royal Society of Chemistry. He received the National Academy of Sciences Award for Initiatives in Research in 1981. His research interests are in the structure and dynamics of molecular systems. He has published more than one hundred papers in journals such as the _Journal of Chemical Physics, Journal of Physical Chemistry, Physical Review Letters, Macromolecules, Journal of Polymer Science and Biopolymers._ Dr. Patterson has written chapters for many books, including _Methods of Experimental Physics, Dynamic Light Scattering, Advances in Polymer Science, Advances in Materials Science_ and _Annual Review of Physical Chemistry._ He has taught a wide range of science courses to chemistry, chemical engineering, biology and physics majors at Carnegie Mellon University. Dr. Patterson has also cotaught a course in Christianity and science in the philosophy department, with support from the Templeton Foundation, and continues to lecture in philosophy of science and philosophy of religion. He worships with Christians who acknowledge Jesus Christ as Lord of all and the Bible as the inerrant Word of God.

Jean Louise Bertelson Pond is formerly visiting associate professor of biology at Whitworth College, Spokane, Washington. Dr. Pond received her bachelor's degree from the University of Minnesota and a M.S. from Oregon State University. An area or emphasis in her master's work was the history and philosophy of science. Her doctorate, received from the School of Medicine at the University of South Dakota, is in microbiology. Her doctoral research, which focused on the membrane lipids of a hyperthermo philic bacterium, was followed by postdoctoral work in molecular biology at the University of Florida. Dr. Pond is currently retired from teaching. Recently she taught a course in the history and philosophy of science at Whitworth College. In 1993 Dr. Pond was awarded the Howard Vollum Writing Award on "Horizons of Science and the Christian Faith" for her article *Catholic Frogs*. She and her family spent a year (1996-1997) in a rural and disadvantaged area of South Africa, where she and her husband volunteered as teachers in St. Mark's School (a junior and senior high school affiliated with the Anglican Church). Currently she is teaching herself ancient Greek.

Howard J. Van Till is professor (emeritus) of physics and astronomy at Calvin College, Grand Rapids, Michigan. After graduating from Calvin College in 1960, he earned his Ph.D. in physics from Michigan State University in 1965. Dr. Van Till's research experience includes both solid-state physics and millimeter-wave astronomy. During the past two decades he has devoted a considerable portion of his writing and speaking efforts to topics regarding the relationship of science and religion. Having concluded that the usual creation-evolution debate is the product of serious misunderstandings, Van Till's goal is to encourage a nonadversarial and mutually informative engagement of Christian theology and the natural sciences. He is the author of numerous books, book chapters and essays on this theme and has spoken at many universities, colleges and churches. He is a member of the American Astronomical Society and the American Scientific Affiliation. Since 1992 he has served the John Templeton Foundation as a member of its advisory board and has assisted the foundation in the administration of several programs in science and religion.

Richard F. Carlson is currently professor of physics at the University of Redlands, Redlands, California, visiting scientist in the department of radiation sciences at Uppsala University, Sweden, and visiting professor of theology and science at Fuller Theological Seminary, Pasadena, California. He has received a B.S. (University of Redlands), M.S. and Ph.D. (University of Minnesota) in physics, and an M.A. (Fuller Theological Seminary) in biblical studies and theology. His physics research interests are in experimental nuclear physics, and he has done postdoctoral research at UCLA. While teaching at the University of Redlands he has continued his nuclear research at UCLA, the University of Manitoba, University of California,

Davis, and currently at Uppsala University. Dr. Carlson has published over fifty articles in physics research journals. Recently his interests have shifted to the area of science and Christian faith, and he has taught a number of science and theology courses at the University of Redlands and Fuller Theological Seminary. His courses at Redlands and Fuller have resulted in two Templeton Foundation prizes. He also teaches a course on backpacking at Redlands.